Praise for
Claudia Chan and
THIS IS HOW WE RISE

"Claudia Chan's book provides a blueprint for addressing one of the most urgent issues of our time—gender equality—on both a personal and societal level. *This Is How We Rise* is a must-read for any person or organization who wants to start a movement that empowers women."

    —RESHMA SAUJANI, founder of Girls Who Code

"This is the century of women. Few recognize and support the empowerment of and community building between women and men with as much dedication as Claudia Chan through her book *This Is How We Rise.*"

    —HARVEY KARP, MD, creator of *The Happiest Baby on the Block*

"Claudia Chan is a revolutionary who understands how important women's release from diminishing social expectations are to everyone's prosperity. She inspired me to launch my financial services company when she asked me 'Who are the banks that support women?' When I couldn't answer her, I realized I had to do it myself. She's an instigator to many women stepping up into previously unimaginable roles of power and influence. This book will do the same for you."

    —AMANDA STEINBERG, founder and CEO of DailyWorth.com and WorthFM

"Along with Sheryl Sandberg and Sallie Krawcheck, Claudia Chan has been one of the instrumental leaders fueling the popularity of feminism we are seeing today. Her vision of mainstream empowerment and work to make it more globally accessible through S.H.E. Summit and this book has been impressive and courageous. And she is extremely thoughtful about educating women to recruit men in her work."

    —JOHN GERZEMA, *New York Times* best-selling author of *The Athena Doctrine* and CEO of the Harris Poll

"This masterful book provides you with a window of clarity into your life, your purpose, and your leadership. After reading it, you will have no choice but to realize your potential as an incredible agent of change."
—DAYLE HADDON, founder and CEO of WomenOne

"Claudia Chan is one of the most inspiring female entrepreneurs I know. This book is critical for mainstreaming and modernizing women's empowerment."
—ALI BROWN, entrepreneur, mentor, and angel investor

"In a masterful and personal way, Claudia Chan has written an enlightening manifesto that shows every person that the only meaning to a truly successful life is to align with our soul's purpose and cultivate our gifts in service to others. As you read this book you'll feel called to rise to action for the better good of all."
—AGAPI STASSINOPOULOS, author of *Wake Up to the Joy of You*

"I can't speak highly enough of Claudia Chan's extraordinary ability to inspire women to aim high and act on our passions not just for ourselves alone but to help all women rise. This is an important book that combines Claudia's movement builder's heart with her businesswoman's savvy. It's a book all women need right now."
—GLORIA FELDT, cofounder and president of Take the Lead and author of *No Excuses: 9 Ways Women Can Change How We Think About Power*

"Claudia Chan is a force of nature for women looking to rise in their careers and lead, while constantly pulling one another ahead to realize their fullest potential. Claudia has galvanized women and started a movement with S.H.E. Summit that empowers, inspires, and connects the dots for women to be powerful and successful in their lives and careers. Her thought-provoking book goes under the soil and pulls back the curtain on topics that women most often feel are off-limits, but that are the fundamental keys to success."
—LAUREN MAILLIAN, entrepreneur, marketer, best-selling author, and television personality

"Claudia continues to inspire everyone with her passion and purpose. Her book challenges each of us to reflect on our personal mission, rise to our fullest potential and provoke others to do the same."
— **MARIE CLAIRE LIM MOORE, executive director of development at the Women's Foundation Hong Kong**

"This book is a creative blueprint for every woman looking to own her leadership power and channel it for good! If you are seeking real advice on how to realize your potential, maximize your talents, and make meaningful change in this world—look no further. This is a must-read for all future and current change makers."
— **AMY HEPBURN, adjunct professor at Duke University and George Washington University**

"It is time for women to tell our new story. Claudia is a role model herself of a woman who went after her dreams to live her own truth."
— **ZAINAB SALBI, founder Women for Women International**

THIS IS
HOW WE
RISE

THIS IS HOW WE RISE

Reach Your Highest Potential,
Empower Women,
Lead Change in the World

CLAUDIA CHAN

Da Capo
LIFE
LONG

Da Capo Press
Hachette Book Group
1290 Avenue of the Americas, New York, NY 10104
www.dacapopress.com
@DaCapoPress, @DaCapoPR

Printed in the United States of America

First Edition: October 2017

Published by Da Capo Press, an imprint of Perseus Books, LLC,
a subsidiary of Hachette Book Group, Inc.

The Hachette Speakers Bureau provides a wide range of authors for speaking events. To find out more, go to www.hachettespeakersbureau.com or call (866) 376-6591.

The publisher is not responsible for websites (or their content) that are not owned by the publisher.

Editorial production by Lori Hobkirk at the Book Factory.
Print book interior design by Cynthia Young at Sagecraft.

Library of Congress Cataloging-in-Publication Data has been applied for.
ISBNs: 978-0-7382-2002-4 (hardcover), 978-0-7382-2003-1 (ebook)

LSC-C

10 9 8 7 6 5 4 3 2 1

To my father in heaven, Wallace,
and my mother on Earth, Vivian,
thank you for my life and for fighting for
the extraordinary education and privileges
that have come with it.

To my brother, Robert,
your protection of me when we were young
enabled me to fly.

To my husband, John,
you are my rock and my dream come true.

To Jackson and Arya,
my capacity to love has no limits because of you.

CONTENTS

AUTHOR'S NOTE

I believe our world is not operating at its full potential because human beings are not operating at theirs. I wrote this book to provide you with a new perspective of your life and what it might mean for the world. It is a call-to-arms for every woman and man to rise to a new definition of leadership and create change in the world. *It is important to read the book in chronological sequence, starting with the Introduction, which sets the context for the rest of the chapters.*

Please also note that I wrote this book based on my personal journey, which has taught me that creating social change is weak without leadership development. Leadership development is weak without personal growth. Personal growth is weak without spiritual growth. I have learned that humanity needs a far greater motivation that transcends our limited, precious time on earth to truly contribute our best while we are here. In the last year of writing this book, during which I've experienced both the death and loss of father and the birth of my second child and daughter, this has become more apparent than ever. The diagram on the next page illustrates the life journey that each of us must go on in order to fulfill our highest destiny.

Therefore, I will be alluding to a higher power throughout the book as the source that powers our existence and the existence of humanity. Because my higher power and ultimate source is God, I often refer to God. But because every person has their own beliefs and stance on spirituality, please replace God with whatever you define as your life source—some popular ones I have heard include spirit, the universe, destiny, consciousness, and nature.

I also want to call attention to the fact that our modern understanding of gender is radically different from that of previous generations. We no longer view gender as a biological reality but instead as a social construct. More important, not everyone identifies with the binary categories of

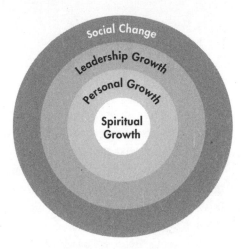

Source: Claudia Chan International, Inc.

female and male, which is why a multitude of sexual identities have been embraced under the umbrella of LGBTQIA (lesbian, gay, bisexual, transsexual, queer, intersex, asexual).

Additionally, as someone who identifies as a heterosexual woman and has a partner who identifies as a heterosexual man, most of the examples in this book look at intimate relationships through that lens. I chose to use these examples not to exclude other identities and experiences, but simply to stay true to my own lived experiences. Feel free to reimagine these scenarios to fit your specific set of circumstances.

Introduction

I stood in the ladies' room of our West Soho office and tried to catch my breath. It was 2009, the market had tanked, and my business was beginning to follow suit. I had just come out of another frustrating executive meeting with my business partner, Chris, where we spent several hours finger pointing and arguing childishly to the point where I lost track of what we were even talking about. I'm sure our voices reverberated through the sterile, white-walled office; the rest of our team likely heard it and probably thought, *There they go again.* The ladies' room was the only place I could escape to, so I washed my hands and threw water on my face. But the person I saw in the mirror was nearly unrecognizable. My constant negativity about work was infecting everyone in my personal life and wearing down my soul. When I looked in the mirror I felt disappointed with the person staring back at me. *I don't like you*, I thought. *I don't like who you've become.* That was the moment when I knew something in my life had to change, and it sent me on a journey of personal learning and leadership development that has completely altered the trajectory of my life. Deep inside I also knew that I had to embark on this radical change for a greater purpose that could help other people. I didn't know what that purpose was yet, but when I did realize it, I felt like I finally began to live the life I was meant to. Let me explain.

WE'VE HAD IT BACKWARD

Most of us go through life in a rather reactionary manner. In the beginning of our lives childhood circumstances and parents shape our perceptions of success and failure. As we get older, additional factors like school, friends, bullies, media, wins, losses, and other events influence the development of our beliefs—our core belief systems as well as what we believe about ourselves. And these beliefs influence who we become: the choices we make, the careers we pursue, the relationships we invest in, and the quality of self-worth we nurture. We journey through life thinking we know who we are based on these beliefs.

The problem with this reactionary journey is that we are living in a constant state of lack or negativity characterized by one—or more than one—of these:

- **A when/then mindset:** "When X happens, then I will be happy."

- **Self-doubt:** "What if I can't do this or I am not good enough?"

- **Self-consciousness:** "What will others think about me?"

- **Comparison:** "They have it better than me."

- **Scarcity:** "I have limited money, time, peace, joy, stuff."

- **Overwhelmed:** "I have too much pressure and responsibility."

- **Guilt:** "I should have been better at X or done more for Y."

In this reactionary model we never obtain a consistent, unwavering sense of personal worth and peace. After investing fifteen years in various kinds of personal work, leadership development, and spiritual growth, I have come to learn that we never get to this permanent state of fulfillment when we live our lives guided by serving ourselves first before anyone or anything else. We go about every day centered in the self. A more straightforward way to say this is that our natural human tendency is a "me over we" mindset rooted in the ego that subconsciously traps us in a self-obsessed way of living. Think about it: if life were a theatrical stage and the spotlight was always on *you*, everything attached to *your* sense of self-worth—like money, appearance, popularity, job title, accolades, love from or being seen by others, what others think about you, and so forth—becomes your subconscious idol and obsession. In this way of living you will always be concerned with what other people think.

My own wake-up call didn't come until I was thirty-five years old, when I finally made the change to the "me for we" mindset and made a commitment to serve something bigger than myself. Prior to that, I lived in a reactionary, self-centric manner because I was naturally shaped by the cir cumstances I had been born into.

> "Our natural human tendency is a 'me over we' mindset rooted in the ego that subconsciously traps us in a self-obsessed way of living."

My parents embody the classic immigrant story: they came to America with next to nothing in the 1960s after surviving the war in China and growing up in Taiwan. They scrimped, saved, and worked themselves to the bone to provide the best quality of life and education for my brother and me. They succeeded in giving us the opportunities they didn't have. They became the owners of several successful Chinese restaurants, which afforded us a very comfortable, middle-class lifestyle. The struggles they overcame and the success they created with limited education and broken English humble me every time I think about it. And though I am forever grateful for and immensely respectful of my parents for their provisions, this upbringing ingrained in me somewhat of a survival mode and scarcity mentality that naturally valued self-centric securities like making enough money to have a good life and dressing the part to be accepted by the white, upper-class networks. Because my parents had been discriminated against as Chinese immigrants, this is what my brother and I needed to do in order to "make it in America," and looking back they were not wrong.

Fast forward to ages twenty-five to thirty-five, when I found myself at the pinnacle of this dream: president of Shecky's, a women's entertainment company that I had spent the last ten years building into a multi-million-dollar business. It was the era of *Sex and the City*. Chick lit and chick flicks were all the rage. In the wake of the dot-com crash and

9/11, which still had New York City reeling, people retreated into a world of frivolous, cheap thrills. For women it was all about living fabulously—meeting Mr. Big, wearing Jimmy Choos, and jet-setting around the world in style. Shecky's capitalized on this trend by launching Girls Night Out, ticketed events where women could discover new fashion brands and beauty products all while sipping cosmos with their girlfriends. Thousands of women showed up to our first couple of events and waited in long lines that wrapped around city blocks. At the company's height we were running eighty event days a year across fifteen cities with 150,000 annual attendees.

Shecky's was a huge success. On paper I was the ultimate success story, the triumphant child of hard-working immigrants. I had money, public esteem as the female face of Shecky's, and the material accoutrements that come with living the glamourous life, yet I was the living embodiment of exactly the kind of self-centric mentality I've talked about. I was so caught up in achieving a superficial image of success measured by the savings in my bank account, the brand names I dressed in, and the VIP forums I was invited to—I thought this meant "I made it."

Yet even with all these things, I wasn't happy. Throughout my ten years at Shecky's I co-led the business with a partner whom I never fully agreed with when it came to our business's vision and culture. Our business soared in the early years because we were at the right place at the right time, but toward my later years at the company our arguments became more public, our innovations more stagnant, and our incompatibilities more detrimental to the business and culture. My worth was so tied to the business that my fear of losing everything I had worked to accomplish—reputation, social status, financial stability—overwhelmed me. It became all about me and my fears as opposed to worrying about something more meaningful and purposeful. As the business declined, so did my integrity. I found myself always putting Chris down, placing all the blame on him, and propping myself on a pedestal in defense of his attacks on me. Then in the summer of 2010 I hit rock bottom. I was on the phone with him, having the same argument we'd had a hundred times before, but this one did me in. I felt completely depleted, desperate, and miserable with negativity and exhaustion. Reaching this low point was the trigger that sent me out into the world searching for more meaning and kicked off what has now been a seven-year journey of spiritual discovery, personal growth, leadership development, and social impact.

The deep unhappiness and misery I felt led me down a path where I would discover one of my life's greatest *ahas*: our natural, "self-centric" way of living as human beings is totally backward, and it is only when we lead a life guided by something so much bigger than ourselves that greater peace, satisfaction, sufficiency, and self-love start to become more permanent feelings. Instead of a "me over we" mindset, we must learn to cultivate a "me for we" mindset that conveys our existence in the context and support of the greater society and planet. When we focus on serving and contributing to something much bigger than just me, myself, and I—our innate habits of self-judgment, comparison with others, caring about what others think, and when/then mentality start to disappear, and life can become more relaxed and fulfilling. If we can replace our own self-centric goals on our life's grand stage with a greater purpose that impacts a larger part of humanity, then all the worth we spend our lives trying to validate actually starts to become a reality in the most miraculous way. I will explain this more in upcoming chapters; be patient with me.

Now if you've done the work of personal growth, therapy, or coaching, the idea of serving others before serving yourself may sound ludicrous. We've been taught that we need to put ourselves and our self-care first in order to bring our best selves to our careers, families, and causes. I believe and preach this message too. But there is a difference between self-love and being self-centric. Self-love is keeping your bucket replenished and full so you can bring your most fit self to the external realms of your life like family, workplace, community, and neighbors. It is optimizing the health of your physical, mental, and financial state so you can best serve your life's purpose. Conversely, being self-centric is investing in all of these areas but for the sole purpose of serving yourself. Self-centric people mainly put themselves front and center on their own stage and spend their lives consumed in establishing their image, as defined by the societal clichés of making more money, being more popular, having more social media likes, wearing the right brands, living in the fancier house, and so on. In reality, the more we chase these superficial things, the further away we get from having sufficiency and peace. The satisfaction that comes from gaining the material is always temporary.

VIEW YOUR LIFE FROM
AN OUTSIDE-IN PERSPECTIVE

The self-centric and "me over we" mindset is a result of an inside-out view of life where we see the world and understand its events entirely from *our* personal perspective. Our opinions are formed based on our personal experiences, characteristics, and belief systems and no one else's. It is no surprise that we human beings get absorbed in our small perspectives because we go about every day forgetting that our human existence and the planet we reside on were created by a higher power that no human can ever fully understand. As I mentioned in the Author's Note, I refer to this higher power as God. Whether or not you are a believer of God or spirituality, please replace my mentions of God with a word that best describes your life source as you read this book, whether that's the universe, destiny, nature, karma, or another force.

Now allow me to stretch your perspectives and replace your inside-out view of life with an outside-in lens. Envision seeing your life from the viewpoint of this larger force: looking down on this planet and seeing yourself as one of the 7.3 billion people that were created to inhabit, share, and nurture the earth for your limited time here. Can you imagine that before you were even born, God or the universe had a vision for the greatest version of your life? That you were born with the birthright to be extraordinary and that your time and presence on earth would mean extraordinary achievements beyond your wildest dreams? That you would move mountains, leave a dent on the universe, and even change the world in a very specific way? And that the key to this success would be discovering not your purpose for yourself but the big-picture purpose for you beyond your day-to-day life?

So that your purpose will be fulfilled, two people came together to conceive and create you and give you the genetics you have. Every gene, every natural-born skill, every positive and negative experience, every relationship, every thought and feeling in your life has happened *for* you, not *to* you, to bring you closer to this purpose. Imagine if this source of power was watching your every move and listening to your every thought, sending you clues or signs in the form of visions, gut feelings, literature, people, and circumstances to see if you would take the bait to draw you to see this greater purpose. Sometimes challenges are thrown your way not to stop you but to direct you, protect you, or mature you in order to prepare you for your tremendous destiny and to build your integrity, strength, intellect, and character. For example, when conflict arises it is human nature to understand it solely from our personal perspective and to react with frustration, defensiveness, or disappointment. But if we see it from the outside-in perspective (what are the circumstances of the person that is upsetting me or what might this challenge be trying to tell me?), then we give that conflict more compassion and flexibility. If you think about it, the two most profound life experiences are birth and death. We start off as crying babies who are completely dependent on others and lack maturity and wisdom. It is our human journey to continually grow, learn, and develop throughout every life stage until we reach the end of life.

> "Every gene, every natural-born skill, every positive and negative experience, every relationship, every thought and feeling in your life has happened *for* you, not *to* you, to bring you closer to this purpose."

Having an outside-in lens on life shifts how we see ourselves, putting our individual identity in the context of the whole world so we can then be more considerate and conscious of what our being means for the whole world. If you can believe that you were created for a specific contribution to this world, then you're able to start thinking of your dreams, goals, actions, careers, and choices with not a self-centric mindset but a purpose-centric one. You shift away from your natural-born "me over we" instinct to a "me for we" one, and it is this way of living that provides the greatest form of fulfillment and self-worthiness that you can ever have. Just think of how good you feel when one person or a larger group of people tells you how profoundly you have helped them. There is zero insecurity, judgment, or lack in that feeling because it wasn't about you; it was about the other person or people you made a difference for. Instead, that feeling comes with abundance, power, sufficiency, worthiness, and pride—and you can have a life filled with these everlasting securities if you switch to a "me for we" mindset. The greatest lesson of my life was when I realized that *only* the purpose-centric path can lift us to that massive potential.

In fact, I believe the problems we face in today's world culture (violence, economic instability, terrorism, discrimination, sexism, poverty, divisive politics) exist as a result of people acting out of a self-centric, "me over we" mentality. I love using an organization as an example to convey this point. Imagine the planet is an organization. In order for the organization to thrive, it is the individuals, not the entity, who determine its success. These individuals who make up the organization must show up and put in the effort that ultimately enables the whole entity to thrive, and the better they are at doing this, the more each individual thrives inside of the organization. The more individuals thrive, the more their personal families and local communities thrive. Thus, everyone's success is a result of the quality of everyone's contribution to the whole organization. Similarly, if the entity functions poorly, then leadership at all levels is weak and morale is low. We need individuals at all levels, from the most junior to senior, caring and working to solve problems.

BEGIN WITH A "ME FOR WE" MINDSET

My true transformation began in 2010 when I started to learn about the "me for we" path driven by purpose and contribution to the greater good. But what would my purpose be? All of my discoveries pointed toward the global need for women's equality and empowerment:

- Leadership and business conferences I attended lacked women on stage and in the audience.

- Women's mentorship programs I attended limited their agendas to topics of work-life balance and networking.

- The women's forums that I did see focused on innovation, disruption, leadership, and gender equality and were either too elite and expensive for the average woman or too siloed and scattered to reflect the more mainstream set of modern women I fell into (too pink, too old-school women-in-suits, too feminist, too industry or topic specific).

- Mainstream female publications and outlets focused primarily on what makes women look good superficially (fashion, beauty, trendy places to shop and party), not on the substance that actually makes up women.

I had attended all-girls schools growing up as well as Smith College, so the feminist within me reawakened as I immersed myself in everything I could about the state of women. Reading Nicholas Kristof's and Sheryl WuDunn's book, *Half the Sky*, in 2010 opened my eyes to the devastating global oppression of women and girls, especially those in the developing world, and how they have been subjugated, enslaved, and killed for the simple fact of being female. The authors argue that if the abolition of slavery was the defining movement of the nineteenth century and the defeat of totalitarianism the struggle of the twentieth, then ending the oppression of women and girls globally is the fight that will define this century.

Sheryl Sandberg's commencement speech at Barnard's Class of 2011 sobered me to the stalling statistics of women's status:

> But the promise of equality is not equality. As we sit here looking at this magnificent blue-robed class, we have to admit something that's sad but true: men run the world. Of 190 heads of state, 9 are women. Of all the parliaments around the world, 13 percent of those seats are held by women. Corporate America top jobs, 15 percent are women; numbers which have not moved at all in the past nine years. Nine years. Of full professors around the United States, only 24 percent are women.[1]

So I left my role at leading a women's entertainment company to build a women's empowerment company, S.H.E. Globl Media, which officially launched in 2012. Today it is a leadership organization devoted to inspiring a new generation of thriving change agents. Through an annual experience of connection, education, and activation, we develop and empower female and male leaders to *rise* to their highest potential and *lift* others in the process so that gender equality is accelerated and achieved by 2030.

At the heart of my work today is taking individuals on a leadership growth journey, the same one I put myself through when I left Shecky's. First of all, I deeply asked myself, "What do I want in and for my life?" By this point I was already *committed* to getting it and most importantly, believed in myself that I could get it no matter what. So when I defined what I wanted, I realized that the "what" required a purpose, service, or positive impact greater than me. This, obviously, became empowering women, but empowerment in the very specific way that I had experienced it and with my professional knowledge of how to create and market event programming for women. Then I got brutally honest with myself about the internal and external factors, people, and habits that didn't serve this greater vision, and I took action to remove, distance myself, or forgive them. I invested my time in reading, coaching, conferences, yoga, and meditation as well as in a faith practice and attending church on Sundays. All of this strengthened my natural instincts to discern which lessons to keep and which to discard. Through these actions I developed a value system to live by and a mission statement to guide me; these continue to evolve and form as I continue to grow as a leader. I promised myself to always stretch instead of settle and choose courage over comfort because the glass ceiling is thicker in our minds than it is in the outside world. I journaled incessantly as a tool to manage my mind and better empower myself.

The life I'm leading today is so much different from the one I led seven years ago. The incredible transformation I have gone through has brought me the greatest joy, confidence, empowerment, freedom, and abundance that I have ever known. But that doesn't mean things are

> "I deeply asked myself, "'What do I want in and for my life?'"

easy for me now or that this kind of transformation happens overnight. Consciousness is only the first step. I struggled—and still struggle—with many of the negative feelings, self-imposed limitations, and self-centric habits that we're going to tackle in this book. I write this book far from being the perfect model at living this way but instead as a handbook on life and leadership for myself and for all of you. I'm here on the journey with you so that together we can help each other get better at this thing called life.

STOP LIVING YOUR LIFE *IN* THE WORLD; START LEADING YOUR LIFE *FOR* THE WORLD

This is a call to every single living person with basic means to step up their actions and improve the shared society we live and raise our families in. We must stop living our lives in the world (me over we) and instead lead our lives for the world (me for we). Otherwise, problems will continue to catch up with us like they already are. If we don't learn how to do this, we will continue to live in a lose-lose scenario where neither the external society nor the individual person can ever realize their fullest potential. We will never rise to the extraordinary purpose and glory that God (or your higher power) has destined for us.

People sometimes ask, "If there really is a God, why doesn't God simply put an end to conflict, suffering, violence, hunger, or poverty?" Well, guess what? I believe that God created a solution called *people* to do that. It's so easy for our self-centric, reactive, inside-out thinking minds to sit on the sidelines moaning about the issues, expecting others with powerful titles to improve our situations when we actually are and have the power. If we all saw the issues through an outside-in lens and operated from a "me for we" mindset, perhaps we would see that we are on this earth for a short period of time to use our extraordinary power to fix issues that we were created to fix (remember that you were created with a unique set of skills, experiences, blessings, and problems for specific reasons).

This book is a wake-up call to inform you that you are the leader you've been waiting for. The chapters that follow are divided into three parts. Part 1 focuses on how we got here and why we need people like you to lead. Leadership is not just politicians and CEOs; it's ordinary people seeing a problem they can help solve and doing something about it by becoming an agent for change. We'll discuss how personal issues become political issues and vice versa, why what happens everywhere else in the world affects and matters to you, and what the current state of feminism and masculinity looks like today. We also look at how empowering women and embracing feminine traits can help bring positive change and improve the world by orders of magnitude. And most importantly, we define the macro-movement, the collection of causes, campaigns, and organizations that are each contributing to the greater good.

After you've committed to owning your potential as a leader in Part I, we work on building the foundational habits that will free you from the egoistic, self-centric mindset and ignite your passion and purpose in Part II. It's human nature to live from the ego, which is why each of the thirteen pillars teach you strategies to deal with various aspects of daily life. The chapters in this section are like a toolkit and provide you with exercises and mantras you must practice every day. If your mind is a muscle, you need to work it out in order to improve it, otherwise it quickly gets out of shape. By internalizing these essential pillars, you will be setting yourself up with a rock-solid foundation that can withstand whatever obstacles come your way.

Finally, Part III brings it all together by showing you how to actually take action and execute your goals. To make your work as a leader sustainable, we talk about how to treat your life as the organization you're leading to make sure you don't drop the ball on important areas that make your life possible: health, relationships, and financial well-being. Leadership starts where you are, and I explain the ways in which you can make an impact without having to quit your day job or change your entire lifestyle. Finally, we dig into how and why lifting others will be the most important component of any good you accomplish.

The new leadership calls on all of us, both women and men, to live authentically and contribute meaningfully to the world we all share. At its very core, this way of leading is rooted in the belief that only when we lift others for a greater purpose can we rise to our highest potential. Earthly life is temporary, but each of us was brought here to do something incredible with our limited amount of time: make the world a better place before we leave it. So get ready to take on the challenge of your life and show the universe what you're made of. This is how we rise.

PART I

WELCOME TO
THE MACRO-MOVEMENT

1

Why You Can and Must
Lead Change in the World

"It falls to each of us to be those anxious, jealous guardians
of our democracy; to embrace the joyous task we've been
given to continually try to improve this great nation of ours.
Because for all our outward differences, we all share the
same proud title: Citizen."

—BARACK OBAMA, FORTY-FOURTH PRESIDENT
OF THE UNITED STATES

In day-to-day life we are mainly consumed by our personal lives and families and think less about the external world we live in, and this makes it easy to forget that we have the individual power and ability to change what we feel is wrong or broken in the outside world. We get so preoccupied with managing everything on our plate that it's natural to think, *Who the heck has the time to take care of other people's problems when I can barely stay on top of my own?* I understand where you're coming from. (Life can get so busy that you feel you're just operating in survival mode, which is why Part II of this book will give you thirteen foundational tools ranging from how serving others will actually simplify your life to how defining what matters allows you to manage it all.)

It's critical that each and every one of us acknowledge our personal power in our communities. As a resident of your neighborhood, a parent at your children's school, an employee at your organization or company, a professional in your industry, and a citizen of your country, you have a shared interest in the success of these communities. All of us can agree that too many things are broken in this world; I believe that the movement for gender equality provides the best starting point to address almost all the issues afflicting the world, and I'll tell you why in the chapters to come. Right now what's most important to realize is that every day is an opportunity for you and me to step up and solve a problem.

The reality, however, is that most people don't step up. The majority of us can be complacent, passive, and inactive when it comes to stepping up for the greater good. Instead we expect those with titles like president, CEO, owner, VP, congressman, or mayor to lead our schools, workplaces, cities, states, and countries—or we expect organizational structures like government, corporations, activists, and NGOs to keep everything just and running. Yet when something disturbing or disastrous happens, we are quick to blame those traditional leaders and entities. We can blame and complain without the self-awareness or consciousness that maybe we can be the leaders to create the change we want to see. And we certainly don't examine our own role in the issue.

To put this into perspective, consider this: the most basic, low-effort opportunity we have to improve our country and stand up for issues that matter to us is using our voting power to put the right candidates in office. Yet voter turnout in the United States is routinely low and trails behind most other developed nations.[1] In the 2016 US presidential election voter turnout plummeted to 57 percent of eligible voters, down from 61.6 percent in 2008. Interestingly, voter turnout levels remained the same in states that voted for Donald Trump and dropped an average of 2.4 percent in states that voted for Hillary Clinton; however, turnout surged in competitive states, and the majority of those voters cast ballots for Donald Trump.[2] If more voters had showed up in swing states and realized that their votes do matter, the election might have resulted in a different outcome.

Another example of citizen inaction is the decline in the number of people volunteering their time for issues that relate to a personal vulnerability or experience. For example, if someone has been a victim of sexual assault or discrimination in an industry dominated by one gender or because of their sexual orientation or race, how often will they publicly support an organization related to that cause? According to a US Bureau of Labor Statistics study, volunteerism dropped to a ten-year low in 2014, at 25.4 percent of the total population; the drop was especially large among educated people with a bachelor's degree or higher, though education is usually the best predictor that someone will volunteer.[3] Civic engagement has also fallen globally, so the average voter turnout in presidential and parliamentary elections throughout the world is not much better, at 66 percent.[4] It amazes me how certain citizens can kick and scream about the change they want, yet many of them fail to take advantage of their most essential right—that of the ballot.

One of the biggest reasons people are not participating is fear—fear of failure, fear of being criticized, fear of making decisions, and fear of having to take responsibility when things go wrong.[5] But we should be more afraid of what happens when we don't participate. When you fail to act, you're actually giving up your power and letting others make decisions for you and your families on a public policy level and a personal lifestyle level. You're letting others decide your right to get paid after having a child, the quality of food served at your kid's school, the corporate culture you work in, the career growth opportunities available to you, and the public safety of your neighborhood. When you fail to use your voice, you are letting somebody else speak for you.

"Have you ever considered that you could be the leader you and your community have been waiting for?"

It's easy to forget that it is the individuals who comprise entities, not the entities themselves, who move progress forward and drive success and innovation. We forget that change happens only when some*one* stands up and takes the initiative to lead. Have you ever considered that you could be the leader you and your community have been waiting for?

And if you haven't, can you take a few minutes to ponder why not? Is your answer good enough to satisfy you?

WHY LEADING CHANGE IN THE WORLD MATTERS TO YOU

It's clear I'm trying to convince you to become a purpose-centric leader and lead your life for the world. If the benefit to the world at large seems too abstract, consider these three major reasons why leadership should matter to you. They may help to illustrate the immediate effect that leading change can have in your own life.

1. **The Family Reason.** If we don't act, speak up, and fight against injustices, we let others who may lack integrity and our best interests in mind to determine the living standards of our current family unit as well as our children's family and the next generation to come (and the next, and the next). You see, the quality of your character and achievements shapes the quality of what your children's characters and achievements will become and that continues to get passed on. If you are a hard-working, loving parent who provides well, that's great. But what if you could stand for something more, like being someone who really made a difference for the greater good? Imagine what that role modeling could do for your children and their generational lineage? Or, if you don't have children of your own, for nieces, nephews, or other children who may look up to you?

2. **The Humanity Reason.** Can you imagine that the world is a body and that you and every human alive right now are a part that body? When you lead a positive external change—something that is not just good for your personal self but for others too—the whole body and universe benefit. Whatever the issue you take action on, think about the number of people who experience that issue and how many of them you could

personally help. Sure you can say, "Well, other people are living selfishly, so why shouldn't I?" But answer this: Which person do you want to be in the world—the selfish one or the courageous one?

3. **The Spiritual Reason.** For those of you who are spiritual in some way, you believe there is a greater existence or power outside of your pure physical being, right? One of my favorite pastors, Rick Warren, likes to use this analogy: imagine that the nine months you spent in your mother's womb prepared you for earthly life (the phase you're in now), but what you do with your earthly life is meant to prepare you for the next phase of spiritual life, which may even be eternal. If you say you are indeed spiritual, then owning that commitment means you believe in a greater consciousness that is always watching and tracking your integrity, contributions, and impact for the earth. For those of you who are not spiritual, consider it this way: what you do in this lifetime determines the legacy you leave behind. Regardless of whether you believe there is a next life after this one, don't you want people to remember you in a positive and impactful way?

We owe thanks for all the privileges, rights, and innovations we enjoy today to those with "me for we" mindsets—individuals who fought wars against slavery, persevered through physical violence and political persecution, and created inventions and products to advance civilization and improve lives. Really absorb this point. All the opportunities and blessings you get to experience today are owed to your ancestors and courageous, purpose-centric leaders. Because of suffragettes like Susan B. Anthony and Elizabeth Cady Stanton, who began campaigning in the 1840s, American women gained the right to vote in 1920. Marie Curie's pioneering research on radium and uranium lead to the modern X-ray, and she became the first woman to win a Nobel Prize. In the 1960s Martin Luther King Jr. fought to end segregation and secure civil rights for all Americans, regardless of the color of their skin. Rosa Parks refused to give up her seat to a white passenger on a bus in Alabama and sparked a nationwide movement against the segregation of public facilities. Gloria Steinem and Betty Friedan led second-wave feminism in the United States and paved the way for career women.

Each of these people has made history by standing up for a greater, societal good they believed in. As you read through the rest of this book, these are the kinds of role models I want you to compare yourself to. Not to the ordinary, but to the extraordinary. You have one shot at this earthly life, and I don't want your attitude to be *Who am I to do this?* but instead *Who am I* not *to do this?* I humbly implore you to consider a life of leadership because for every human who fails to take action, there is a humanity progress deficit. When you don't contribute your destined, natural-born talents, the world misses out big time on your effort.

> "When you don't contribute your destined, natural-born talents, the world misses out big time on your effort."

THE PERSONAL IS POLITICAL

Many of us think the personal problems we deal with are just that: personal. In reality the issues you confront in your everyday life are also political issues, and you're probably not the only one suffering from them. If you're a working parent, you or your partner may have had to take unpaid leave when the baby arrived because of paltry maternity leave policies. If you are a member of the LGBTQIA community, you didn't have the right to legally marry your same-sex partner until 2015, and it's still unclear which public bathroom you should use if you're transgender. Maybe you or a friend has been sexually assaulted at some point, and that has deeply affected your self-esteem and ability to form healthy relationships. You might suffer from a chronic health condition like lupus but can't get healthcare coverage, or you developed asthma as a child because of exposure to pollution. Perhaps you are racially profiled by the police on a regular basis simply because of the way you look. Someone in your family might be struggling with mental illness or an addiction of some sort, but they're afraid to seek help out of shame. Maybe you were raised by a single parent or are a single working parent yourself who is struggling to make ends meet. Do any of these scenarios sound familiar to you? Each one of these challenges represents a social issue (childcare, LGBTQIA rights, healthcare, racism, unconscious bias, mental illness, job creation), or what I like to call *movements*, that needs fueling. Working to achieve gender equality and address women's issues has implications for each of these movements.

Because my career is centered in women's empowerment, let's focus on women's issues for a moment. Historically women were meant to be seen but not heard, and the problems and concerns that affected them were often kept hush-hush and considered inappropriate for polite conversation. The taboos around many female difficulties—menstruation, miscarriage, postpartum depression, fertility issues, body image, domestic abuse, sexual assault—are still pervasive in the twenty-first century. We all know women continue to experience gender discrimination and inequality in all spheres of society, but what we may not know is how much of this you or your close friends are unconsciously experiencing and affected by.

For example, if you're killing yourself to impress your boss and get a promotion, guess what? The men at your company already get paid more to do the same amount of work. If you're a woman who wants to start a business and raise capital, guess what? From 2010 to 2015 only 10 percent of venture dollars globally went to start-ups with at least one female founder.[6] Women outlive men in every country around the world, yet because of the pay gap, they're more likely to retire with less money saved. In fact, both young and old women are falling far behind in financial literacy because they are undereducated and underrepresented in the industry[7]; 86 percent of investment advisers are men.[8]

"The personal is political" was actually a rallying cry for the women's liberation movement in the sixties and seventies because it highlighted the links between lived personal experiences and the corresponding need for social and political change. "Personal problems are political problems. There are no personal solutions at this time. There is only collective action for a collective solution," Carol Hanisch wrote in her 1970 essay that established the term.[9] My intention is not to tell you something jaw-dropping and new but simply to put the sentence at the front of your mind. Personal problems won't get solved unless you and I are courageous enough to take positive action (the chapter on courage will prepare you for this).

POLITICAL ISSUES ARE
YOUR ISSUES

When you read the news it's easy to think that problems in far-off places—or even problems in the same city but on a different street—don't affect you. But whether or not you feel the effects now, the man who was shot because of his skin color or the girl who was raped on her way to school does threaten you. Here's why: the ripple effect of inequality gets back to all of us, and eventually you or someone you know will suffer because of one of these problems. As Martin Luther King Jr. famously wrote in his "Letter from a Birmingham Jail" in 1963, "Injustice anywhere is a threat to justice everywhere. We are caught in an inescapable network of mutuality, tied in a single garment of destiny. Whatever affects one directly, affects all indirectly." The World Economic Forum puts it this way: "We live in a fast-paced and interconnected world where breakthrough technologies, demographic shifts and political transformations have far-reaching societal and economic consequences."[10] No country, state, or town is an island in today's globalized world where everyone is just a Wifi connection or plane ride away. The ripple effect works both ways: positive action works to improve the world for everyone, and negative actions cause problems that hurt everyone in one way or another.

THE MULTIPLICATION BENEFITS
OF YOUR LEADERSHIP

When you decide to lead change in the world, your actions will multiply benefits. First, the people who are impacted by the cause you're leading change for will obviously benefit. If you champion a corporate culture initiative that brings women and men together to create a more gender-diverse culture, those employees will start feeling more represented and supported in their careers and will probably perform better. If you run an organization that aims to curb food waste by delivering leftovers from events or businesses to people in need, you're giving someone a hot meal and making sure they don't go hungry. If you're an environmental activist fighting for stricter restrictions on pollution, the results of your work will make the world a healthier place and preserve the earth for the generations to come. When we call attention to an issue that affects a marginalized group or topic, what we're really saying is that these groups and topics are important and their issues are worth fighting for. By naming a problem and giving it airtime, we start to chip away at the social stigma that exists around it.

Second, your act of leading will model what it means to be a leader. Many people can consume inspiration from you, realize it may not be so inaccessible after all, and then in turn want to inspire others like you do. They decide to step up and become leaders too. I have to imagine that every entrepreneur, leader, and change maker out there are products of the role models they looked up to. In fact, as Liz Wiseman's work on *The Multiplier Effect* has shown, the best leaders are those who produce more great leaders by amplifying the intelligence and abilities of those around them.[11] Multipliers are leaders who not only know how to attract and cultivate talent but also inspire and challenge others to stretch their potential and deliver results that exceed expectations.

Last, your service as a leader will make you feel more fulfilled and affirmed. Service not only makes you feel good but is also good for you. For example, adults who regularly serve others or a larger cause are more likely to have lower blood pressure and longer lifespans.[12] On top of the health benefits, serving others boosts self-esteem, psychological well-being, overall happiness, and a feeling of connectedness—communities with lots of service-oriented people are better places to live.[13] You know what I mean. Think about that feeling you get after you receive a thank-you letter or email of appreciation for helping someone, when people rush up to you after a talk or speech you've given and express how much your words inspired them, when you learn about a fruitful collaboration that has formed between two people you introduced, or when you witness a massive achievement by someone you mentored.

Today 7.3 billion people make up this world. Imagine what society would look like if every one of them committed to lead a positive change. Could innovations occur every minute; climate change be solved; wars, terrorism, and acts of violence ended; global poverty obliterated, clean drinking water made available to all, girls and boys be valued equally, and so on? This has to start somewhere. It needs to start with you and me pursuing leadership, acting as role models, initiating its ripple effect, and making the desire to fulfill one's purpose so contagious that we will unleash the potential of this population.

2

Gender Equality and the Priority to Lift Women

"Women speaking up for themselves and for those around them is the strongest force we have to change the world."

—MELINDA GATES, COCHAIR AND TRUSTEE OF THE
BILL & MELINDA GATES FOUNDATION

In the last chapter we talked about many social problems that need solving, but when I think about the most efficient starting point—that is, a big-tent social issue that, if addressed first, could create a ripple effect of progress across most other issues—it's the acceleration and achievement of global gender equality.

UTILIZING OUR WORLD'S GREATEST UNTAPPED NATURAL RESOURCE

To me gender equality is an effective place to start.

Hillary Clinton famously said, "Women are the largest untapped reservoir of talent in the world." Similarly, one of the most successful businessmen in the world, Warren Buffett, has claimed that one of the reasons for his success is the fact that he's had to compete against only half the population.[1] If we apply the outside-in lens to the state of the world's nations, communities, institutions, and governments, we realize that none of these entities have ever operated at their full potential because they're not utilizing one of the greatest natural resources that humanity has always provided: women and the diversity of opinions, traits, and talents that they bring.

Research shows that feminine traits are a new form of innovation because it gives leaders a competitive edge.[2] After interviewing and surveying thousands of people around the world for the book *The Athena Doctrine*, authors John Gerzema and Michael D'Antonio concluded that "people had grown frustrated by a world dominated by what they saw as traditionally masculine thinking and behavior: codes of control, competition, aggression, and black-and-white thinking that have contributed to many of the problems we face today, from wars and income inequality to reckless risk-taking and scandal."[3] In fact, two-thirds of their respondents, including the majority of men, felt that the world would be a better place if more people embraced typically feminine traits and more women participated in government leadership. Interestingly enough, Gerzema and D'Antonio discovered that the traits most closely identified with successful leaders—humility, cooperation, empathy, patience, flexibility, candor, vulnerability, reliability, and trustworthiness—also demonstrated "aspects of human nature that are widely regarded as feminine."[4]

> "Moreover, when we empower women, we unleash their talent for compassion, collaboration, and communication, which can then be applied to solving other issues in our communities."

A coalition of nations is now banking on the "Third Billion"—the population of women in both developing and industrialized countries poised to enter the economic mainstream in the coming decade—to fuel economic growth and stability.[5] This group of women is an enormous, untapped economic force that rivals the populations of China and India, countries with more than a billion people each. If we look at things strictly based on the global numbers, it's easy to see that the world is not benefiting from a huge segment of its human population.

When we think about inequality today, there are countless diversity groups fighting for causes related to ethnicity, sexual orientation, gender, physical ability, poverty, addiction, and abuse that we want to empower and that absolutely need representation. So why start with gender equality? Rooting our activism in gender equality and lifting women first actually impacts the greatest number of people and reaches the broadest spectrum of identities because the issues that affect women also affect the same people who make up the diversity of groups listed above. If your cause is women of color, women veterans, or equal pay, we need to make the case that *all women* are equal first. If your cause is lifting people out of poverty and hardship, women and girls make up 70 percent of the world's poor.[6] If your cause is aiding people who face violence, abuse, and sexual assault, one in three women worldwide experiences physical or sexual violence, most commonly from an intimate partner.[7] If your cause is sanitation and clean drinking water in developing countries, the task of fetching water (sometimes hours away) disproportionately falls to women and girls.[8] If your cause is education, there are 62 million girls in the world who are not in school today because of poverty, lack of healthcare, forced marriage, or simply because they are girls.[9] On the positive side, if your cause is innovating within an industry like healthcare, government, or finance, there is an enormous population of untapped talent available to you. When it comes to environmental sustainability, women "have emerged as a force, not only in support of proper environmental management, but also in demands for better quality of life and greater social equity.[10] Moreover, when we empower women, we unleash their talent for compassion, collaboration, and communication, which can then be applied to solving other issues in our communities. Although I am encouraging you to center your leadership through a gender equality lens, in Chapter 4 I will provide you with a visual context for how you can lead change behind specific causes that are most authentic and passionate for you.

GENDER EQUALITY IS CRITICAL FOR EVERYONE— NOT JUST FOR WOMEN

When you hear the term *gender equality*, it's easy to assume it only addresses advancing women when, in fact, it's critical for everyone. Michael Kimmel, founder of the Center for the Study of Men and Masculinity at Stony Brook University, asks, "Why do we automatically think of women when we hear the word gender?" in his TED Talk on gender equality. Despite perceptions, gender equality is not a zero-sum game where one sex wins and the other loses. Creating true parity between the sexes will bring about a win-win situation for all.

GENDER EQUALITY IS CRITICAL FOR MARRIAGES AND MEN. According to Kimmel, egalitarian relationships between women and men lead to greater happiness and higher levels of marital satisfaction for both partners. Surveys show that men, especially younger men, want to balance work and family life by being part of a dual-career, dual-caregiver couple. They also want to be involved fathers. Men are healthier, smoke and drink less, are more likely to do routine checkups with their doctor, and are less likely to get treated for depression when they share housework and childcare responsibilities. Best of all, when men share work equally with women, they have more sex.

GENDER EQUALITY IS CRITICAL FOR CHILDREN. The traditional family institution is composed of women and men raising the girls and boys they bring into the world, and though we now live in an era when parenting can also comprise LGBTQIA couples and single parents and when gender norms are shifting, especially in the eyes of young people, it's critical that we role model how all sexes are equal and have equal opportunities so that our sons and daughters can grow up believing they can be anything they want to be. There's a great saying that "you cannot be what you cannot see," and it's our responsibility to shape a society that reflects the diversity of who is in it. That means learning and addressing challenges that each sex faces.

GENDER EQUALITY IS CRITICAL FOR COMPANIES. When women lead in greater numbers in the professional world, companies benefit economically and socially. A 2016 Morgan Stanley report suggests that gender-diverse companies yield more profits; among the stocks ranked at the top of their global stock selection, stocks with higher gender diversity outperformed those with lower gender diversity.[11] Research also shows that more gender-diverse companies have less job turnover and lower rates of attrition, employees are happier and more productive, and recruiting efforts are more successful when workplaces are more gender equal.[12] The more female executives a company has, the better it performs,[13] and according to Catalyst, companies that have women directors on their boards attain a significantly higher financial performance.[14] Moreover, if there were more women in executive, decision-making roles, corporations would have an imperative to create better paternity-leave policies.

> "The global movement to lift and empower women to equality is not only a priority; it is also a necessity for the well-being of our families and the innovations of our nations."

GENDER EQUALITY IS CRITICAL FOR COUNTRIES. The positive effects of gender equality carry over to the national level too. It turns out that countries that are more gender equal score higher in overall happiness, and their citizens have longer life expectancies.[15] Myriad studies show that when women have equal access to education, work, and healthcare, they help sustain a more peaceful and prosperous world.[16] If there were more women elected to government, chances are we'd be fighting fewer wars, making more commonsense compromises, and channeling badly needed resources to health and education. When it comes to economics, a larger workforce leads to greater stimulation and increased GDP. As it turns out, if American women didn't enter the workforce in the millions like they did, then US GDP would have been 11 percent lower in 2012 (that's $1.7 trillion dollars lost).[17] On a global level, securing equal economic opportunities for women could raise the world GDP by $28 trillion before 2025.[18]

All of the evidence points in the same direction: leveling the playing field between genders in the workplace, at home, and in society will benefit everyone. After all, feminism is not the advancement of women over men but "granting women political, social, and economic equality with men."[19] The global movement to lift and empower women to equality is not only a priority; it is also a necessity for the well-being of our families and the innovations of our nations.

WELL OVER ONE HUNDRED YEARS AWAY

Progress has been made toward advancing women in society and the workplace over the last several decades, giving them control over their educations, careers, finances, relationships, and reproductive rights. But don't be fooled: we are light-years away from getting to global gender equality. According to the World Economic Forum, the global economic gap between men and women has narrowed by only 3 percent in the last ten years. True equality across health, education, economic opportunity, and politics is projected to be another 170 years away.[20] And one in four Americans thinks that humans colonizing Mars is more likely to happen before half of all Fortune 500 CEOs are women.[21] Unfortunately, the rest of the world would likely agree with that sentiment.

Women face alarming barriers to equality both in the developed and developing world. Keep in mind that the issues women in developed nations face can vary drastically in comparison to the issues women in still-developing countries contend with.

In the developed world women have experienced inequalities or injustice in the realms of career (equal pay, maternity leave), relationships (gender roles, household responsibilities), safety (domestic abuse, rape), and health (sexuality, pregnancy). The pay gap in the workplace is real; on average, American women make 20 to 30 cents per doller less than men do.[22] Sexual harassment continues to go unchecked in many organizations, with minimal consequences even when inappropriate behavior is brought to light. When it comes to self-esteem, women are also the more self-critical gender. Because they're taught to be perfect, they frequently avoid taking risks that would lead them down the path of leadership.

Girls are under more pressure than ever not only to excel in school but also to conform to unrealistic standards of beauty. The following tables offer a deeper look at women's issues relating to confidence, the workplace, financial literacy, and entrepreneurship:

TABLE 2.1.
WOMEN AND CONFIDENCE

- Only 4 percent of women consider themselves beautiful.

- 53 percent of thirteen-year-old American girls say they are "unhappy with their bodies." This number skyrockets to 78 percent by the time girls turn seventeen.

- 74 percent of girls feel pressured to please everyone.

- 90 percent of eating disorders are found in girls.

- An eight-year study that analyzed data from 985,000 women and men across forty-eight countries concluded that men have higher self-esteem than women regardless of country or culture.

- The confidence gap between men and women is greater in industrialized nations than in developing ones.

- Women and men begin their careers equally confident about reaching top management, but women's confidence declines with experience.

Sources: Confidence Coalition (2017); Dove (2013); Heart of Leadership (2017); Nextshark (2015); Warrell (2016).

TABLE 2.2.
WOMEN AND THE WORKFORCE

- In the United States the pay gap across all occupations is 77.5 percent, which means women earn about 77 cents to every dollar a man earns.

- As recently as 2016 women made up only 4.4 percent of Fortune 500 CEOs in the United States.

- The higher a woman is promoted, the less likely she is to earn the same amount as a man.

- 50 percent of law school students are women, yet women make up only 20 percent of law firm partners.

- Women account for only 26 percent of people employed in computer and mathematical occupations.

- The average working woman will have lost more than $430,000 during her working lifetime compared to men due to the wage gap.

- Mothers are the sole or primary source of income in more than 40 percent of US households.

Sources: Catalyst (2016); Catalyst (2017); Henson (2015); Schwartz (2015); US Department of Labor (2017).

TABLE 2.3.

WOMEN AND FINANCIAL LITERACY

- Only 45 percent of working women in the United States participate in a retirement plan.

- Men tend to have higher average account balances across all employer retirement plans.

- 42 percent of women lack financial security.

- Less than 20 percent of women feel "very prepared" to make wise financial decisions, yet only 35 percent use a professional financial adviser.

- Lower lifetime earning potential combined with longer lifespans leave many women unprepared for retirement. Three out of five women over sixty-five are unable to cover their basic needs.

- 86 percent of women don't know how to invest or choose a financial product.

- 50 percent of millennial women compared to 61 percent of their male counterparts have started saving for retirement.

_____

Sources: Go Girl Finance (2016); The Money Post (2016).

TABLE 2.4.
WOMEN AND ENTREPRENEURSHIP

- Women started only 36.8 percent of new businesses in 2015, while men started 63.2 percent.

- 94 percent of the decision makers at venture capital firms are male.

- Start-ups that have at least One female founder account for only 18 percent of all start-ups in the United States.

- The number of women entrepreneurs is approaching the twenty-year low that was recorded in 2008. There was more gender equity in this respect in 1996 than there was in 2017.

- Palo Alto and San Jose—in the heart of Silicon Valley—have the smallest percentage of female founders. Las Vegas has the highest, at 26 percent.

- 90 percent of the $114 billion invested by venture capital never sees a female founder.

- According to the National Women's Business Council, men start their businesses with six times the amount of capital as women.

- Nearly half of female founders say that the dearth of mentors and advisers is holding them back.

Sources: Calhoun (2015); Dishman (2015); Entrepreneur (2004).

TABLE 2.5.
WOMEN GLOBALLY

- 2 million girls disappear from the world every year due to gender discrimination.

- Every two minutes a woman dies during pregnancy or childbirth.

- Women do 66 percent of the world's work but earn only 10 percent of the world's income and own 1 percent of the world's property.

- 700 million women alive in 2017 were married as children (below eighteen years of age).

- 1 in 5 women will experience rape in her lifetime.

- In 2017 there are 200 million women and girls who have undergone female genital mutilation across thirty countries.

- Around eight hundred thousand people are trafficked across international borders each year, of which women and girls make up 70 to 80 percent.

- 74 percent of new HIV/AIDS infections are in women, primarily between the ages of fifteen and twenty-four.

- More than 855 million adults, 70 percent of whom are women, are illiterate.

Sources: Gross (2016); Kristof and WuDunn (2010); UN Women (2016); WHO (2016).

On the global scale in developing worlds the problems women and girls face make first-world problems look like a walk in the park—these women have to deal with threats to their existence on a daily basis. I'm talking about walking hours to collect clean water, lacking proper medical care during pregnancy, getting raped on the bus to work, or being kidnapped while looking for firewood. Women in developing countries are routinely subjected to violence, slavery, and discrimination simply for being female. The reality is that more girls have been killed from "gendercide" over the past fifty years than men were killed in all the wars of the twentieth century. Poverty is sexist; women make up 70 percent of the 1.4 billion people who live in extreme poverty globally.[23] In addition to working for a salary, women also do more unpaid domestic labor than men in every country in the world.[24] In sub-Saharan Africa, Oceania, and Western Asia, girls still face barriers to entering both primary and secondary school, and women around the world are much more likely to be illiterate.[25]

DON'T GET FRUSTRATED— GET MOTIVATED

The cold, hard facts of how disadvantaged women really are is sobering and deeply discouraging. But try not to get too down thinking about it because, in fact, we are still early on in the history of the women's movement.

We are currently in what I consider to be the fourth wave of the women's movement. For me it started when the book *Half the Sky* was published in 2009 and opened our eyes to this era's most pervasive human rights violation: the oppression of women and girls in the developing world. The late 2000s and 2010s have birthed and continue to birth a high volume of powerful movements through events, organizations, campaigns, and books that lift women in some capacity. Everyone experiences history differently, but for me the following timeline clearly marked a new era of the women's revolution.

2009—*Half the Sky* by Nicholas Kristof and Sheryl WuDunn comes out and uncovers the oppression, violence, and poverty women and girls around the world experience. The book becomes a national best-seller and has a huge impact on readers, ranging from people like Tom Brokaw and Melinda Gates to Angelina Jolie and George Clooney.

2010—TEDWomen launches and creates a cross-disciplinary program to explore who today's women leaders are and how they are reshaping the future.

2011—The documentary *Miss Representation,* directed by Jennifer Siebel Newsom and Kimberlee Acquaro, highlights the underrepresentation of women in roles of power in the United States and the media's portrayal of them.

2012—Anne Marie Slaughter's article "Why Women Still Can't Have It All" in the *Atlantic* goes viral and sparks controversy and discussion in communities across the country about the work-life balance challenges that working women still deal with.

2012—Malala Yousafzai, a Pakistani activist, is shot by the Taliban on her way to school for being an outspoken proponent of girls' education. She becomes an international symbol for girls' rights and later receives the Nobel Peace Prize in 2014 at age seventeen for her work to promote the right to education for all children.

2012—Lena Dunham's show *Girls,* which chronicles the career aspirations and love lives of four millennial friends in New York, premieres on HBO and becomes a controversial hit for representing modern feminist culture.

2013—Sheryl Sandberg's book *Lean In,* based on her 2010 TED Talk, becomes a best-seller and reveals that the situation for women in corporate America hasn't improved as much as we think it has.

2014—Pop music's most famous icon, Beyoncé, closes the MTV Video Music Awards with a medley performance of songs from her self-titled album and ends with an emotional rendition of "Flawless" with the word FEMINIST in all caps emblazoned across the screen behind her.

2016—Hillary Clinton becomes the first woman nominated for president by a major party in American history and runs a tireless campaign against her rival Donald Trump. Although she loses the Electoral College, she wins the popular vote by more than 2 million votes.

2017—The Women's March, the largest protest in American history, takes place in Washington, DC, and cities around the world the day after Donald Trump is inaugurated as the forty-fifth president of the United States.[27] Nearly 5 million people—women, men, and children—participate across all seven continents, including Antarctica.[28]

I believe the invigoration and energy around women's rights that we've seen in the last few years is so progressive and pervasive that this fourth wave might be the final one to get us to equality—but only if we keep fueling the fire. We're seeing active participation from media coverage to fashion magazines, corporations to governments, grade school classrooms to universities, celebrities to male CEOs. Actor Jeffrey Wright captured the current sentiment perfectly when he tweeted, "May the election of Trump bring forth the fiercest, smartest, toughest generation of ass-kicking women this country could possibly imagine," which has been retweeted almost eighty thousand times.[29]

THE ROAD TO THE FOURTH WAVE

The best way to navigate the path ahead is to understand the road that got us here in the first place.

The first wave of feminism, which gained momentum in the 1800s thanks to leaders like Elizabeth Cady Stanton, Susan B. Anthony, and Sojourner Truth, sought to increase women's political power by securing the right to vote. Suffragists rejoiced when the Nineteenth Amendment was finally ratified into law in 1920.

The official legalization of "the pill" in 1960 ushered in the second wave, which focused on issues around sexuality and reproductive rights. Radicalized feminists, spurred by trailblazers like Betty Friedan and Gloria Steinem, began shedding what they called the oppressive artifacts of the fairer sex—bras, girdles, high heels, and makeup—in exchange for greater personal and professional freedom. A set of landmark cases, *Roe v. Wade* in 1973 and *Planned Parenthood v. Casey* in 1992, legalized and affirmed a woman's right to abortion.

Despite all the great progress made during the second wave, a backlash against the movement and its purported male-bashing set in during the late nineties. For third wavers feminism became a dirty word. This new generation of women was characterized by their individuality and distanced themselves from the "messy legacy" their mothers left behind.[26] In 1991 Anita Hill brought public attention to sexual harassment in the workplace when she made an accusation against Clarence Thomas during his Senate confirmation hearings for Supreme Court justice. But because of the third wave's individualistic slant, the movement lacked cohesion and never truly took off. The underground feminist punk movement Riot Grrrl made waves in the Pacific Northwest in the early nineties, and Eve Ensler's *The Vagina Monologues* gained some momentum following its 1996 off-Broadway run, but in the late 1900s and 2000s mainstream culture was hooked on *Sex and the City* and focused on women's vanity, rather than on women's equality.

Though the current state of women and inequality presents a painful and frustrating reality, we can all turn pain into progress and become motivated to create a new reality. We forget just how early on in the movement we are. In the United States, the most powerful country in the world, women haven't even had the right to vote for a hundred years. That milestone is still three years from now, which means you and I have the opportunity to be a part of a critical, "earlier" generation that helped make gender equality a reality. I love to look into the future thirteen years from now and imagine that the global goal of reaching gender equality by 2030 (set by the United Nation's Sustainable Development Goals) was made possible because of my current generation's efforts, which built upon the work of the feminists who came before us. In 2030 I will be fifty-four years old, my son, Jackson, will be fifteen, and my daughter, Arya, will be thirteen. They will live in a world where girls have the same opportunities as boys, especially in areas like science and math—and they can't even fathom anything different. They will know that their mom made a big contribution to this equality, along with countless others who had the will to fight. If you want the same thing, don't feel frustrated—feel motivated. Don't feel exhausted—feel exhilarated.

THE NEW FEMININE POWER

The amazing news is that the time is *now* for you to start that corporate initiative, speak up in your workplace, launch that business, build a viral campaign, write that book, start that blog or website, jump back into the workforce after stay-at-home caregiving, and volunteer more time to that cause. There is a new feminine power today that women innately possess, and a new generation of women and men are relying on these feminine traits to innovate. The twenty-first century is the most feminine generation we've seen in history, characterized by a millennial/gen Z culture that rejects all gender stereotypes. Not to mention that social media overflows with new women's hashtags every day, building on the #LeanIn, #GirlBoss, and #LikeAGirl slogans to remind us that the "future is female."

Right now in the fourth wave there is a spectacular momentum for women characterized by opportunities I've outlined below. And if you don't have a life vest, it's okay: there are plenty of women's communities that will jump in to support you.

- **Increased resources and investment funds for female entrepreneurs.** A recent boom in the number of female-focused venture-capital firms has helped stimulate more investments in female-founded tech start-ups. Today there are more than half a dozen female-run venture capital funds, like Female Founders Fund, Aspect Ventures, and Cowboy Ventures, that actively seek out and invest in female-founded companies.[30] There are also numerous investment funds and accelerator programs specifically targeted at women, such as Goldman Sachs's 10,000 Women Initiative and Circular Board, as well as conferences like DWEN, Summit by Dell and digital courses like Marie Forleo's B-School.

- **Increased coaches and coaching platforms to empower women in business, confidence, health, and fertility.** Authors like Gabby Bernstein offer free content online for women in addition to mastermind classes, online courses, and webinars. Rha Goddess platform, Move the Crowd, helps women and men become social entrepreneurs, whereas women's wellness experts Aimee Raupp and Alisa Vitti give advice on fertility and hormonal health.

- **Increased empowerment or femme marketing campaigns.** The traditional fashion ad with too-tight jeans and spilling cleavage might just go the way of the dinosaurs because advertisers are finally getting smart and connecting with women on substantive topics. Companies that sell beauty and feminine health products are also tuning in to issues that impact women. The brand Always created the #LikeAGirl campaign to stop the confidence-drop girls face when they reach puberty, while

Dove's Self-Esteem Project empowers women to have a positive relationship with the way they look.

- **Increased celebrities drawing attention to women's rights and social change.** Celebrity endorsements are the best advertising a campaign can get. By drawing attention to women's issues in real life and on the screen, stars like Angelina Jolie, who has done humanitarian work with the UN, and Jessica Alba, founder of the entrepreneurial venture the Honest Company, are diversifying their talents and demonstrating that they're more than pretty faces. Whether it's Beyoncé making a statement on marital infidelities with her visual album *Lemonade* or Patricia Arquette broaching the topic of equal pay in her 2016 Oscar Award speech, celebrities are making feminism popular and trendy for the masses.

- **Increased female dominance on social media channels.** Women are legion on the Internet and more active on social media sites like Facebook, Instagram, Snapchat, Twitter, and Pinterest than men.[31] For example, on Facebook women have 55 percent more posts on their walls than men, and women post an average of 394 posts, compared to 254 posts on average for men. Women leverage these channels to ensure that female voices are heard, commenting on what they like and don't like.

- **Increased rise of single women and influence over financial, social, and political issues.** Rebecca Traister's 2016 book, *All the Single Ladies*, highlights the demographic rise of single women in America. Single adult women now outnumber married women for the first time ever in US history.[32] Unmarried women have more time to devote to work and more disposable income to spend, making them an increasingly influential and valuable demographic (employers and advertisers are all paying more attention to these women). Plus, their growing political sway—unmarried women constituted 23 percent of the electorate in

2012—is going to make it difficult for politicians and lawmakers to continue ignoring their needs.[33]

- **Increased government attention and policies for women globally.** In the United States, under the Obama administration, a White House Council on Women and Girls was established, and First Lady Michelle Obama launched the Let Girls Learn initiative, which aims to keep girls around the world in school and help them attain a quality education.[34] In Japan Prime Minister Shinzo Abe submitted a bill to require all public-sector institutions and companies to develop concrete action plans for increasing the participation and representation of women as well as parent-friendly policies.[35] Women still lag far behind men in Rwanda, but President Paul Kagame has committed to eradicating gender-based violence with a zero-tolerance policy and by improving access to medical, legal, and psychological services for victims.[36]

- **Increased men campaigning for women.** Women aren't the only ones standing up. Men too are getting behind gender equality, contributing to the dialogue, and investing their businesses in women. In 2014 the UN launched the HeForShe initiative for people everywhere to support gender equality, with celebs like Jared Leto, Joseph Gordon-Levitt, Harry Styles, and Nigel Barker publicly supporting it.[37] Male-led companies like Refinery29, Netflix, Bustle, and SHE Knows Media are funneling resources toward creating feminist content.[38]

Ladies, what is that idea that you've wanted to start, build, or create for some time now but have been too afraid or complacent to act on? There has never been a better time for you to rise and embrace this new feminine power, which history's bravest women have afforded you. And if you are female, you *must* represent the female sex, because if you won't stand up for your own kind, how can you expect others to?

Gentleman—especially those who understand female potential as fathers, brothers, sons, or partners—what action can you take for women and girls that will help achieve the equilibrium you know our societies and families need to thrive? If you're not yet sure, let's venture into the next chapter focused on men!

3

Including, Engaging with, and Empowering Men

"I believe partnering into the future is the only way humanity will survive. This is a global human issue, not a women's issue. But, of course, while it affects us all, it's crushing female life force."

— PETER BUFFETT, COPRESIDENT OF NOVO FOUNDATION

Gender inequality affects all of us, but because women have historically been the more disadvantaged sex, the initial interests and activities of the gender equality macro-movement have focused largely on women and girls. That leaves a big, fat elephant in the room: What about men and the role they need to play in this movement? Women, we can't do this alone. Consider all the courageous and supportive men you know and the important roles they play in your life. I write this chapter as a wife to a husband, a daughter to a father, a mother to a son, a sister to a brother, a friend to many men (gay and straight), a CEO of a leadership platform focused on gender and diversity, a program curator of gender topics, and an observer and listener of countless male behavioral stories at work and at home. I write from these experiences and perspectives, but my greatest passion for this topic comes from my role as a wife and mother—I've been growing in partnership with my husband, John, for nine years and in my role as a mother to a son and daughter who are both under two years old; I think a lot about how we can shape their relationship to other genders.

SYNERGIZING THE SEXES
TO SERVICE SOCIETY

Before I go any further, I want to again acknowledge that not everyone identifies with the binary categories of female and male or woman and man. Luckily, we live in a new gender-pluralistic era that embraces the many different identities that make up the LGBTQIA (lesbian, gay, bisexual, transsexual, queer, intersex, asexual) community. However, for the purposes of this chapter, I'm going to refer to the traditional categories of woman and man in a heterosexual context.

When I rise above to see society from the outside-in perspective, I realize that society logically can reach its full potential only when all the sexes synergize and work together in harmony to service it. This is not too different from a mother and father raising their children, in which the better both parents work and communicate with each other, the more their children thrive. Our world's innovations and problems need this kind of dual-gender nurturing too. The foundation of humanity is made up of two sexes, yet one of the sexes has been valued far less for most of history. For the whole body of society to sustain, succeed, and thrive, men *and* women both provide their own unique values. I find it paradoxical that the more devalued sex happens to be the one responsible for the physical creation of all humanity. The 280-day human gestation period occurs in a woman's body. In the early stages of bringing a new person into the world, it is *she* who takes the lead in managing the biological process of conceiving, carrying, birthing, and feeding.

Now most of you know the extraordinary emotional, physical, and intellectual labor that motherhood demands, if not from being a mother yourself or being in partnership with one, then from your experience as a child of the mother who raised you. I would venture to say that the traditionally feminine traits of vulnerability, empathy, resilience, patience, collaboration—along with the sheer stamina and strength it takes to birth and raise society's population since the beginning of time—may benefit our current leadership structures. I would bet everything I have that history might have experienced less conflict, greed, violence, corruption, slavery, and devastation if women had shared more leadership positions of power with men.

Each sex needs the other, and society needs both for the different qualities they each bring. Though when you think about it, in all the time that we have existed on the planet, have women and men ever fully figured out how to best coexist with each other in all societal spheres from home and family to the workplace? I would venture to say no.

Let's look at the roles both sexes have been traditionally expected to play. Dating back to the earliest Homo sapiens, the male role has been to hunt, protect, provide, conquer, always have a plan, and be strong in the face of adversity,[1] while the female role has been to gather, bear children, nurture, love, feed, and manage everything related to family life and the domestic sphere. Every culture spanning the seven continents has had its own variations of these gender roles, but for the most part these male and female roles have been remarkably universal.[2] And due to thousands of years of war, disease, slavery, migration, religious conquest, technological breakthroughs, political revolutions, economic depressions, and oppressive regimes, most people have just been living in survival mode, rendering them unable to try to improve gender relations. Fast forward to modern times: even today, there are no forums designed to help women and men synergize better, other than marriage counseling. Whether it's in the context of marriage, the workplace, or the community, women and men enter and operate into these with assumptions about each other based on gender. Instead, we must throw gender stereotypes out the window and start with communicating with each other to fully understand the other person's genuine needs, challenges, and desires in order to make the whole entity successful. To do this, women and men must instigate conversations or "therapy sessions" in a way that sets everyone up to succeed.

This suggests that in all of the contexts in which women and men engage—culturally in nations, socially in friendships, professionally in workplaces, and emotionally in intimate relationships and families—these relationships are functioning far from their potential.

In order for men and women to thrive in relationship with each other, both sides must bring their most mature, highest-integrity selves to the relationship, and this requires individual personal growth *first*. When I say *thrive*, I refer to the confidence and betterment that men and women develop when they feel affirmed about themselves on all levels—emotionally and physically, and financially. There is no doubt that each sex achieves this feeling in different ways, nor that getting there is easy. For one thing, men are more likely to equate money with status and power, so they try to acquire as much of it as they can, while women more commonly relate to money in terms of how it can help them and the people they love.[3] To me, this level of happiness and stability is not possible without each sex undergoing the process of personal growth. In order for the societal spheres of family, workplace, and government to reap their best human resources, each person has to undergo personal growth to synergize successfully with one another. As with marriage counseling, when you enter the mediation process, you discover characteristics about yourself that create disharmony with your partner. To resolve these, both people need to do some personal work to understand the source of the issue. Once you and your partner can see and name patterns, you'll both be able to create synergy.

> "In a sense, all of society has to undergo some serious marriage counseling, but for that to be successful, each party needs to do the inner work first."

TODAY'S WOMEN'S MOVEMENT MUST INCLUDE, ENGAGE, AND EMPOWER MEN

So let's talk more about personal growth. In all my fifteen years of doing the work—be it therapy, life coaching, leadership education, church going, reading, writing, and meditation—I have learned that the journey of personal growth begins by doing the inner work of defining your deepest desires, fears, and shames, and understanding where in your past they come from so that you can determine how best to live your life in the outside world. This requires humility, courage, a time commitment, and the willingness to ask for help. It's far from easy work and can be a lifelong process; after all, everyone hopes to grow in wisdom with age. Reflecting on the research I have done on the state of women and men for this book, I see that each sex is on a totally separate trajectory of inner growth.

More often than not, women have undergone more therapy and coaching, attended more well-being retreats, and consumed more self-help resources. They have taken advantage of mentorship progams, women's clubs, workplace events, and mommy networks and realize they have a higher value and untapped potential to fulfill. Because the women's movement has afforded women these resources, many women made personal empowerment and self-reflection journeys. Ad campaigns and women's empowerment articles are launched regularly to remind women of their power.

You see, society expects women to be openly vulnerable, emotional, and transparent—even though it often chides women for these traits, such as when a woman may cry at work. Yet for many men it's the opposite. Studies confirm that men are much less likely to seek psychological help when they need it.[4] In the UK 62 percent of patients referred for counseling for anxiety and depression in 2013 were women.[5] Men have been raised not to show anything that implies weakness, whereas women have historically invested a lot more in self-help.[6] For example, women are usually the first partner in a relationship to see a couples counselor and then they bring in their male partners.[7] Men, however, routinely bottle up their emotions and tell no one of their troubles; they believe they must find a solution on their own.[8]

Jack Meyers, author of *The Future of Men*, explains that while women have been mobilized by Sheryl Sandberg's "lean in" mantra, men are experiencing a serious lack of positive role models and messaging. "We're creating a 'lean out' generation of young men who are caught in the crosshairs of a historic gender shift," Meyers says. Men and boys are not receiving the same kind of social encouragement and positive messaging that society has embraced for women and girls. There are no "girl power," "the future is female," or "like a girl" slogan equivalents for men. In fact, despite shifting gender roles, men are still expected to "man up" and "be a man."

Yet in many ways men struggle with the same issues women struggle with—self-worth, purpose, comparison, the pressure to please others. Often, a man's worst fear is failure, which can be summed up in many ways: getting rejected, not making enough money, being laughed at, feeling irrelevant and unneeded, and, worst of all, disappointing the woman he loves.[9] Traditionally, they have been taught to lock up these emotions, hide their vulnerabilities, and maintain the charade that their value comes from being macho and dominant at all costs. Connor Beaton, the founder of ManTalks, calls this the "mask of masculinity." On his blog Beaton gives readers a revealing look at just how far the pressure to conform to the male ideal can go:

> "Men struggle with the same issues women struggle with—self-worth, purpose, comparison, the pressure to please others."

> In the past, I would have tried to face [the death of a friend] on my own because, like many men, I thought that I would be less of a man for talking about the real, messy shit going on in my life. I would bottle it up, stuff it way down, put on the armor, and go out in the world pretending I had it all together. But I've started to realize something: not talking about these things doesn't make you a man. Holding in all of your anger, sadness, grief and loss doesn't make you strong. It makes you weak—and not in a metaphorical way. We're literally weaker when we're alone. Pretending that you are invulnerable is the ultimate vulnerability because it is the ultimate blindspot.[10]

Beaton is one of a growing group of inspirational men modeling the new masculinity and bringing men together to combat the stigma there still is around talking about male emotions. Men need to address male-centric struggles with other men, but they haven't had the advantage of belonging to groups and attending events where it's safe to share vulnerabilities, problems, and fears the way women have. The closest thing to these groups and gatherings that men have traditionally had involve business trips, sporting events, or meeting on the golf course—not the best place for having deep conversations about your feelings. A

British study revealed that 51 percent of the men surveyed said they had two or fewer friends outside the home, and 12.5 percent said they had none at all.[11] Because relying on community and opening up to others about personal problems are seen as showing weakness, men are not encouraged to open up in peer-to-peer friendships, making it challenging for them to get help during tough times.

Not being able to vent and heal emotionally also has physical and mental effects. For example, women are outpacing men in higher education, with men making up only 40 percent of undergraduates and 38 percent of graduate students in the United States.[12] Boys are also 10 percent less likely to graduate from high school than girls.[13] Lack of education not only hurts men's job prospects and lifetime earning potential but also affects their likelihood of marrying and starting a family, especially for working-class men outnumbered and outranked by educated women.[14] Men's overall health also lags behind women's: men are three and a half times more likely to commit suicide than women,[15] more men die due to smoking and alcohol than women, and male life expectancy is lower than female life expectancy in every country in the world.[16]

I'm fortunate to have a supportive and collaborative husband. We have an extremely close relationship where we equally share the responsibilities of raising our children, keeping the house in order, ensuring our pantry is stocked with nutritious food, and paying the bills. We even advise each other on our businesses; I help him with business development, while his company, Mighty Insights, helps me with technology and digital marketing. He's often reminding me that man-to-man emails or conversations can't be as transparent as mine are. And when he's communicating with women, he has to be appropriate and can't be as overly friendly as I can. But how can any of us get the best help from a mentor or friend when we can't fully explain our concern? Women are pros at this because we are taught and even expected to be vulnerable. But for many men, to be vulnerable (or anything that implies feminine) is to be weak.

Even though today's female generation has in many cases done more inner work than men, they haven't sorted out how to approach their male counterparts and include them in the conversation around gender issues on both a personal and societal level. And many women have trouble understanding how deeply males might be struggling. In my assessment women are more absorbed in their female issues and emotions—and rightfully so! However, although men do have an extraordinary amount of power in the world, many have probably not invested much time or had the opportunity to understand men's side of gender issues. At the same time, women can't successfully bridge the gender gap unless men agree to open up and participate—so we need to be smart and patient about how we include men on conversations about gender.

"Women are experiencing a fourth wave of the women's movement, while men are experiencing the first wave of a new men's movement—one that is redefining masculinity."

Of course, I am fully aware of the reality that women are discriminated against and that a huge imbalance in power between sexes exists, but I have witnessed the negative effects of sexism on men and boys too. Gloria Steinem voiced a similar concern when she noted, "We've begun to raise daughters more like sons . . . but few have the courage to raise our sons more like our daughters." The stereotypes and biases sexism instills cut both ways.

From my outside-in perspective, women are experiencing a fourth wave of the women's movement, while men are experiencing the first wave of a new men's movement—one that is redefining masculinity. And when it comes to figuring out how to include, engage, and empower—yes, I said empower—men, women must learn to do this if they want equality to be a reality faster.

Inclusion means psychologically shifting the way we think about our agendas to include and involve men. Engagement, the next step, is physically reaching out to men (family members at home, coworkers in the office, or friends in social settings) for coffee, meetings, and casual conversation to ask them questions about the issues that affect them (oftentimes they're issues women care about too) and what their perspectives on gender are. Finally, empowerment is the act of truly wanting to help men on their journey of growth by providing them with introductions, resources, and invitations to events. And confident people don't need to tell someone they're helping them—many have a hard time accepting help or admitting they have issues. Instead, know the personality you're dealing with and try to get them there humbly.

If we want men to champion gender equality, it's women who need to help men get their feet in the door. Excluding and ignoring men means we're not doing everything we can to support the full potential of our husbands, fathers, brothers, and sons. How can we, as women, expect to stimulate growth, expansion, and possibility for all people without also investing in men? The men who get it need to try to get more men to join, but to get those men there in the first place, we need women to keep encouraging them.

MEN MUST BE PARTNERS, NOT ADVERSARIES

Traditionally the women's movement has come from a place of lack. Women have been oppressed, marginalized, and discriminated against for thousands of years. That is the reality of our history. As a result, the energy women bring when tackling gender issues can sometimes be negative and cast men as adversaries rather than partners in our fight. Now ladies, the last thing I want to do is pile on another burden for women to carry, but understanding the problem starts with compassion, and that goes for both sexes. The majority of female attitudes I have heard in reference to today's gender-equality movement tend to fall into these categories:

- defensive and adversarial (*That guy was such a chauvinist asshole!*)

- complacent (*There are women building companies and running for president—we're already there.*)

- demoralized and victimized (*Everything bad happens to women—men have it so easy.*)

- motivated and energized (*I don't care if people call me bossy or ambitious—I'm going to keep fighting for what I deserve.*)

Men's empowerment groups have also discovered that some male attitudes fall into these categories, especially among millennial and young men:

- defensive and adversarial (*Women are outperforming us—we're supposed to be the ones in control.*)

- confused (*I don't get it: women are running circles around men these days—they have all the power.*)

- empathetic (*It's not right that women are always harassed and discriminated against—I wish I could do more about it.*)

- motivated and energized (*The women in my life are rock stars—I back up my female colleagues in the workplace and share the load with my wife at home.*)

In all these scenarios we often respond based on our inside-out perspective. We make assumptions and then move on with sets of opinions based only on our own views without conversing with the other side. Great leaders try to hear all sides before they form opinions and act on them.

A NEW MEN'S MOVEMENT

We've arrived at a time that is in desperate need of a new men's movement that embraces vulnerability, redefines masculinity, and better collaborates with women to create the equilibrium our society needs to thrive. Of course, the last chapter of this book (and many other chapters) casts women's issues as exclusively the province of women. It's time to ask: What are men also struggling with?

A lot of issues that were once seen only as women's issues are now seen as men's issues too. In 2016 men were just as likely as women to say parenting is "extremely important" to their identity, and 48 percent of working fathers say they'd prefer to stay home with their kids if they didn't need the income.[17] Still, men need women's support—in the same way that women need men's support. While nearly 2 million men were stay-at-home-dads in 2012, surveys show that only 8 percent of Americans think a child is better off with a father at home as opposed to 51 percent who think a child is better off with a mother at home.[18] In a poll conducted by Deloitte of one thousand working adults, fewer than half feel that their company promotes a culture where men feel comfortable taking parental leave.[19]

When we think about the two sexes as a partnership, we can start to see how both sides need to be supported and nurtured for either to be successful. In a heterosexual marriage where both partners work, a woman might not be fully supported in her needs—maybe she needs help with childcare in order to step it up at work and get that promotion—if her husband is struggling with the idea that he can't be a real man if he's taking time off to care for the kids and giving up his position as the family breadwinner. The question we should be asking is not how men can support women but how the sexes can support each other. If we don't synergize, resentment always builds up on one side, stalling progress for everyone.

Thankfully we are starting to see the first wave of a new men's movement. This movement is in its infancy, but many are already breaking down the stereotypes around what it means to be a man in the twenty-first century. They are becoming stay-at-home dads at greater rates; building organizations, platforms, and consulting practices that challenge society's expectations of machismo; and tapping into their less-explored, emotional selves through therapy and life coaching.

Before Simon Isaacs even became a father, he went online to check out parenting websites, but he quickly realized there was nothing out there for men, in contrast to the more than 4 million mommy bloggers.[20] He co-founded Fatherly, a parenting resource for men where new and expecting fathers can go for advice and insights from other men.[21] Likewise, Tom Matlack founded the Good Men Project in 2009 with the intention of starting an international conversation around "what it means to be a good man in the twenty-first century."[22] By sharing stories from men on manhood and the defining moments in their lives, the Good Men Project is fostering a safe space for this deeply needed dialogue. Former NFL player Wade Davis completely broke the mold when he came out as a gay man—a taboo that's rarely talked about openly in the sports world—and became an activist for LGBTQIA and women's rights. Now he's using his celebrity to speak out against misogyny and traditional notions of masculinity and to promote equality for LGBTQIA athletes as executive director of You Can Play. Davis believes that "feminism, gender equality, closing the wage gap—all of these things are thought to be a woman's job," he said. "We need to turn to men and say, 'This is our job. We're all in this together.'"[23] There are also millennial men like JuVan Langford who are connecting with younger generations of boys and men; Langford created the MENtour to empower young male teens nationally and confront "the academic, social, emotional, and behavioral gaps" they experience in high school.[24] These men are leading the charge by educating and connecting with other men and creating forums where men and boys can openly discuss their struggles and be empowered..

WOMEN AND MEN ARE STRONGER TOGETHER

When it comes to improving gender relations, we simply lack the forums, communities, educational programs, and events for dialogue and exchange that would allow women and men to engage in a way that is mutually beneficial. The closest thing we have to this is the traditional structure of couples counseling and maybe gender- and diversity-themed events, but even those have nominal male turnout, often because men aren't invited.

Clearly we need a new way of cohabitating that necessitates this new gender collaboration model. Whether man or woman, we each need to do the personal work of understanding our inner issues while also seeking to understand the other sex and being action oriented and open-minded so we can best empower the other.

Change will benefit all sexes, but we can't get there alone. By empowering men, women not only gain allies for their own issues but also set the stage for a much-needed movement for men and boys. By empowering women, men, and boys will benefit greatly too. We're all on the same team, so it's on each of us to create a safe space where women *and* men can explore our challenges side by side. Both genders need to rise and lift together so the whole world can thrive.

4

Calling on a New Breed of Leaders

"Presenting leadership as a list of carefully defined qualities (like strategic, analytical, and performance-oriented)
no longer holds. Instead, true leadership stems from individuality that is honestly and sometimes imperfectly ex-
pressed. . . . Leaders should strive for authenticity over
perfection."

—SHERYL SANDBERG, COO OF FACEBOOK AND
FOUNDER OF LEANIN.ORG

By now I have painted a picture of why society needs you to lead change
and how you in fact were created with the potential and destiny to do
that. I hope I have convinced you to see social issues—which are really
your issues—through a gender-equality lens because when you lift
women, you lift countless other issues at the same time. And I have
given you my perspective on how both sexes must cohabitate more synergistically to serve society, a goal that requires today's women's movement to be proactively inclusive of men and empower them to start a
new men's movement that redefines masculinity to enable that synergy.
This final chapter of Part I is about making the commitment to do all of
the above. Our society, workplaces, partners, children, family lineage,
and future need you to get up off that chair and raise your hand to become a leader.

CHANGE YOUR RELATIONSHIP
TO THE WORD

So how do we become leaders? First, to really see yourself as a leader, you need to change your relationship with the word. The word *leadership* is often used in the context of corporate America or political office—it has an elusive and inaccessible feeling to it. You might think of a head of state or a middle-aged male CEO, but leadership is so much more than the traditional notion of taking on a dauntingly stressful role, having "all eyes on you" pressure, and snagging a fancy title that comes with a fat paycheck. We need to redefine the term to mean something *every* citizen aspires to. Many people say certain people aren't built to be leaders, but I disagree. To me leadership is not something anyone is born with but something one works on becoming. And just as the words *successful* and *wealthy* denote things all people aspire to be, we need the word *leader* to convey the same allure and desirability. Yet when you choose to lead and your heart is rooted in the right reasons, things start to happen for you and everything you desire personally becomes that much more attainable. In fact, it's interesting to note that people maximize their chances of being successful and wealthy when they embody leadership attributes. But it's as if most people subconsciously want the success and wealth without putting in the hard work it takes to attain them.

What the old-school concept of leadership really needs is a brand makeover you can relate to. I like to call this new brand S.H.E. leadership, which stands for "SHE and HE Empower" because this new breed of leaders are essentially empowerment agents in the world. Think of this new definition as going beyond business and impact. Think of it as leading your whole life well: your health, finances, family, parenting, job, social change, and more. (I have a whole chapter devoted to this later in the book!) The new definition is also a diverse one, so you can be a teenager or a senior citizen, an immigrant or a veteran, and any skin color, learning and modeling leadership. The new definition also becomes more accessible to you when you realize that everything has happened for you so you can lead. Remember those dreams and curiosities you have about doing something more meaningful in life? That's God tapping you on the shoulder, hinting at your destiny. And best of all, if your leadership is inspired by a true purpose and the greater good, it will be your most fruitful path. This may seem counterintuitive, but the selfless path of serving others is actually the most fruitful path because it effortlessly delivers all the things you desire. I'll explain that more in our chapter on Purpose. In the meantime, will you commit to joining this new breed?

REACHING YOUR POTENTIAL IS THE CLIMB OF YOUR LIFE

It's important to know that the leadership journey is a lifelong process. Just like any form of growth, it's not something that happens overnight, and your work is never done. This book is called *This Is How We Rise* because it's about what it takes to rise to our highest potential—and about how our personal rise can empower others. For me what it has taken is an upward life journey of spiritual discovery, personal growth, and leadership development. To help you visualize this process and why it is both difficult and rewarding, I'm going to use the analogy of a mountain.

FIGURE 4.1. Your Life Potential

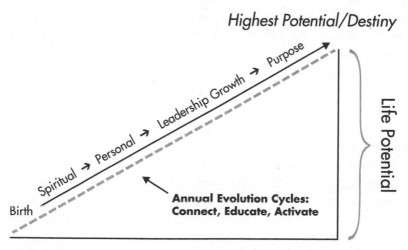

Source: Claudia Chan International, Inc.

The graphic on page 61 charts the trajectory of an individual person's life, from the beginning to the end of earthly life. Growing spiritually, personally, and as a leader to push your purpose forward is the activity required to rise to the top of the mountain (the peak of your potential). The journey of scaling and climbing the mountain, which can sometimes be treacherous and at other times effortless, is the length and duration of your lifetime. You will accelerate ahead through blocks of time when you are focused on a few specific goals; I call these elevation periods (we'll talk more about them in the Productivity chapter), which you see illustrated by the "dashes" beneath the line representing your leadership development trajectory. Ultimately it is your job in life to define what purpose means to you and devote your time on earth to lifting it—and the people and causes you care about—up the mountain.

> "Ultimately it is your job in life to define what purpose means to you and devote your time on earth to lifting it."

WELCOME TO THE MACRO-MOVEMENT

So how do you know what issues, people, and causes to lift? Given the many issues I've highlighted in the previous chapter, I understand if the climb feels daunting. You shouldn't feel pressure to take them all on. I want to introduce you to the term *macro-movement*, the umbrella under which all other movements, causes, issues, and campaigns fall. When you think of gender equality, feminism, or any other social issue, you tend to think of it as one movement. In reality, each movement is made up of a large collection of submovements. If all people in society could identify one or more problems that they have a great passion for or a personal connection to and then apply their unique talents toward solving them, this would generate a massive ripple effect of positive change across the globe. That is exactly what the macro-movement seeks to do: launch thousands of social movements that fuel each other and work together to solve the world's problems.

The illustrations on the next few pages will help you visualize examples of the landscapes and some of the submovements that make up the larger macro-movement. As you review them, think about your own interests and experiences and what submovement you might be most passionate to lead change in.

Within the gender-equality macro-movement there are a multitude of issues and movements that have sprung up around them. They occur

FIGURE 4.2. **Gender Equality Macro-Movement**

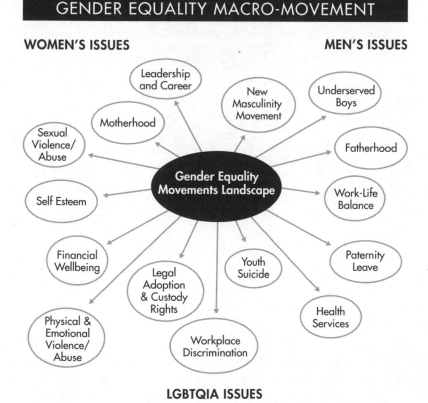

GENDER EQUALITY MACRO-MOVEMENT

WOMEN'S ISSUES

MEN'S ISSUES

Leadership and Career

New Masculinity Movement

Underserved Boys

Motherhood

Sexual Violence/ Abuse

Fatherhood

Gender Equality Movements Landscape

Self Esteem

Work-Life Balance

Financial Wellbeing

Youth Suicide

Paternity Leave

Legal Adoption & Custody Rights

Physical & Emotional Violence/ Abuse

Health Services

Workplace Discrimination

LGBTQIA ISSUES

Source: Claudia Chan International, Inc.

FIGURE 4.3. **Women's Macro-Movement Landscape**

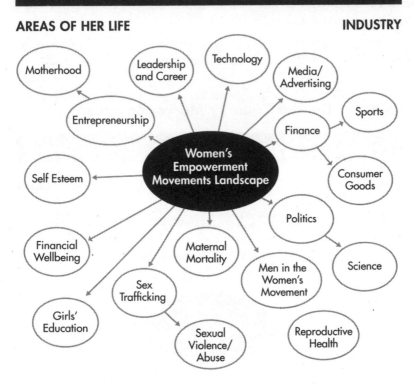

Source: Claudia Chan International, Inc.

largely within the categories of women's issues, men's issues, and LGBTQIA issues. If you have committed to working toward gender equality, aim to lead a cause that belongs in this landscape.

But it doesn't stop there. If you are serving a cause in the women's issues category, the landscape of women's issues is so big that it has its own macro-movement, so I have divided it into three main categories with example causes: the areas of a woman's life (self-esteem, financial well-being, relationships, career, motherhood), the industries in which she works (politics, sports, media, technology, consumer goods, finance), and the social and cultural issues that affect her gender (access to education, maternity care, sex trafficking, etc.). Note that these are just my views of how my left brain organizes the issues—you can make adjustments of your own.

To further show just how many specific issues exist within a macro-movement landscape, there are submovements under each issue. For example, take a look at the following organizations driving purpose and impact for girls' education or women's financial literacy.

TABLE 4.1.
GIRLS' EDUCATION

- **Malala Fund** puts programs in place in the developing world to help girls receive twelve years of safe, quality education.

- **SHE Innovates** provides sanitary pads to school-aged girls in Rwanda. Menstruation, because of taboos associated with it, is a major barrier to education for girls.

- **She's the First** provides scholarships to girls in low-income countries, fostering first-generation graduates.

- **Let Girls Learn** leverages public and private partnerships globally to address the range of challenges preventing adolescent girls from attaining quality education.

- **The Oprah Winfrey Leadership Academy** selects high-potential, high-performing adolescent girls from disadvantaged backgrounds in South Africa to attend boarding school, where they will receive many more opportunities.

TABLE 4.2.

WOMEN AND FINANCIAL LITERACY

- **DailyWorth** works to get all women to view money not as a source of stress and anxiety but as one of freedom and empowerment.

- **Ellevest** is a digital financial adviser that takes women's unique, lifetime salary curve, preferences, and longer lifespans into account and helps them make prudent investments for the future.

- **The Wage Project** creates programming to help end discrimination against women in the American workforce.

- **Prudential** has started the initiative #OwnMyFuture to inspire women to own their financial security and offers free resources and education.

- **Purple Purse Foundation** provides financial tools to empower women in abusive situations and help them break free by becoming financially literate.

Behind each submovement are passionate, empowered social change agents (what I want you to raise your hand to) making a difference for one subset of people who will create a ripple effect of good for others. Because there is so much work to be done, there is plenty of room for others to join in and concentrate on unaddressed aspects. I know you have seen white spaces in the past that you have contemplated filling, but as you now contemplate what that may be, stay focused on who you want to help and why rather than the fame you might gain from it. Stay in the purpose-centric mindset—because God cares more about your *why* than he does about your *what*.

Tammy Tibbetts, a first-generation college graduate, took an issue she was passionate about and built it into a submovement under the umbrella of girl's education when she founded She's the First, an organization that funds scholarships for girls in developing countries. An intense volunteering experience in Liberia at age twenty-two deeply inspired her, and her work is one of many amazing nonprofits that support girls' education around the world. For Jacqueline Ros, who launched her company, Revolar, which manufactures a safety button that people can wear anywhere and use to call for help if they find themselves in dangerous situations, her *why* was having a younger sister who was assaulted twice before the age of seventeen.[1] What started off as a device to protect women against rape culture now also benefits the elderly, single travelers, and people in high-risk jobs like taxi drivers. Her cause falls into the submovement around sexual violence and abuse against women and other vulnerable people.

These are just a few examples of how everyday citizens are already contributing to the macro-movement. Following their lead, you can drill down from the massively broad macro-movement and explore the more specific landscapes and their submovements to see where your own passion and expertise might lie. Start with the group of people you want to help. Think about the region, industry, or segment of the population that needs a solution in this area and will benefit from your work. What's the specific problem or issue they are experiencing? What's unique about your personal experiences and expertise that will improve their situation in the most time- and cost-efficient manner?

The macro-movement is all inclusive, encompasses many different needs, and tackles issues big and small: equality in the workplace, reproductive rights, racial profiling, single-parent families, sexual assault, access to education, professional mentorship, safe neighborhoods, third-world poverty, and so on. At one point or another all these topics touch us either directly or indirectly. Maybe you're a woman working in the male-dominated tech industry where your male peers get promoted twice as quickly, or your close friend just confided to you a story of sexual assault, or perhaps a recent trip to Nigeria opened your eyes to the maternal mortality rate and lack of quality healthcare in third-world countries. When experiences like these strike a chord within us, God is giving us something to ponder. It may not be a career in maternal health, but it may be to pursue that women's empowerment project idea you've had. Even though you don't have it completely fleshed out yet, these events that touch the heart are signs to keep fleshing it out.

MISSION TO MOVEMENT

Let's take a moment to differentiate between a mission or purpose and a movement. A mission or cause starts with one individual or organization moving a purpose forward. A movement is your mission multiplied by the number of people who join it; it's progress toward a collective goal, which occurs only when you create so much meaning and relevance around an issue that others find them-

"Define your mission with the intention to turn that mission into a movement."

selves caring about it and want to get involved as well. Movements are powerful because they single out complex issues and make them accessible to the masses, who in turn are mobilized to take action. They often take on lives of their own, go viral, and become a part of the culture, sometimes to the point where you can't even control them. If you can aim to create a movement, you will extend and prolong the impact of your mission or purpose (we'll talk more about this concept in Part II). Think of the infinite potential— movements trend on social media; get widely covered on mainstream news; inspire initiatives at schools, conferences, and meetups; and anyone can join.

Sheryl Sandberg didn't just write a best-selling book called *Lean In*; she created a broad-based Lean In movement that empowers women to step into leadership roles, whether they're corporate professionals, moms, students, military members, or millennials. Rooted in the belief that "when a woman helps another woman, they both benefit," the Lean In organization has run a number of successful campaigns: #leanintogether (mobilizing women and men for gender equality in the workplace), Lean In Collection at Getty Images ("a library of images devoted to the powerful depiction of women, girls, and the people who support them"),[2] #banbossy (a social media campaign to encourage girls instead of criticize them), and the formation of Lean In Circles (small groups of women who meet "to learn and grow together"). Sandberg didn't reinvent the wheel when it came to jumpstarting her own movement; instead, she mobilized her strengths and insights as COO of Facebook, the most influential social media company in the world. It was quite natural for her to expand the message in *Lean In* to myriad social campaigns, both online and in person. Thanks to her grand vision, there are twenty-nine thousand Lean In Circles meeting in 147 countries, and most members credit their circle with a positive change in their lives.[3]

Always, the Proctor & Gamble company that makes feminine hygiene products, decided as a well-known brand to tackle an issue that aligns with its products and the greater purpose of its company by creating an ad campaign that talks about what happens to girls at puberty. As their bodies change, teenage girls' confidence plummets and they drop out of sports, which is a critical activity for building confidence.[4] People often use the phrase "like a girl" as an insult—"You hit like a girl" or "You run like a girl"—further reinforcing stereotypes that girls aren't as able as boys when it comes to sports. Always didn't like what it was hearing, so it changed the conversation and rolled out a series of commercials that exposed this social gender bias and flipped it on its head by using the #LikeAGirl hashtag. Now people use the phrase to reinforce the idea that girls are badasses, and similar hashtags have cropped up such as #LikeABoss. By focusing on an issue they saw their target customers experience, Always fueled a movement that has changed the way people talk about girls. It did this not by starting a new organization but by tapping into its customer base and using the advertising channels already available to it. The first #LikeAGirl commercial aired at Super Bowl XLIX to more than 80 million viewers worldwide.[5] Subsequent videos have been produced as part of the series, and Always now partners with the International Olympics Committee, UN Women, and TED to expand its reach on this topic.

Girls Who Code brought attention to a very specific issue within the women in industry submovement, aimed at closing the gender gap in STEM and tech careers. Reshma Saujani launched the nonprofit by inviting twenty girls in New York for a coding summer camp, and since then it has grown exponentially to ten thousand girls across forty-two states, which is the same number of women who graduate with a degree in computer science each year in the United States. By thinking big and seeking to spark a submovement by appealing to tech companies and corporate sponsors like

> "Leadership is a never-ending process of climbing up the mountain—there is always more to learn and new challenges to take on."

Adobe, AT&T, and Prudential, Reshma was able to secure more than ninety corporate and charitable partners, many of whom host their clubs and drum up financial support and other resources to promote Girls Who Code.[6] This is exactly what leaders do: they draw upon their natural-born strengths and enlist others to join their movement. As you set out to join this new breed of leaders and ponder where you want to effect change, define your mission with the intention to turn that mission into a movement.

CONNECT, EDUCATE, ACTIVATE

Like I mentioned earlier, leadership is a lifelong process that requires constant work. In order to keep forging up the summit, we need to be continually evolving through a cycle of connection, education, and activation.

I call this the S.H.E. Leadership Evolution Cycle. Say you're a female professional who wants to grow in your career. You know you're meant to do something better, that you're not being valued for all you bring to your current role. A woman you highly respect at your firm informs you about my S.H.E. Summit Conference (connection) and get educated about all these topics that have silently been influencing your everyday life (education). One specific topic or speaker ignites you to make a bold decision to take an action in your workplace (activation). The following diagram better explains how this leadership path up your mountain is a continual cycle of actions that you must be proactive about taking.

Connections provide community, support, and exposure to education. Education creates consciousness and care for issues, which leads you to activation. Activation is then the process of deciding to take positive

FIGURE 4.4. **The S.H.E. Leadership Evolution Cycle**

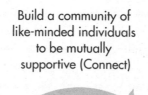

Build a community of
like-minded individuals
to be mutually
supportive (Connect)

CONNECT

EDUCATE

**THE S.H.E.
EVOLUTION**

Take action
that moves
your mission
forward
(Activate)

Exposure to
inspiring role
models and
leadership
development
(Educate)

ACTIVATE

Source: Claudia Chan International, Inc.

action. This is a process I personally like to plan once a year. It becomes my New Year's resolutions, if you will. Every holiday season moving into January I like to give some deep thought to how I will advance up my summit this year. What are new connections I need to make, and who are people I need in my life? What do I need to learn more about and gain more wisdom in so I can be more effective in leading my whole life up the mountain? How can I amplify my movement and activate further so I can improve the lives of more people with every step?

Connections are meeting new people who embody the values you respect and provide an expertise your purpose needs. I'll walk you through all this and teach you how to build your own tribes in the Community chapter. To gain these relationships you must seek out relevant introductions, events, groups, and communities. Education is not just attending a course or learning program; it's also reading books and articles, signing up for webinars, and working with coaches and advisers. Activation is making a commitment to the new goals you set and acting on them. Once you get the virtuous cycle of education, connection, and activation going, they all lead back to one another, reinforcing and building upon the foundation you started with. But the process is something you must be proactive and intentional about. Leadership is a never-ending process of climbing up the mountain—there is always more to learn and new challenges to take on. But this is what builds wisdom and endurance, which in turn builds character, and character shapes you as a leader. So will you raise your hand and make an oath to join this new breed of leaders? Everything in your life has happened FOR you to help you find this path so that you can make a lasting impact on the world. It is your destiny; don't be like the majority and abandon it.

PART II

THE THIRTEEN
FOUNDATIONAL PILLARS
OF PERSONAL LEADERSHIP

Now that you have made the commitment to rise to your highest potential by lifting and contributing to a larger purpose in the world, let's build what I call your "foundational leadership pillars." One of my mentors says, "If you want greatness, you will experience great challenges. If you are average, you will have average problems." This means that if you pursue the massive greatness your destiny has planned for you, I guarantee you will have seasons of great challenges in life.

To survive, advance, and thrive through these rough events, you must first plant some deep roots with leadership habits and principles that will keep you strong through the storm. I always use the example that a tree with deep roots can stay standing through the roughest weather, whereas a tree with flimsy roots will get blown over with the slightest wind. When things don't go how you want or there's repeated resistance, most people throw in the towel too early or revert to immature human patterns (remember, we're born focused only on the self and lack maturity) because they aren't rooted in anything formal.

Part II of this book includes thirteen foundational leadership pillars that are roots for you to plant so you can be the most productive in the proactivity of your goals and the reactivity of circumstances. Think of these habits as your personal leadership toolbox, equipped with powerful tools to help you navigate the many obstacles of life. Just as any house needs a solid structure of high-quality materials to ensure a long life or as a business or organization needs a strong strategy and values set to maximize its success—people, too, need these foundations. The next section of the book is like your life's foundation of values.

Every chapter covers a distinct value to cultivate, with examples that illustrate the principle at work and guide you in reflecting upon the ideas discussed. To learn and incorporate these pillars into your life, I've included homework for you—questions to ponder and answer—at the end of every chapter. The best way for you to respond to these questions is by journaling the state of mind you're in and how you're relating to the material. I encourage you to get a journal or notebook and dedicate several pages to each of the pillars in the following chapters. So for the first chapter, which is on Purpose, you would write "PURPOSE" at the top of the page and journal any insights or thoughts that come to you as you read through the chapter. You should also use this space to answer the homework questions. Whenever you need to strengthen one of the pillars—like Resilience, for example—you can go back to your Resilience notes and plug back into all the tools you learned about. In a way your journal will become your leadership life coach. Call it your S.H.E. Leadership journal.

These leadership values are also designed to combat the reactive tendencies humans fall back on until they've done the work of personal growth. I discussed some of these in the Introduction—recurring self-criticism, caring about what others think, comparison, never feeling sufficient or enough, and so on—and how these tendencies are rooted in an ego, self-centric mentality. No matter how successful anyone is, we have all struggled with the same emotions and moments of doubt. I have had clients say to me, "What is wrong with me? Why can't I get rid of this bad habit of putting myself down?" or "I'm always feeling insecure!" (or whatever their core limiting belief is). They are frustrated because they can intellectually acknowledge the negative pattern but can't seem to eliminate it for good in practice.

I have found that the more you know your bad habits, prepare tools to combat them, and keep practicing those tools, the faster they eventually dissipate and you become a new and improved version of yourself. For example, if you know your body tends to get belly fat, then you create a diet and exercise regimen to keep that body part leaner, and the more you make it a part of your lifestyle, the more it becomes what you naturally do. This practice becomes a part of you and your makeup as a person, and what's even cooler, what you model to your children and friends will positively impact others. Psychological and emotional habits work in the same way.

Action is everything, and you get out what you put in. More clarity, joy, freedom, success, money, and confidence don't just happen to you; in fact, we are born with none of these things, and God then throws us all kinds of good and bad things—skills, events and circumstances, people, and so on—so we can experience life and grow in different areas. Again, think of it from an outside-in perspective: your life is perhaps seventy to one hundred years of discovering, learning, and maturing, and the sooner you learn the right values and habits of a great character, the more you will reap in the years you have remaining. If you build a strong foundation at thirty-five years of age, the greater success and life quality you will have for another fifty-five years, assuming you live to ninety. No matter what age you are, it's never too late to start. So let's get started, shall we?

5

Purpose

"What we really want to do is what we are really meant to do. When we do what we are meant to do, money comes to us, doors open for us, we feel useful, and the work we do feels like play to us."

—JULIA CAMERON, TEACHER AND AUTHOR OF
THE ARTIST'S WAY

Hopefully you are fired up and ready to begin your journey of leadership development because you now understand how urgently we need diverse and passionate leaders like you. If Part I laid the groundwork by giving you a cold, hard look at all the problems the world faces—inequality across gender, race, socioeconomic background, religion, and countries—Part II will introduce the internal foundation and structure that you will build your leadership on. Let's start by establishing your purpose.

The word *purpose*, defined in the dictionary as "the reason for which something is done or created or for which something exists," has been around for a long time, but it has been used more often in recent years, especially among women and millennials who seek fulfillment above all else. Many terms are used interchangeably for the concept of *purpose*. Some label it as "your calling," Tony Robbins often uses the term "peak performance," and we've heard Oprah refer to purpose as "fulfilling the highest, most truthful expression of yourself as a human being."[1] What I aim to do in this chapter is to give you a more profound, mind- and heart-challenging definition of purpose that will hopefully change the course of your life. Here we go.

FINDING YOUR *HOLISTIC* PURPOSE IS YOUR LIFE'S ASSIGNMENT

Let's be honest: most of us think purpose is just what we're meant to do in this world so our personal lives and families can thrive. For those of us who have more of a social awareness, when our self-centric actions can help others thrive too, that's the cherry on top. In the Introduction of this book I asked you to stop viewing your existence solely from your own perspective (the inside-out lens) and, instead, try to understand your individual identity within the context of the universe (the outside-in lens) so you can be less obsessed with *what I will get for my life in the world* and more passionate about *what your life means for the world*. One of my favorite leadership teachers, Bill Hybels, had his life changed when a mentor asked him, "What will you do that will outlive you and all of those earthly accomplishments?" Can you ponder this question? You can't take your material things or money into the grave. What are you leaving behind that really matters come the end of your life? Now, I am not necessarily referring to legacy, estates, or endowments; I am referring to what mark or contribution you can leave behind that will last way past your time here. I am defining this impact and legacy as your holistic purpose.

Purpose is much more than building success in your personal life; it also encompasses the external social good your life contributes to. Then *together* the whole of your personal and social contributions give your life the greatest meaning and significance there is. In fact, let's just start using the term *holistic purpose*. The more you realize your holistic purpose, the more you become the person the universe intended you to be. Think of it as your life's assignment—the reason you are here on this place called Earth—and once you start to understand what it is, it becomes the *why* that steers all the decisions you make in your future. This assignment determines how you will use your life and the gifts you've been given to serve not only your personal realm (family, children, health, joy, well-being) but also the social realm (positive change in your community, fighting injustice, educating the next generation, lifting people out of poverty). In this definition the social realm is a not just the cherry on top; it becomes *equally* important to your personal realm. One exercise I do to help me see this is to imagine viewing things from the perspective of the universe's creator:

> Looking down at 7.3 billion people across Earth, I see Claudia Chan in the crowd, working her way up her life's mountain. Claudia's holistic purpose is not just to fulfill a self-centric life focused on her own desires for her personal comfort, joy, and family but also to serve the greater good during her time here in a way that will have a lasting impact beyond her years.

In the **personal** realm Claudia's purpose is to serve

- *her highest integrity and character development (the more she invests here and strengthens her pillars, the better she can show up in all areas of life);*

- *her spouse and marriage (the more her marriage thrives, the better she and John can show up for their children, relationships, vocations, social contributions, and more); and*

- *her children (she can raise and shape children with extraordinary character who will become contributors to the world).*

In the **social** realm Claudia's purpose is to serve

- *her relationships and community (the individuals she can make a small to significant influence on in her circle of friends, extended family, coworkers or even strangers), and*

- *her social movement or contributions (right now she is clearly focused on activating individuals and organizations to realize their highest life potential and to lead change, but this will evolve over time because I have some big, unexpected assignments ahead for her—let's see how she does with this one).*

Most people's definitions of purpose fall either into only the personal realm (*I live to provide for my family and children, period*) or into a siloed social realm (*It's my calling to be an artist who uses art to spark dialogue on political issues*). As we define purpose for ourselves, we must be careful not to confuse it with the pursuit of personal popularity, money, and accolades. These things may help us to serve and carry out our greater purpose, but they are a means to an end, not an end in themselves. Pause for a moment and think about what motivates your desire for that next career or life milestone. Is it because you want that promotion and higher pay, or is it because you will be in a higher position to lead change and impact hundreds or potentially millions? If you start feeling inadequate because someone who is doing similar work is getting one hundred times more recognition than you in the form of social media likes, press, and accolades, what would make your purpose feel more adequate? Investing more in promoting awareness of your personal brand or focusing on the positive results of the mission behind the work you do? Even if you commit to the purpose-centric life and mindset, you need to fend off the self-centric tendencies all humans have. I push you to challenge yourself and your motivations because that's how change agents and social movement drivers think. We are not striving to be average; we're striving to be trailblazers and game changers.

Remember the image of the summit we discussed in the last chapter? Your holistic purpose is your north star that will guide your lifelong journey up the mountain; the top of the mountain is your highest potential or what you are destined to achieve. But it's up to you to decide: How high do you want to go? Where will you end up in this lifetime? You need to aim for the highest point and believe that your potential is exponential, immeasurable. When you live this way you will be blown away by what you can accomplish, from the children you will raise to the volume of people whose lives you can improve in the specific way you're meant to. The more you allow this holistic purpose to guide your personal and vocational decisions and strategies, the more agile, exciting, and fulfilling your journey will be.

START WHERE YOU STRUGGLE

Some of you may already have strong clarity around your purpose, while many of you may have only an inkling or a sense, and for the rest of you, perhaps purpose hasn't hit your radar yet or you've been struggling with it and wondering, *Why on earth is it not clear to me? There are too many things my purpose may be.*

Use the example of my holistic purpose as a launching point to think about your own. What might purpose mean in your personal realm and in your social realm? If your purpose is still unclear or only partially known, I implore you to invest the coming year or as much time as you need to discover what purpose means for you. Unleashing your purpose in the personal realm is a matter of building your character and cultivating a lifestyle that supports your values. Oftentimes this is closely tied to the people who hold the greatest significance in your life, whether they're family members, partner, children, closest friends—these are the people whom your existence has great meaning for in the long haul.

Discovering your purpose in the social realm can be a bit trickier, but here's an unexpected way to think about it. One of the most profound things I have ever heard was from Pastor Rick Warren, who said, "The very thing you're most ashamed of in your life and resent the most could become your greatest ministry in helping other people. Your pain is your ministry. Your life's mess is your life's message."[2] Remember in the Introduction when I asked you to believe that everything in your life forms part of the picture of your life assignment? Maybe one of those hardships happened for you to overcome so that you could help others overcome it too. Or perhaps you witnessed something unjust so that you could do something about it. This is not to suggest that the universe intended bad things to happen to you but instead to say that drawing from personal experience can lead you to be passionate about a cause, to speak up from a place of experience, and to empathize with others who are going through similar challenges. Often the most powerful thing you can do when you've experienced pain, adversity, or loss and persevered through it is to do something that will help others going through the same experience. Often for so many—myself included—it is our greatest pain that can lead us to our purpose.

Let it become your motivation and the strength that keeps you going when the obstacles come. Too many people experience and witness pain and either allow the event to defeat them or abandon the opportunity to do something about it. By focusing on how to heal or prevent others in that area of pain you've experienced, you not only help others going through it and make the pain hurt less by doing something good for it, but you also create meaning and understanding for why you had to experience that pain in the first place. You can end up even being grateful for the pain. You realize it was a part of your life mountain and helped shape your north star or purpose.

There are many women and men who are already putting their purpose and mission into practice by addressing issues they have faced personally and overcome—their painful personal experiences have been the fuel for their greatest contributions. Take model Ashley Graham and her campaign to remove the "plus size" label. In 2016 she gave a TED Talk titled, "Plus Size? More Like My Size," in which she revealed her fraught relationship with the fashion industry. Her message to women was this: embrace your body and own your back fat, thick thighs, and cellulite because they are what make you beautiful, sexy, and empowered.[3] Soon after this talk, her modeling agency dropped her, but that didn't stop her. Since then she's been featured on the cover of *Sports Illustrated*'s swimsuit edition and launched her own lingerie line, and she continues to promote body positivity through the Plus Is Equal campaign that calls for equal representation of body types in the media (67 percent of American women are sizes 14 to 34).[4]

Juno Dawson is another incredible role model who didn't realize she was a transgender woman until the age of thirty when she met an eleven-year-old named Charlie who had decided she was going to start school as a girl when she was just seven. Since then she has been publicly documenting her transformation into a woman as a columnist for *Glamour* in order to show an alternative to Caitlyn Jenner's glammed-up reveal on the cover of *Vanity Fair*. For most, Juno says, the road to transitioning is "slow, and hard, and frustrating."[5] As an award-winning author of YA fiction in the UK, she has also had a huge impact on young readers by introducing them to issues around gender identity, sexuality, and mental health, most notably with *This Book Is Gay*, a manual for teens and young adults in the LGBT community.[6]

For entrepreneur Lisa Nichols, her pain-into-purpose moment came when she went to withdraw money from the bank to buy diapers for her baby and realized she had only $11 left in her account. From that moment on she knew she had to turn her life around. She downsized her home, sold unnecessary possessions, and lived frugally. She began writing checks to her savings account under the heading "funding my dream" until, after three and a half years, she had amassed $62,000—enough to start her business. Today she is a highly sought-after motivational speaker who speaks to audiences about how to discover their untapped talents and take control of their financial lives.[7]

Now I'm going to ask you to do something you might not like. I want you to cycle back through your entire life, go back to the very beginning, and ask yourself

What have been some the most painful events and circumstances of my life?

How did I overcome and conquer the situation?

How does it still affect me? Did it make me a stronger person?

How did it shape me into the person I am today?

What has happened to you happens to other women and men. Start where you struggle the most. That's where you are meant to lead. We can help each other by sharing the knowledge we have learned from the experiences we have had to overcome. When you find a constructive way to tap into your discomfort and use that suffering as fuel, your pain transforms into progress, power, and positive impact.

Then think about the talents and skills you have been blessed with and how you can utilize them to help solve the problem you've experienced.

What can you uniquely create or contribute? If you're a writer, your talent is sharing stories through the written word and putting your art and creativity out into the world. If you're a corporate professional, you might be in a position to become a junior employee's mentor or start an internal diversity initiative.

"When you find a constructive way to tap into your discomfort and use that suffering as fuel, your pain transforms into progress, power, and positive impact."

As a lawyer you could do pro bono work for people who can't afford legal representation, or as an accountant you could help a nonprofit get their taxes in order. If you're a mother and have dreams beyond being a mom, you need to pursue them. Performers like Charlie Chaplin or Judy Garland or Beyoncé have the gift of connecting with others through music and film. Nelson Mandela, Mother Teresa, and Mahatma Gandhi were skilled community organizers who used their leadership to rally others and call for social change.

God has assigned a purpose to you that harnesses both your natural-born gifts and the unique experiences you've had. For example, I was born with tremendous social skills, have always had a business sense, and know how to simplify and popularize complex concepts for a mainstream audience. The circumstances of my life—growing up with immigrant parents in a scarcity mentality, attending all-girls schools, the books I read, the conferences I attended, running a women's entertainment company for ten years, the chauvinism and sexism I experienced in the workplace—all happened for me. Why did I do these things? What I'm meant to do is create events for women, and because I have shifted to the "me for we" perspective, my

"God has assigned a purpose to you that harnesses both your natural-born gifts and the unique experiences you've had."

work at S.H.E. Globl Media is focused on women's empowerment and gender equality. At a certain point you start seeing the messages life is sending you. All the events that have happened in your life are like the pieces of a puzzle you put together.

PURPOSE IS THE PATH OF LEAST RESISTANCE
AND MAXIMUM JOY

The best way for you to maximize your potential and succeed is to live in service—the act of helping or doing work for others. You unlock your potential only when you start serving, which manifests in several ways. The more you lift others, the more you lift yourself. If life is a karma bank, the more you serve and give back, the more karma points you collect. When you look back at your life at twenty, thirty, fifty, ninety years old—or however old you live to be—what will your efforts have resulted in? Your contribution and the good you effect are the results of your life's work and the legacy you leave behind. When you're rooted in serving the greater good, all the personal goals—relationships, money, fulfillment—you aspire to attain end up happening for you because your actions are driven by the right motivations, which bring more positivity and abundance to you. Personal good becomes the by-product of working for the greater good.

Moreover, the holistic purpose you are serving becomes your evaluation tool and the thing you use to screen every action you take. If you are struggling with a big decision, simply ask yourself *Does this align with my purpose in either realm?* Answer this question, and you'll easily know what to say yes and no to. You will have clarity.

Remember when you were scared to do anything because of what others might think about you? The purpose-centric path takes the spotlight off you and puts it on the change you hope to bring, so you stop falling prey to that critical inner voice and find the courage to make bold moves. Whenever I get stressed or nervous about a meeting (i.e., *What if things don't go well?*), my strategy to regain my confidence is to know that I'm doing something good. If my desire is to impact meaningful change and I'm doing what I truly believe is the right thing, I know the outcome will eventually result in something massively positive. Plus, the fact that you are doing something to help others will bring you so much satisfaction and self-worth. It's hard to feel bad about yourself when you're doing good for the world.

In contrast, the more we're focused on personal gain, the more life feels like we're constantly hitting a brick wall and going against the grain. This is when we start to compare ourselves to others and feel like we're not enough. We get caught up in all the wrong metrics and begin to judge ourselves by the values we think are important to others: how much money we make, how pretty we are, how many social media likes we have, and so on. When ruled by our egos, the milestones we set up for ourselves lock us into a hedonic treadmill of never-ending desires. You tell yourself *If I can just get that six-figure promotion or that Fendi bag at Bergdorf's or that house in the Hamptons, then I'll be happy.* The reality is that day comes and goes without much fanfare because the goalposts keep moving. Your ego will never be satisfied.

The most successful people have flourished largely due to their dedication to service. During the early days of Oprah's talk show, she felt pressure to create programming that would drive up ratings, so she aired a show where a woman learned of her husband's infidelity in front of a live audience. After witnessing how humiliating that moment was, Oprah decided she would never again do something that demeans another human being.[8] She shifted her programming to empowering and uplifting others and, as a result, became one of the richest and most admired women in America.

After living the glamorous life in New York City as a nightclub promoter, Scott Harrison realized he was superficially rich but spiritually poor. He left his former life behind to volunteer with Mercy Ships in West Africa, which forever changed his life and opened his eyes to the dire poverty people suffer in other parts of the world. The experience inspired him to found Charity Water, a nonprofit that brings clean and safe drinking water to people in developing countries. Since the organization was founded in 2006 it has raised more than $2 million for nineteen thousand water projects in twenty-four countries, impacting more than 6 million people.[9] These stories are evidence of how leading a life of service and doing the right thing will unleash your limitless potential. The miracles hit like crazy, and your wildest expectations come true.

SUPERCHARGE YOUR PURPOSE
BY DEFINING ITS SOURCE

I remember asking my dear friend, collaborator, and mentor Rha Goddess, "How do you stay immovable in your purpose and confidence?" She said, "Oh, you mean what is my source?" I've brought up the word *source* several times already, and this is what I mean by it. To climb your mountain with uncommon courage requires a source that is bigger than your human understanding. Your life's assignment comes from a source you truly believe in (God, the universe, spirit, etc.) that is calling on you to serve and will be your ongoing fuel, especially when you want to give up. We live and think too small. We need to think of our lives in the context of the universe. If purpose is the why behind your vision and life, then your source is the why behind your purpose. In the same way that you plug a lamp into an outlet to gain power, plugging your purpose into your source, the universe, God, or a higher power renews and electrifies your motivation to new heights. It also brings you back to an appreciation for how incredible and vast the world is.

Some of you may be spiritual, and some of you may not be at all. However, spirituality does not have to be religion. Some people may not be spiritual at all, while others consider themselves spiritual but not religious. Others prefer to understand the world from a scientific perspective or from nature's point of view. Regardless of your beliefs, the universe is a miraculous place, and there is too much in life that we have no good explanation for. What's behind the unexplained? Why do miracles happen? Is it just by accident and chance? I feel that people have simply given up on spirituality too soon. How much time and attention have you devoted to thinking about this? This is your life we're talking about. Now, how much time have you wasted on worrying about what other people think? I don't plan to convince you to be spiritual or to believe in certain things, but I encourage you to at least consider them. There are many different things to believe in; choose what works for you.

Purpose is what drives us more than anything else in our lives. You can choose not to be spiritual, but I want to give you my perspective on it: you will not realize your highest potential without it. Your source, the power that created the universe, is what charges your purpose and gives you clarity. While purpose guides you and lights up the path ahead, the pillars discussed in the following chapters will shape your character and give you the tools you need to carry out that purpose. If you are the captain of your ship, then purpose is the compass that helps you find north.

When the road ahead gets rough—and it will get rough—your purpose is meant to remind you that your work has a vital importance in this world and that we're all depending on you to succeed.

HOMEWORK

Ponder and answer these questions in your journal:

- What will you do on this planet with the gifts, talents, and experiences you were given?

- What is your purpose in the personal realm and social realm? Look at your life from God's perspective. What do you think you're on this earth for? Be as specific as possible on the good you want to manifest.

- Write your purpose statement that puts your goals into action. Think of your purpose statement just like a personal business plan. Let this message be the overarching mission of your life.

- Now visualize your life mountain and mark where you might be on it. Celebrate the fact you are exactly where you're meant to be, then let the distance to the top motivate you to take more courageous steps.

6

Vision

"The creation of thousands of forests is in one acorn."

—RALPH WALDO EMERSON,
POET AND ESSAYIST

Now that you have reflected on your holistic purpose and have hopefully gained some clarity around it, it's time to take actions to achieve your goals. I would like you to think of *vision* as the "work structure" through which you live out your purpose in the social realm (for the rest of the book I will refer to *purpose* as it relates to the social realm) because what you choose to work on will dominate most of your waking life. Did you know that adults spend 30 to 40 percent of their lives working, which adds up to nearly twenty-five to thirty years of their entire lives?[1] Keeping in mind the magnitude of how much time you devote to work, you want to be extremely intentional about what it actually produces during your lifetime. So how exactly do you know what structure to build or pursue?

First, I want to break down the many work structures out there that we can use to fulfill our purpose. It's important to understand the various options and the differences between them because when we are more intentional about the structures we want to work within, we can move up our purposeful mountains faster.

PURPOSE-CENTRIC PROGRAM, PROJECT OR INITIATIVE. These are the smallest structures that one can use to devote time to a greater purpose. Perhaps you have a full-time job in digital marketing at a company, which has been your career path and area of professional expertise. It's what you do to pay the bills. Your purpose isn't 100 percent clear yet, but you know it's in the line of advancing women and girls, which your current full-time job doesn't have any connection to. Therefore, to serve that area of social good, you might volunteer on weekends as a Big Sister at a Girls Club, join a women's initiative in your workplace, mentor students interested in your field, do pro bono work, or serve on a volunteer committee for an amazing nonprofit that is tackling an issue you care about. In total the project takes about five to ten hours per month of your time. This kind of structure can also include workplace initiatives, marketing campaigns, product launches, and other volunteer opportunities, but it mainly requires only a short-term commitment or a smaller portion of your professional time.

PURPOSE-CENTRIC JOB. This is when you have a full-time job at a corporation or foundation whose work directly contributes to a cause you believe in; however, your purpose may not be completely aligned with your organization's cause, and this single job is only a first step toward building a career devoted to your purpose. My friend Genevieve spent most of her career in the magazine industry, and it wasn't until 2016 that she decided to take a sabbatical and work full-time for Hillary Clinton's campaign for president. Her job at the campaign could be a first step toward changing career paths and aligning with a cause that supports her purpose.

PURPOSE-CENTRIC CAREER. A career is a body of work that you have developed over a series of jobs in the same field or industry; while each job may have entailed different kinds of responsibilities, because they were a part of the same industry, you were able to build up an expertise and skill set. Your career may not always line up with your greater purpose. Maybe you have built a career in advertising—that's where your professional expertise and knowledge is based—but your true passion is impacting social change through nonprofit work, so you sit on the board of directors for nonprofits in your free time.

PURPOSE-CENTRIC VOCATION. When the individual jobs you have held and the career that they constitute align and lead you to devote most of your working life to your purpose, it's called a vocation. Originating from the Latin word *vocare*, which means "to call," vocation is the highest form of work you can aspire to. It's the realization of your purpose through the work you do each day. Dina Powell built her first career in government and then went on to manage Goldman Sachs's investing business, where she launched initiatives like 10,000 Women to provide resources for women entrepreneurs in developing countries. Now she is serving as a senior counselor to President Trump on economic initiatives, which combines her expertise in government and finance and puts her in a position to influence the economic policies of an entire country—a role that is likely the realization of her life's purpose.

If you are sure of your purpose, it makes sense to choose a structure where you can maximize your work time toward that cause, and this means devoting your entire career or vocation to it (however, don't quit your current job until you find or start the right opportunity that hits you in your stomach). But if you are in the early stages of figuring out what your purpose is—not to mention, finding a financially lucrative path to do it, which takes time—then you can start by taking on a few purpose-centric programs, projects, or initiatives that will demand less time as we referred to above. These structures, which mirror the stages of your journey to discovering and pursuing your purpose, will evolve and shift over time. Whether you're a full-time mom, freelancer, or corporate employee, your purposeful work can be inside a corporation, a nonprofit organization, or an entrepreneurial endeavor that you start. In Part III, I will give you more specific examples of how to lead change from where you are. Regardless of its context, it's important to not minimize your purposeful work as "hobbies" but instead to proudly own them as your purpose-centric projects or work you're devoted to right now. As I get back to using the word *vision* in this chapter, remember that it is these work structures that I'm referring to when I use the word.

VISIONS ARE ALWAYS
BEING CAST ON YOU

So how do you know what visions and work structures to pursue? I believe that God casts visions on us all the time. Whenever you experience curiosity or an idea that comes to you out of the blue—*Wouldn't it be awesome if . . . A more effective way to combat this issue or innovate is . . . Someone should invent a product or service like . . . because it simply doesn't exist*—pay attention because these thoughts might be components of your vision. Whatever you feel extremely passionate about, that thing that comes so easily to you, those are clues for your vision too. When you're inspired at a conference or an idea sparks from reading or watching something, that's your destiny giving you hints, luring you toward a vision to pursue.

"The problem is that most people abandon the visions cast on them. They ignore the taps and turn a blind eye to the clues."

Author and spiritual teacher Sanaya Roman says, "You are constantly being sent signs from the universe on what path to take. Part of sensing energy is seeing the messages."[2] The problem is that most people abandon the visions cast on them. They ignore the taps and turn a blind eye to the clues, dismissing them as silly or random thoughts. But if you can imagine from your outside-in lens that a higher power is sending signs to you, your eyes and ears will begin to give these thoughts the serious attention they deserve. That's why "follow your instincts" or "your instincts will never steer you wrong" is such a commonly given piece of advice.

However, not every idea or instinct should be taken seriously, so how do you know which ones should be acted on? Evaluate and reflect on whether your ideas are in alignment with the purpose statement you defined for yourself in the last chapter, and ask yourself some hard questions like the following:

- Does this vision (e.g., the move I want to make, the action I want to take, the initiative I want to start) serve my purpose?

- What's my motivation? Am I interested in doing this because it will build my wealth and promote my status (ego/self-centric), or am I motivated by the cause and the lives I will improve if I take this on (purpose-centric)?

- If I was tremendously successful at bringing this vision to life, what would its positive impact or result look like? How many people could I possibly impact? Could I start a ripple effect?

Allow the answers to shape your vision, giving special attention to the final bullet point—the potential positive impact of your work should be the driving force behind your motivation. We live in a social media–dominated era where everyone is obsessed with or encouraged to build their personal brand. I don't have a problem with this term except that it prompts people to become more self-centric and superficial. As with money and fame, establishing a great personal brand or platform should not be the end goal but rather the means to establishing the end goal of your purpose. If you're alive on earth for ninety years, use your talents to achieve the positive impact you were put here to create, and your personal brand will naturally flourish in ways you never could have imagined. Ultimately the excitement and passion inspired by your vision will hit your gut so hard that it may throw you off your chair, so don't worry about not seeing it.

TRUST YOUR TESTED VISION AND BREAK THE MOLD

People are like sheep: we follow the herd and play it safe because we get caught up in the routine busyness of life and forget—or never stop to consider—the significance we were created for. We lack the self-esteem, courage, and motivation to break away from the mold and decide, *I will just do what everyone else (other moms, people my age, classmates, professionals in my field or company, etc.) is doing and blend in with the crowd, then I don't need to hustle that hard. That way I'll minimize the risk of wasting time on the unknown.* Now imagine your higher power or creator, who designed you to be extraordinary, looking down at you and how apathetic you seem. Don't settle for mediocre just because it's safe and easy; instead, pay careful attention to your visions. If they align with the sense of what you think your purpose might be, speak to your passion and skills, and can transform your past experiences—good and bad—to give them meaning, then by all means, break away from the herd and pursue the vision that is not yet visible to others. You just may do the impossible.

SEE THE INVISIBLE; DO THE IMPOSSIBLE

In 2010 what inspired my vision to create S.H.E. Globl Media was the phrase, "You cannot be what you cannot see." After I had absorbed the depressing statistics and realities of women and girls in the world, I felt I needed to create something to mobilize all the affluent, educated, and privileged women in America (starting where I live and the community to whom I have the most access) to care about this. Because my ten-year professional background at Shecky's was creating events and online content to attract masses of women, I quickly realized there were no accessible, modern, and fashionable events or websites for women focused on empowerment. At the time mainstream magazines for women were all focused on traditional categories like fashion, beauty, home, food, and design. The events I attended that were held specifically for women were either too fluffy (sample sales and shopping parties), too exclusive and expensive (Fortune's Most Powerful Women's Summit, Forbes Women's Summit, TED Women), siloed to a narrow topic (parenting, fashion, career, health), or specific to a particular industry (women in tech, women in media and communications, etc.).

I'm not saying these events or media channels weren't necessary, but I saw a tremendous white space for a new kind of women's leadership and lifestyle conference and media platform that would be beautiful, modern, affordable, and accessible, and would cover topics that would empower women in every area of their lives (leadership, business, career, confidence, money, relationships, health, etc.) while also teaching and activating my newfound purpose around women's issues in an exhilarating and innovative way. I wanted to create content and conferences that would unleash women's potentials in their own lives as well as in their actions for other women. I had a vision of building a brand with an Oprah-meets–Gloria Steinem voice because nothing else like that existed yet. In March 2012 I launched ClaudiaChan.com to publish hundreds of open and honest interviews and mentorship advice from leading women, which was followed by my first S.H.E. Summit conference that June. Just five years later we have impacted thousands of people around the world through our events by activating thousands of women to start or support specific movements.

> "If you can see an invisible need, then you can and must do the impossible— make it a reality."

A mantra I like to share is this: if you can see an invisible need, ideally something that you or others would clearly benefit from once solved, then you can and must do the impossible—make it a reality. The invisible can also be a pain that needs to be healed or prevented, a white space that needs to be addressed, or a hole that needs filling. I know it's scary and requires you to make a radical departure from the herd, but remember: innovation means doing what has never been done before. Disruption is radically changing or interrupting a norm, often by introducing a new product or a new way of doing something. The new normal, innovation, and disruption are all terms used in game-changing leadership forums where everyone aspires to make an impact. More reward comes with risk than safety. Keep viewing your existence from that outside-in, "me for we" lens to remind yourself that you were created to contribute something unique, something only you can do. The sooner you start believing in this, the sooner you will start executing your vision and fulfilling the purpose God has planned for you.

THE BIGGER THE VISION, THE BIGGER THE STEPS YOU TAKE

Once you shift to perceive God's expectations for your life and the grand vision God has for you, it's easy to see how the steps you're taking can be a lot more courageous, daring, and bold. Let's go back to the image of the summit. The top of the mountain is your life's highest potential. It's the maximum number of people you empower through your purpose, the amazing kids you raise, and the quality of life and meaningful experiences you have in your lifetime. If there was a long, winding staircase to climb to the top, would you take one step at a time or try to take several steps at a time, knowing that your time is limited? Similarly, when we envision, we should envision the biggest, grandest version of what we hope to create so we take the bigger steps actually needed to get there. This is especially true for women who tend to be more conservative, especially in stressful scenarios.[3]

The bigger your vision, the bigger the steps you must take. This is how you can achieve more than you ever imagined possible. If your vision is exaggerated, you're going to be that much more fearless and daring.

From the very beginning of S.H.E. Summit I set out to create not just a New York–based event, which is where I am located, but a global conference that millions of people can access through our livestream and meetups. I envisioned building an archive of evergreen videos and written content that corporations and organizations interested in the advancement of women could leverage and build community around. I envisioned creating a model where corporations could activate their own S.H.E. Summit events by leveraging our catalog of programs and speakers. I envisioned the aggregate of millions of people being impacted by the movements that I could encourage women to start. I envisioned multiplying leaders by inspiring more people to become leaders. I also envisioned modeling the best attributes of some of the biggest brands out there. Platforms like TED inspired me to scale content visibility, the music and technology conference SXSW inspired me to organize pop-up events around the world, and Oprah inspired me to maintain the vulnerability and authenticity of my voice and the voice of our speakers. My point is that I always try to push myself to think of the biggest, boldest vision of what I can create, and wherever I land in my build-out is what is meant to be because although we can't always realize our vision in full, we can sure get close—we end up much further along than we'd be if we started with a baby vision.

Your purpose requires execution, otherwise it's pointless. Vision provides the working structure for you to execute your purpose. Executing vision is not only one of the most creative pursuits in life but also one of the most exhilarating because it is the act of acknowledging the purpose God had in mind for you. Deciding to act on your vision is like raising your hand to the universe and saying, "I accept my life's assignment."

HOMEWORK

Ponder and answer these questions in your journal:

- Based on the purpose you are starting to see for yourself, what structure would make sense for your current circumstances, talents, and experiences? Should you start with a small project, aim for a new job, or invest in building a career or vocational path?

- What visions have you had in the last few years that you have abandoned and still feel exciting to you?

- What have been the biggest risks you've taken in your life? Were the outcomes good or bad? If risk-taking has not failed you before, let that help you invest in your new vision.

7

Faith

"Surrender to what is. Let go of what was. Have faith in what will be."

—SONIA RICOTTI, AUTHOR AND LEADERSHIP COACH

If vision is seeing and pursuing the invisible, faith is believing and trusting in the invisible. If you've said yes to your big, bold vision, now you've got to double down on faith and sustain it for the rest of your life. Humans are wired to control things, demand answers, hedge their bets, and maximize security, so it is no wonder that having faith is one of life's most difficult practices to cultivate. Because we have a natural tendency to lack faith, it is one of the leadership muscles that you need to be the most proactive about exercising and stretching throughout your life. This means relentlessly believing and trusting in your goals and your ability to manifest them. Faith, trust, and belief are underestimated powers because we don't invest enough energy into them. Here's a visual that may help you build these muscles better: imagine a large energy force field that draws its battery power from you. The purpose of this energy field is to help you move your vision, purpose, and dreams forward. Now imagine this force field is fueled by the amount of faith you have, and the more belief and trust you feed the energy field, the more powerful it grows to do your heavy lifting. Do you see the significance in believing and trusting? Without it, you're depleting the greater force that exists to support you. Without it, you're denying God's desire to help you.

You see, God designed you for such a big purpose and vision that God couldn't have possibly intended for you to do it alone. God's plan has always been to support you up the mountain and be a partner in your journey, but you have to truly believe in God to get God's help. "The universe has your back" is an expression for a reason. For a less spiritual analogy, imagine there is a talent agent in your life famous for spotting hidden abilities and strengths. She sees a magical gift in you that's so big that you wouldn't believe it. She sees your limitless potential and offers you overly generous free advisory, introductions, and other favors to bring you closer to your destiny. Not having faith in your grand potential and vision is essentially ignoring your agent's offer, help, and generosity. Why would this agent want to waste her time on you? Faith is believing and trusting in what is invisible. These kinds of outside-in analogies can provide the visibility we need to cultivate faith.

THE STRONGER THE FAITH, THE LESS YOU WORRY

I find that often people can be disappointed with the outcomes they receive because they cling to the idea that they can wield total control over their futures. From their inside-out points of view they try to force their way as the only way and believe they have full control over their destinies when, in reality, they have an invisible partner who wants to help them. Again, if *God* doesn't work for you, call this partner destiny, nature, the universe, or your ancestors in heaven. Just know that your being and will alone are not enough to achieve your life's potential.

The great thing about having this kind of faith is that it enables you to surrender your fears and imperfections; it enables us to achieve more by doing less. That sounds like a game we would all be down to play! Faith loosens the grip that worry has on us, eliminating the psychological struggle and resistance that only slows us down. Every step up the mountain is hard enough. Faith and the confidence and assurance it gives us make each step lighter and less forced. Another practical way to think about this is through one of my favorite mantras: You can become only what you believe, so your power to believe is your greatest power. *How much* you accept something (your vision, self-worth, significance, purpose, etc.) as true determines *how much* of it you will manifest.

So how do you know when to loosen your grip more and let the universe do its work? If what you're doing feels forced, exhausting, and even miserable, consider how you might soften your expectations and instead surrender to whatever the universe has in store for you. If you're trying to get that new job or sign investors for a new venture but keep receiving constant rejection, know that sometimes God wants you to take a different approach and may be intentionally preventing you from receiving what you want to help you grow or realize something you may have overlooked. Maybe your *why* is in the wrong place.

"You can become only what you believe, so your power to believe is your greatest power."

My friend Laura went through a rough time when she decided it was time to make a career change. She had the perfect résumé, with an undergraduate degree and MBA from Ivy League schools, substantial work experience at well-known consulting and financial firms, and many other accolades. But her then-current job neither compensated her adequately nor recognized the quality of the work she did there, and on top of that, they had her working almost twelve-hour days on deal closings. She spent her very limited time outside the office applying to jobs and interviewing, but she couldn't seem to catch a break, and this went on for more than a year. With each rejection she became more and more depleted by her work situation, lack of sleep, and career opportunities. Finally, I said to Laura, "I think you need to take a leap of faith and quit first. Take some time off, regain your positive spirit, and get inspired again." Luckily she and her husband were financially stable enough for her to quit, so she did, and soon after she discovered a health issue that, if left unaddressed, could have really harmed her fertility; it took her several months of doctor's appointments and self-love activities to recover both physically and emotionally. And that's when the miracles began to appear: a venture-capital fund reached out to her, and soon she was earning the same money for less work as a consultant, her husband was offered his dream job in DC, which was totally doable because of her now-flexible working arrangement, and shortly after they moved into their new home Laura got pregnant with their first child. When I look at Laura's story from an outside-in lens, I believe this plan was always in store for her and her husband, just as I believe we all have a greater power and partner above us helping us climb the mountain—we just need to have faith that this force exists and has always been there for us. Faith truly is trusting in something invisible.

WHEREVER YOU HAVE THE MOST SCARCITY, DEVELOP THE MOST FAITH

As I have mentioned, extraordinary challenges happen to those meant for extraordinary greatness. If you're going to take on the big visions you're destined for, you must be prepared for big obstacles, rejections, adversaries, and naysayers. Think of these as the inevitable rough patches and storms you must weather as you climb to the summit. We tend to experience the most scarcity during our roughest seasons of life. Unless we've sorted these issues out through personal growth work or therapy, we *all* have scarcity areas in our lives, whether it's with money, health, career, or relationships. Maybe it's trying to meet a significant other and every date you have backfires, or gaining customer traction for a venture and all you hear is *no*. You may go through a period of time when you feel you keep failing and find yourself waiting anxiously for a *yes* to arrive in your email inbox. It's moments like these when we need to double down on faith. Vincent van Gogh combatted self-doubt by espousing this belief: "If you hear a voice within you say 'you cannot paint,' then by all means paint, and that voice will be silenced." It's precisely when we are going through our most difficult periods that we must summon up the most faith and fight the urge to give up. The next chapter will focus on navigating obstacles along with the miracles and good they bring, but the point I want to make here is that all we need is to allow faith to pull us through tough times and navigate the way forward when the path becomes hazy.

Two weeks before S.H.E. Summit 2013 I was on the phone with my life coach at the time, Mimi Duvall. I was freaking out about all the details that had yet to come together: closing last-minute sponsorships, finding amazing speakers to fill open panel spots, selling enough conference tickets to cover margins. It was clearly a moment when I had spiraled into complete control-freak, micromanagement mode, which overwhelmed any of the faith I had. I didn't want to leave anything to chance. I'll never forget what Mimi said to me after I finished my rant of worries: "Claudia, it just sounds to me that you're lacking faith." Her comment was so simple and obvious. I had done all that I could to prepare for the summit up to that point. My team and I had put hundreds of hours into planning over the prior months. On top of that, there was a large community of partners and, of course, God helping to move the event forward, but I didn't trust any of it because I couldn't see it. For all of us there comes a point at which you've put so much love and energy into something that you just need to surrender and let the universe run with the momentum you've already generated. The alternative is allowing your anxieties and worries get the best of you, and then your actions will be ruled by fear and insecurity.

> "For all of us there comes a point at which you've put so much love and energy into something that you just need to surrender and let the universe run with the momentum you've already generated."

This is an example of a reactionary response to life's unpredictabilities. Today my faith is much more proactive. From the get-go my purpose and vision is clear and rooted in a "me for we" mindset. I have big visions for my next year and S.H.E. Evolution Cycle of who I need to connect with, where I need more education, and how I want to be further activated. Because I worry less, I put fewer hours into second-guessing my decisions and can actually work less to gain a bigger result. And I worry less because I have more faith. It's just a lighter path we should all work toward.

If there's one thing I have learned time and time again, it is that our power to believe is everything. It's so simple yet so complicated. Believing sounds easy, but due to all the obstacles, the anxiety of knowing how much there is to get done, and the massive subconscious self-doubt, having faith requires daily work. The more we ignore faith, the more we lose God's help. The less we exercise our belief and trust muscles, the more these muscles atrophy. The climb gets more difficult because we're trying to do it all alone.

When we give in too much to our fear of failing, that is the reality we create for ourselves. Reverse this path today and choose to believe the universe is on your side—faith widens your possibilities.

HOMEWORK

Ponder and answer these questions in your journal:

- Where do you have the most scarcity in your life and need to build more faith?

- What goals have you set in motion already and now need to surrender all concerns to? What fears can you replace with faith?

- As you sit in the waiting rooms of your life waiting for faith to produce results, what can you be working on to grow as a leader? What skills and experiences can you cultivate for when the day comes? God often keeps you in the waiting room to build you—that's in our next chapter on resilience.

8

Resilience

"The gem cannot be polished without friction, nor man perfected without trials."

—CHINESE PROVERB

When you choose to rise to your highest potential, you will naturally face more resistance and obstacles. That's just the law of physics. If you're climbing the mountain with a hard-to-reach destination in mind, there are more steps, more pressure in the ears, more storms to endure. Going further increases the risk of scrapes and even injuries. But as you rise, the rewards get more spectacular and you develop more strength, agility, and resilience. With every difficult step, you're building a new muscle. With every major storm you weather, you learn how to handle the next one better. That's why Resilience is the fourth pillar of personal leadership.

Setbacks are an inevitable aspect of life, so if you want to become a leader and trailblazer who achieves extraordinary things, you must be resilient in the face of obstacles because they will only continue to come your way. In this chapter we'll discuss what it means to be resilient, so I will be focusing a great deal of our attention on obstacles—failures or anything that conveys pain—physical or emotional. These are the things we all fear, try to avoid, and find unpleasant; for example, research shows that the pain of rejection can actually affect people in ways that are similar to physical pain. We're going to reframe your relationship with obstacles from the negative to the positive: obstacles are actually leadership- and character-building experiences to embrace in all areas of life.

REFRAME YOUR RELATIONSHIP WITH OBSTACLES TO SEE THEM AS YOUR BEST TEACHER

We all experience disappointments and setbacks in life—getting rejected from a job interview, breaking up with a significant other, losing a loved one, falling ill or getting injured, running out of money to fund your business or even keep the lights on, unfair treatment because of discrimination, a lawsuit, trauma from an accident, and so on. Obstacles are both inevitable and endless. The trick to mastering obstacles is how you view and respond to them. Instead of complaining, deferring to negative thoughts, or simply giving up, shift your perspective to see obstacles as opportunities to build, protect, direct, and mature your character.

"Treat obstacles like obstacle courses that build specific strength muscles required for leaders."

There's a reason people so often repeat the maxim, What doesn't kill you makes you stronger. Psychologists Richard Tedeschi and Lawrence Calhoun coined the term *posttraumatic growth* to describe the positive changes many people report after experiencing a traumatic event. In the 1980s they conducted a study with six hundred people and found that those who reported positive changes also noted other surprising improvements: stronger relationships, more compassion for others, greater wisdom, self-acceptance, less materialism, renewed spirituality, and a new philosophy of life.[1] The key for these survivors, though, was not the traumatic event itself but the struggle to understand it and find the meaning in it.[2]

OBSTACLES BUILD YOU

One way to reframe your thinking is to treat obstacles like obstacle courses that build specific strength muscles required for leaders. These muscles can include

- **Resilience.** When highly disappointed, you are upset for a period of time, but then you bounce back to persevere again.

- **Perseverance or Persistence.** When you get constant rejection, you keep pushing through until you get what you're after.

- **Courage.** When you know you're embarking on something highly challenging, you need to access great confidence and courage to take the next actions.

- **Decisiveness.** In the face of a threat or loss, you have limited time to choose a path, which forces you to be decisive and go with your best judgment.

- **Creativity.** When one method doesn't work after repeated tries, you must expand your thinking and creativity to define new paths.

- **Insightfulness.** Big challenges can come with a daunting amount of fires to put out or responsibilities to micromanage. It takes insight to weed through the volume and choose what you and your resources should focus on.

Are you starting to see how not getting what you want can be good for you? These examples sound so obvious, yet it's our human tendency to immediately become negative when challenges hit. This is especially relevant to those of you who will embark on a riskier path. When we are ready to go after our big visions, we almost always think that the path will be easier than it actually is. Due to our unique experiences, perspectives, and research, we are so convinced of why our vision is necessary that we think it's the most obvious thing in the world. Our passion is so off the charts that we see the benefits so clearly and want buy-in *now*. Unfortunately, those we need to get buy-in from are not always where we are, and it often takes a lot of convincing. Some will never even get it. We forget that being a visionary means "seeing something way ahead of its time." So although being told "we need to hold off," "maybe next year," or "we're not interested right now" when you pitch them your big idea may feel devastating, you should come to expect these responses as part of the process and realize, "That's okay. This is just an opportunity that will build me and make me more creative, insightful, courageous, resilient, and persistent. I am ready to get stronger!"

OBSTACLES PROTECT YOU

Our family has a golden retriever named Connor who has a very sensitive tummy and has to be on a strict diet of mostly bland dog food. Whenever my husband or I take him out for a walk, he's always pulling and twisting the leash in search of scraps of food left on the street. He'll see a discarded pizza crust and desperately try to snatch it up, all to no avail because we're actively protecting him from something we know will make him sick. My husband once pointed out that from Connor's inside-out perspective, he just sees that delicious-looking pizza crust and wants it now. From our outside-in parental perspective, we are protecting him from harm and optimizing his long-term health.

I know it seems silly to compare our human life to that of a dog, but in a very similar fashion, people see their shiny and desirable goals and want to attain them now without considering that maybe what they want now isn't good for them.

In fact, it could even be harmful or damaging to your emotional state, career, reputation, health, and safety. Maybe getting into a minor car accident is what turns you into a more conservative driver to prevent a larger accident down the road. Maybe that person you really liked who never called you back was a blessing in disguise because they would have caused you tremendous pain in the future. Maybe you didn't win that huge project because you never had the adequate resources from the get-go to deliver on all its promises, saving you from irrevocable damage to your professional reputation. I visualize God as the protective figure watching over us and yanking the leash when necessary for our protection. In this one life you can choose to have faith and believe that problems happen *for* you, or you can continue to insist that all obstacles are against you. You decide which response will create the more productive output.

OBSTACLES DIRECT YOU

Just as obstacles protect you, they can also direct you toward better things, bigger wins, and the remarkable path you were destined for. Following college, you thought you were supposed to go straight down the path, but your destiny was at the right turn, so God threw you an obstacle to make the turn. After being married for ten years and raising two awesome kids, you thought you would relax for a while, but your destiny was, indeed, to be a role model for a much bigger cause than other middle-aged women experienced, so God threw you a shocking obstacle that would turn things upside down but eventually pay off to empower thousands. Sometimes trials, big and small, occur to direct us toward an amazing calling we never knew would be in store for us, and we must have faith that they're part of our life's bigger plan.

Remember, there is only one you in the world with your unique set of experiences, personality traits, and skills. Can you now look at your unique being from the outside-in lens and see that none of these things are random, that it's all been designed for a very specific direction that only you are supposed to follow? This reminds me of a great quote about comparison: "You are the only one running in your race." When we're hustling to make more money, get a nicer home, attain a better title, it's easy to look around you and feel you're trying to keep up with others who have more than you. But this is a waste of time because every person was created with a different destination. Their lives were created to achieve a different purpose and make a different contribution in this world.

This is why, if you think about it, every person is dealt different obstacle cards—because they have different life destinations. We are each meant to grow strong in different areas based on the purposeful paths we were created for. For some, their career thrives but their intimate life is always struggling. For others, they might have an extremely complicated relationship in their life or a personal health problem or are pulling their family out of poverty. Some may cruise through life up to a certain point until a major challenge, loss, or tragedy happens that changes their course. And others still might be handicapped from a devastating event that took place early on; they won't ever heal from the scars until they invest adequate time into the personal work. Whether the biggest challenge in your life has already happened, is happening now, or has yet to come, consider how it may be directing you toward your destiny. What better calling in the future might this event be pulling you toward?

> "Sometimes trials, big and small, occur to direct us toward an amazing calling we never knew would be in store for us."

OBSTACLES MATURE YOU

Maturity encapsulates the leadership qualities that are the opposite of aggression and force. These are qualities like humility, patience, vulnerability, gentleness, and flexibility. In fact, for many these qualities are the more difficult to cultivate. You'll know which ones you're weaker in. Let's explore how obstacles help mature these leadership attributes.

- **Humility.** We are overly confident, think it's never our fault, can't admit our mistakes, have a hard time giving in, or must be affirmed and acknowledged to feel valuable. At some point a struggle will challenge us to the core and force us to be humbled.

- **Patience.** We want what we want now, we care more about making our own point than listening to others so we talk over them, and we're too self-absorbed or selfish to consider why good things come to those who wait. In this case, trials force us to wait and make us more patient.

- **Flexibility.** Sometimes we become set in our ways or too rigid about how we think a problem or situation should be resolved. Inflexibility can prevent us from listening to others with an open mind, seeing all the options available to us, or attending that event that changes our life. In reality, learning how to be flexible will open more doors than it closes.

- **Gentleness.** We tend to be way too defensive, assertive, and stubborn, insisting that it's "my way or the highway." Eventually we realize how we're closing ourselves off to opportunities, even creating unnecessary conflicts and enemies. We realize we must be more gentle in our approach and that we can get further with honey than with vinegar.

- **Vulnerability.** We're so consumed with maintaining the image that we have it all together, yet we're desperately hurting and in need of help on the inside. Eventually the challenge is too much to bear, and we learn that only by sharing our vulnerabilities can we seek the best empowerment, help, and healing.

Maturity is the ability to delay pleasure in the service of a long-term goal. In Stanford University's famous "marshmallow test," children were given one marshmallow with the option of eating it immediately or, if they were willing to wait for twenty minutes, they would receive a second marshmallow. Researchers followed up years later and found that the children who had the ability to delay gratification and wait for that second marshmallow generally led better lives.[3] They even had higher SAT scores and lower body mass indexes thirty years after the study.[4] Therefore, cultivating willpower has demonstrated benefits. But unless you were born with Oprah or Tony Robbins as a parent who has been mentoring you since you were in diapers, most of us learn these things the hard way. Often we are unaware of our immature habits until our circumstances become so miserable and painful that we have to change our ways. The great news is that it's not our fault! Remember: the journey from the beginning of life to the end is a process of being the least mature version of yourself to becoming the most mature version of yourself.

After ten years of successfully securing millions of dollars in cash sponsorships and winning corporate clients for Shecky's Girls Night Out, I thought monetizing S.H.E. Summit and ClaudiaChan.com through sponsorships would be rather easy. I knew that if I could create amazing content and exclusive interviews with leading inspirational women in specific genres (career, confidence, health, time management, finances) for women to consume in a powerful and unique way, brands could sponsor specific genres, as the business of branded content production was booming. For example, like I did at Shecky's, I could structure deals with Dove to be our "women + confidence" partner, Chase Bank our "women + money" partner, and Ann Taylor our "women + career" partner. But in 2011, when I started pitching brands the idea of being partners for our 2012 launch, I experienced a lot of resistance because I was ahead of the curve. Marketers were still of the mindset that all women wanted was fashion, beauty, and celebrity content; they didn't get my vocabulary of words like empowerment, leadership, potential, and mentorship. I got rejection after rejection, but I eventually won clients that have grown incrementally since 2012 to solid five-figure clients each year. I never could have anticipated how grueling and difficult getting back to securing healthy six-figure contracts would be. It wasn't until year five of S.H.E. Summit, the beginning of 2016, that we crossed a major turning point and met my original expectations for year one.

Looking back, I am so grateful for these obstacles. The constant rejections from potential sponsors *built* my resilience and persistence and challenged me to get creative with my tactics. For every *yes* I might get twenty *nos*, so the only way to get to yes was to keep on asking. The repeated nos also *directed* me toward a better business model and corporate strategy because they pushed me to better understand which target customer our services could help the most and cater our offerings accordingly. So rather than trying to be everything to everyone, today we're very specific about our services. And because client wins and dollars came so easily to me at Shecky's, in many ways I lacked humility and patience. Therefore, the struggle to get S.H.E. Summit off the ground, which had my own personal savings on the line, *matured* me tremendously. Without these important lessons there is no way I would have developed on the personal and leadership level that I did.

To conclude, people are not born great; they become great because of what they go through in life. If you are someone who has had everything handed to you on a silver platter, your personality and being will likely lack depth, grit, and many of the leadership qualities I've mentioned.

HOMEWORK

Ponder and answer these questions in your journal:

- Think about the challenges you've faced in the past. Looking back, how might they have protected you? Matured you? Built a strength in you?

- What obstacles are you experiencing now? How can you use these trials to improve you? Find the lesson or teacher in it.

9

Energy

"Part of sensing energy is hearing the messages around you . . . You are like a radio that can receive many stations. What you receive depends on what you pay attention to."

—SANAYA ROMAN, SPIRITUAL TEACHER AND
AUTHOR OF *SPIRITUAL GROWTH*

Many people massively underestimate the leadership pillar of energy, both in terms of the energy they project and the energy they receive. I am not referring to energy defined in the dictionary as the stamina needed to be productive. (I will address that concept more in the next chapter on Productivity.) This chapter refers to energy as the life force that passes between the people we come into contact with.

ENERGY IS THE INVISIBLE MESSAGES EXCHANGED BETWEEN PEOPLE

I want you to think about energy as invisible messages flowing around us, through us, in us, out of us, and between us. Have you ever walked away from a conversation feeling exhausted? Take a moment now to picture who this last conversation was with and why it was exhausting. What about the last conversation that left you feeling elated or exhilarated? Who was that conversation with, and why did it make you feel so good? If you analyze your exchanges with people carefully, you may find that the energy you walk away with derives from the messages they sent you.

Perhaps the people who exhausted you dominated the conversation with all their personal drama or something that has created tremendous stress for them, and they barely asked about you. This sends the message that "I am going to dump all my stress onto you, and we won't talk about you because I am much more significant than you are. I'm going to make you carry all my bags so I can free up my hands to vent." Conversely, the awesome person you had that exhilarating conversation with may have inspired you with some generous advice that you did not expect. She helped you see an *aha* without any condescension, and it came from a very genuine place of wanting the best for you. The message this conveys is "I value who you are. You are special, and I want to help you succeed. I support you."

RECOGNIZING DIFFERENT KINDS OF ENERGIES

There are many different kinds of energy that people can project or convey to you. You must learn how to read the hidden messages and intentions behind them and understand how your heart, body, and mind respond to them. Here's a rundown of the variety of energies you and I have often experienced. As you read through them, consider the people in your community who might represent or emote them.

Negative Energies

SELF-ABSORBED ENERGY. Like my anecdote above, this is the friend who saps your energy every time you see her. She's so consumed by her own goals, drama, or circumstances that she spends most of your conversations telling you what's happening in her life. She always has drama to vent about that she thinks will be equally interesting to you and rarely asks how you're doing. Some self-absorbed people are horrible and can go hours without asking one question about you. Some are slightly better and remember to ask, but maybe your updates get 10 percent of the entire conversation time. You walk away feeling drained and insignificant.

NEGATIVE AND COMPLAINING ENERGY. This is the friend who is always complaining about something. The way he views the world is fundamentally negative and glass half-empty. He's often sarcastic and seems to have the worst luck (though it might just be that he makes a much bigger deal out of the misfortunes he experiences in comparison with everyone else). You walk away from these interactions with their dark cloud over you, feeling a bit depressed and sapped of energy.

> "You must learn how to read the hidden messages and intentions behind different kinds of energies so you know what to allow into your space."

SERIOUS ENERGY. This is the friend who doesn't have a funny bone in her body. Everything is serious to her, which makes it difficult to be spontaneous or creative around her. You feel stifled in her presence, so parting ways is usually a relief.

SENSITIVE AND DEFENSIVE ENERGY. This person makes you feel you like you're always on eggshells around them. He gets overly sensitive or defensive at the slightest disagreement (often a simple misunderstanding). This often leads to anger or conflict, creating an environment that's too toxic for you to be in. You never know what version of this person you're going to get. One minute everything is easy sailing, the next minute he blows up at you.

JUDGMENTAL AND CRITICAL ENERGY. Often a family member or someone close to you, this person always opposes what you say or the ideas you suggest. He always has something critical to say; it's never smooth sailing. Preacher Joel Osteen says, "When someone belittles you, they are being little and 'small minded.'"

ARROGANT ENERGY. This person is completely egocentric and lacks humility. She's a know-it-all who doesn't respect others' opinions and doesn't think they have anything to teach her. When you're with her, you sometimes wonder why you even bother having a conversation—she already knows everything! This kind of interaction can be exasperating and leave you feeling resentful.

Positive Energies

LOVING ENERGY. My mother-in-law, Doris, is a wonderful example of this kind of loving energy; she is always pleasant and projecting love. She asks questions about how you're doing and always wishing or praying for you to have the best circumstances. There's never any pressure or baggage; you walk away feeling light, blessed, and loved.

EMPOWERING ENERGY. This energy often comes from coaches, mentors, teachers, or advisers with endless wisdom to dispense. You can turn to them when you feel stuck on a problem, and they'll send you off with knowledge you need to forge ahead. They often share insights and ideas with you that invigorate and empower you to keep pushing for your visions and purpose. Keep in mind that different strokes work for different folks. A corporate professional mentor in your industry offers very different energy and support compared to, say, a life coach who may have more spiritual/guru energy. Surround yourself with what works for you. I like to be exposed to a variety of empowering energies.

NOURISHING ENERGY. This is my friend Kathleen Griffith, who offers help without my even asking. She's the friend who knows you so well that she knows the weight you carry without any communication necessary. She's so nurturing that you prefer to spend Thanksgiving with her over your own family. Aimee Raupp, who is an acupuncturist and fertility expert, is also a born nurturer. She's always sending me tips on which vitamins to take or popping over to give me an acupuncture session. She genuinely cares for my well-being. If you're someone like me, who's always taking on the world, you need a Kathleen or Aimee in your life.

PLAYFUL ENERGY. This is a friend who you can let loose with and be your silly inner self. Her laughter and joie de vivre are infectious. You can't help but feel energized around her, and you walk away feeling like you need more playfulness, humor, and adventure in your life.

Each of these energies does not necessarily represent one person all the time; rather, they are like modes that we all slip in and out of, some more than others. We can all project these energies, which is why it's equally important to ask yourself, How would other people label you? What are your patterns? Where do you need to lighten up or improve?

I can definitely recall an instance or two when a friend felt pressured and overwhelmed by my impassioned views on women's empowerment. Looking back, I can see them thinking, *Claudia is so intense about women's empowerment that she tries to impose her beliefs onto me.* Similarly, you need to be accountable for your own energy and what you project onto other people. Bad energy can be like slapping someone across the face.

Why must leaders optimize energy? As we discussed in Part I, great leaders are not only powerful role models; they also inspire and teach others how to become great leaders (the multiplication effect). Leaders must manage their own energy in order to sustain their personal well-being and professional livelihoods (we get more into this in the Self-Love chapter) so that they can keep working toward their purpose. In addition, they also have to persuade others to join them and collaborate with outside resources. That's hard to do if you are constantly projecting negative energy—people won't want to work with you, and obstacles will easily spiral out of control as the negative feedback loop snowballs.

With all there is to manage in the world, we could use a lot more of Doris's, Kathleen's, and Aimee's empowering and playful energies in our lives. But be careful not to judge negative energies too harshly—often people are completely unaware of the messages they're communicating, and their energy may not match who they really are inside. We all have that friend who comes across as rude or unfriendly when in reality she's just shy or socially awkward. A person might be projecting what he's really feeling but it comes from a place of insecurity, not because he's a bad person. For example, a naysayer who criticizes or puts others down a lot probably does so on a subconscious level to soothe his or her own feelings of inadequacy. Identify the positive and negative energies in your social circles so you can become more strategic and protective of the messaging and content fed to you, but be compassionate toward everyone. In Chapter 13 we'll talk about how grace can help us do this.

In addition to protecting our own energy and limiting contact with people who diminish it, we must also take responsibility for the energy we project onto others. You see, we communicate so much through the energy of our verbal talk, the tones we use, and physical gestures. Yet most people lack self-awareness of the energy they give off. Being on the recipient side of messages and energy emphasizes just what a big impact the energy that people project can have on others. You and I can really harm someone with our energy without knowing we are doing it. Therefore, we must treat this as a big responsibility, be proactive in evaluating our own energy, and interact thoughtfully with others. When you're talking to someone, make sure it's a dialogue, not a monologue. The adage "be quick to listen, slow to speak" is not only a famous bible verse, but Robert E. Fisher has even devoted an entire book to the topic. He says, "Studies have indicated that the tone of voice may be more important than any other element in our response . . . that we must eliminate nagging with its complaining and contentious spirit because it focuses attention on self rather than on the other person . . . and it is said that those who are critical feel the most self-hate. It follows then that those who practice giving praise and appreciation feel good about themselves."[1]

If you were looking at yourself from the outside-in, how would your gestures and conversational etiquette come across? Be highly intentional and self-aware when you engage with others. If all of humanity were more proactive about this, there would be less misunderstanding and brokenness in the world and much more learning and collaboration.

ATTITUDE IS THE PHYSICAL AND VERBAL EXPRESSION OF ONE'S ENERGY

It's easy to confuse energy with attitude. I see attitude more as the physical or verbal expression of the energy you're emitting. It's the words, tone, expression, and gestures you use to deliver what's inside of you to the outside world. Attitude is different from energy in that it is an actualization, an intentional way of being in the universe; it's choosing what to do with that feeling and energy and how you then outwardly express it. You always have a choice to be positive or negative, and I have learned from spiritual teachers that you get what you focus on. When you have a negative attitude, you focus on creating more negativity (lack, scarcity, regrets, mistakes, unfavorable outcomes). With a positive attitude you focus on creating more positivity (the bright side of things, the silver lining, glass half full).

"You always have a choice to be positive or negative."

The late Dr. Wayne Dyer, who wrote over thirty books on mind, body, and spiritual growth, said about the law of attraction: "You attract what you are."[2] Contrary to popular belief, you can't attract things like wealth and fame by the simple act of wanting them; rather, when you live in service to the universe and revere all life, the universe pays you back in kind—by serving you and revering your life. By the same token, if you live in the self-centric mindset, your world will be limited to self-centric people and problems. I often think of the analogy that if you go into a fitness class thinking, *I'm so fat. I'm not flexible. Everyone in this class is better than me. Why am I here?*, then you're probably going to minimize what you can get out of the class. But if you take on the class thinking, *I'm excited to be here. I want to learn. This is good for my body. The more I do it, the better I'll get*, you're going to maximize the good you can get out of the class. Remember, you're always going to get more of whatever it is you put into something.

The work I did with Gillette for their "Use Your AND" campaign for which I was a spokesperson, which encouraged women to embrace all aspects of their personality, got me thinking about how words have power over us. Tony Robbins asserts, "The words you habitually choose also affect how you communicate with yourself and therefore what you experience. Words can injure our egos or inflame our hearts—we can instantly change any emotional experience simply by choosing new words to describe to ourselves what we're feeling." So in addition to being conscious of the energy you project, if you want to actually shift your state of mind and attitude around a specific problem, the most powerful way you can do that is by putting positive affirmations into words. Here are a few examples of how I talk back to negative thoughts through positive affirmations:

It's frustrating how I always get distracted.

▶ *This is my new normal. I am a wife, mother, and career woman. God has empowered me to achieve professional success and scale with a fraction of time it used to take. I can actually work less now to make so much more!*

Other people have it easier.

▶ *Everyone is dealt a different set of cards for a different path. I could never begin to understand the complexities others need to deal with. I just focus on optimizing my own life and path.*

Housework drives me nuts and is a waste of my value and time.

▶ *I am tending to what shelters and nurtures me and my family.*

If I struggle with such self-critical talk, maybe I am a fraud and am not in a position to grow this company.

▶ *Because I am so hard on myself I am perfect for this work. It's why God assigned me to this path. My imperfection is perfection. Overcoming the struggle is a gift, and I am meant to teach it.*

I am too lazy to be successful and don't act consistently with the motivated person I say I am.

▶ *The moments that feel like procrastination are actually investments in other mental, physical, and emotional experiences that recharge me to get me where I need to be.*

Negative words are restrictive and resist the good things you want for your life. When you transform negative thoughts into positive affirmations, the words create space for miracles to enter. Because energy is invisible, like faith, it is very easily undermined and dismissed, which gives us all the more reason to manage and use it wisely.

HOMEWORK

Ponder and answer these questions in your journal:

- Which people in your life boost and inspire your energy? Which people in your life deplete your energy?

- How can you proactively design your life so you spend more time with people who give off positive energy?

- What kind of energies do you typically project to family members, coworkers, friends and acquaintances? How do you think others would other people describe your energy? Let the answer tell you what you can improve on.

10

Productivity

*"Where focus goes, energy flows. And if you don't take the
time to focus on what matters, then you're living a life of
someone else's design."*

—TONY ROBBINS,
LIFE SUCCESS COACH AND AUTHOR

Many use the word *energy*, as Tony Robbins does in the above quote, to
mean what I call *productivity*: "the strength and vitality required for sustained physical or mental activity." Time and energy are our greatest commodities and also why so many people opt out of leading change for the
greater good. There are only so many hours in the day that you can devote
to personal and professional responsibilities. Plus, as we get older, our responsibilities get larger. This is why having a strategic and proactive approach to your productivity, or what I call a *strategic productivity plan*, is
so important, because how far you make it up your life's mountain, how
much life potential and purpose you realize in your lifetime is the output
of where you invest your time and energy. It is the output of your
productivity.

When things get busier in life, humans tend to become reactive instead of proactive. Pastor Rick Warren says, "Don't confuse activity with
productivity." Because people get so sucked into being busy with activities
coming at them from every side, they lose sight of whether these activities

are even aligned with what's truly important. So how do you direct your productivity for maximum impact? It's important to first look at all the meaningful roles you play in your current stage of life. Stepping back to write these down will help you see what makes up your whole identity and life.

Here's a summary of my roles as a forty-one-year-old woman:

- Wife and life partner to my husband
- Mother of an infant and toddler
- Health and nutrition director for my own life and family
- Financial coprovider for my family
- Household operations comanager
- Leader of S.H.E. Globl Media, its staff, and impact in the community
- Change agent and thought leader in the gender-equality macro-movement
- Daughter
- Sister
- Mentor, adviser, and friend to many

Here's a summary of roles that a single professional may have as a twenty-nine-year-old male:

- Marketing director at an advertising agency
- Friend to many
- Son
- Brother to two sisters
- Uncle to a toddler
- Finance manager for himself
- Health and nutrition manager for himself
- Mentor to three direct reports and young professionals specifically working in advertising and marketing
- Volunteer for the Boys Club, where he serves as a role model for young boys in need
- Writer of a widely read marketing insights newsletter

Lay out each specific role you play, order them in the priority of what's most important, and start identifying your goals and responsibilities under each category. By doing this you will define what productivity means to you and determine what is most deserving of your time and energy.

INVEST IN WHAT REALLY MATTERS

During the summer of 2016 I had a lot to be thankful for. Jackson had just turned one, we actually found out on his birthday that I was pregnant with our second child, my company was tracking to triple its revenues, and this book deal had just been confirmed. But at the same time I was a new working parent navigating the various stages of infant to toddlerhood; racked with the guilt of not doing more for my sick father with stage 4 liver cancer; managing an increasingly stressful relationship with my mother; juggling leadership responsibilities for my team, company, and clients; keeping the house in order and fridge stocked; training our au pair who had just arrived from China; keeping up with my inbox and social circles; bearing increased financial and administrative responsibilities that come with a growing family and business; and to top it all off, John and I had become very combative in trying to manage it all and started counseling. With all these things on my plate, I got hit hard with overwhelming anxiety as if it were all coming down on me at once. I am sure you're familiar with that feeling when you think about everything you need to do at the same time and it feels both paralyzing and overpowering. You lose the ability to compartmentalize and chunk your to-do list, and you rehearse every single fear you have back to back in your head. Pile on the fatigue of being in the third trimester of my pregnancy, and it wasn't pretty.

I got on the phone with one of my advisers, Rha Goddess, and shared my panic about keeping up with it all. She simply said to me, "Claudia, it's not about investing in having it all; it's about investing in what *really* matters. I want you to step back and think about what *really* matters to you. John should do the same, and the both of you should define it together for the family." Just like the call with Mimi I had had a few years before on having more faith, sometimes the most profound *aha* realizations come with the most simple advice. Something inside my heart clicked when she said those three words: *what really matters*. When life gets too busy, we get stuck in our inside-out, reactionary thinking. Everything that everyone else has gets thrown in our face, and we start comparing ourselves and feeling like we need to check every single box. There is always going to be someone with a fancier house, car, office, title, or wardrobe. There are always going to be others who achieve more social media likes, press coverage, revenues, and accolades. There are always going to be parents or people who seem like they have it all down so much more than you. The more we play the comparison game, the more boxes we add for ourselves to check off, the more we care about how we are perceived by others, the more pressure we put on ourselves and our partners, and it all gets out of control.

In order to be productive, we must seize the reins of our rampant check boxes, step back, and define what matters most to us right now and for our futures. Once you've defined your priorities, your job will be to start subtracting, eliminating, and declining the less important things and putting your precious resources toward what holds the greatest significance. Doing this will be so freeing because you can concentrate on a few essential things and do them well versus spreading yourself too thin. When it comes to productivity, less is truly more. Just think about the 80/20 rule, which subscribes to the idea that 20 percent of a business's customers account for 80 percent of sales.[1] In the same line of reasoning, 20 percent of your efforts account for 80 percent of the things that really matter to your health and happiness.

A great way to protect your time is to constantly evaluate the return on investment (ROI) that you're getting with regard to how much time you're putting in to any one task or project. Take stock of what's consuming your days and weeks. What people, projects, personal growth, and education opportunities are you currently invested in? How much time do you waste scrolling through your Facebook feed? Are you taking meetings or calls that really aren't necessary, but you have a hard time saying no? Do household tasks like cleaning or cooking cut into your at-home time when you could easily hire someone to do them for you? Are you always saying yes to friends' social invitations even when you know you need that time to recharge your energy?

Whenever you are considering what to devote your time to, consider the potential ROI of the outcome. Is the time and energy you expend on any one activity today going to yield results that propel you toward your purpose? For example, I prioritize spending quality time with John by scheduling date nights and reserving Sunday evenings to veg out and watch TV together. The relationship you have with your partner trumps everything else and determines your success in your career, finances, health, and more, so the ROI on setting aside that time is a relationship that is thriving and brings us so much happiness. Similarly, when I mentor, train, and develop my team members at S.H.E. Globl Media to lead specific areas of the business and take on more responsibility, the ROI I get from being a good leader is tenfold: the company grows in a positive direction and generates increased revenue, my employees grow and learn to take on greater challenges, and our work continues to impact lives and promote change in the world. Imagine if your hourly rate were $1,000 an hour. What tasks are you leading that really deserve your time? Would you be better served by delegating responsibility to someone else or using additional resources instead?

RELY ON YOUR HEART, MIND, AND BODY TO MANAGE WHAT MATTERS

So how do you know what really matters? Some people know immediately, while others struggle with the answer. One way I learned how to reflect on the things that matter is a framework I learned from Anusara yoga, which is rooted in three areas.

- **Heart.** The first question to always ask is, What do I really want? The answer needs to be rooted in your heart and not your mind. We're often guided by our minds, which tend to overanalyze situations and weigh our options ad infinitum, but the heart needs to drive this answer. What you love, what lights you up and invigorates you comes from the heart, not the head. Beware: if you're coming from a very depleted, exhausted place, the process of discovering your passion can come only out of a state where your bucket is replenished (like my friend Laura from the Faith chapter). So if this is you, take some time to invest in anything that creates positivity for you—travel, adventure, yoga, writing, art, reading, networking, and so on. Clarity on your authentic purpose, vision, and desires can come only from a place of positivity and fullness.

- **Mind.** Once your heart has determined what you want, you can now rely on your mind to lay out the how-to plan for getting there. This is when the organized left brain can kick in to create the strategic plan to get what you want (timelines, projects plans, resources, targets, etc.).

- **Body.** Now that you clearly know what matters and how you will get there, it is time for your body to execute the plan and take the necessary actions. What are your morning and daily rituals? What foods do you need to eat, and what activities do you need to start to keep you mentally sharp and energetic? Where are you doing your work?

Your heart, mind, and body make up your whole being. They are your vessel, the engine that pushes you up the mountain and enables you to rise to your highest potential over the course of a lifetime, which means that your productivity and the many people empowered by your contribution depend on your being fresh, present, and in healthy shape.

What do you have the capacity for? Time and energy are your most precious resources, so you need to be picky about what you concentrate on. Learn to say no. The more successful you are, the more people will be vying for your attention. There will be requests to speak at events and invitations to fancy dinners. You won't be able to say yes to all of them without sacrificing one of your core priorities. With the current macro-movement, the messaging—from role models like Sheryl Sandberg and Beyoncé as well as hashtags like #GirlBoss—has called on women especially to go out and change the world while still managing it all: family, career, finances, health. Beware of taking on too many responsibilities; you can deal only with what fits on your plate. Yes, I'm telling you to do more, but by starting with your most essential priorities and subtracting everything else, you'll be able to arrive at a realistic plan. Go deep and focus on one specific cause instead of spreading yourself too thin. The reality is that you have only so much mental, physical, and emotional capacity. You can't pile on more and more responsibilities forever—that's simply not sustainable.

> "Time and energy are your most precious resources, so you need to be picky about what you concentrate on. Learn to say no."

ELEVATION PERIODS

It would be nice to think that you could set your top three priorities in life and then simply optimize them for the rest of your life, but the reality is that priorities shift constantly, and not just from year to year but from month to month and week to week. It's impossible to plan out an entire year, let alone five, because life has a way of always surprising you. The best way I have found to deal with this practically is to plan in chunks of a few months, or what I call "elevation periods." These are intervals when I identify two or three main priorities that I am going to dedicate my time and energy to, and then I sprint up the next stretch of the mountain to take those priorities to the next level. Your purpose and vision are still the underlying forces driving your one-year or five-year plan, but elevation periods allow you to break up long stretches of time into more realistic and doable chunks of work. Here's a breakdown of how I planned a couple of recent elevation periods:

July 2016 to October 2016

- **Jackson:** Training Lynn, our new au pair from China, so she can create a daily routine for Jackson and ensure that he is happy, healthy, and developing well.

- **Dad:** Maximizing the amount of time I can spend with my father as he battles cancer in and out of the hospital, renting an apartment in Manhattan so we can all be together as a family, and celebrating our father's incredible legacy before his time is up.

- **S.H.E. Summit 2016:** Mentoring and leading my team well so they can each take ownership of specific areas of the business and help us produce the most impactful S.H.E. Summit ever this fall.

November 2016 to February 2017

- **Health and Prenatal Care:** Recovering physically, mentally, and emotionally from the last sprint to S.H.E. Summit 2016 by prioritizing time for self-love and self-care; attending to the health needs of the third trimester of pregnancy, going to all the required doctor appointments, and preparing for the baby's arrival in February.

- **John:** Spending quality time with John and being intentional about scheduling date nights, nurturing our marriage, and cultivating good communication by meeting with our pastor once a month and making sure we do the homework he assigns us so we can continue to work on our relationship as partners and parents.

- **Book:** Writing and refining the content I teach through S.H.E. Summit and dispense to clients into a finished manuscript due to the publisher in January; the book is going to take S.H.E. Globl Media to the next level by sharing these concepts and wisdoms with a broad audience.

- **Visioning:** Every year I make a point to spend the final months of the year, when things slow down for the holidays, to reflect on the year's accomplishments and think about my goals for the coming year: What do I want to achieve? Where do I want to go next on my map? How can I more effectively achieve my purpose? This year I'm challenging myself to double S.H.E. Globl Media's revenue and impact for a second year in a row.

Understand that when you set priorities for a specific elevation period, you are necessarily going to neglect other areas. There's a laundry list of things I want to manage the S.H.E. Globl Media team on now, but I am intentionally choosing not to prioritize that because I have only so much energy. If I'm focused on bringing a new child into the world and finishing a book during this elevation period, then I need to cut back on the amount of time I spend leading the S.H.E. Globl Media team and entrust more responsibilities to each of them. This is where mastering delegation and building your dope squad—the network of people and resources who step in to pick up the slack in areas you don't have the capacity to manage on your own—come in. If you're investing in productivity, then you're investing in delegating responsibilities to others. This also means letting go of some things like perfectionism. If I wrote all the articles and newsletters for S.H.E. Globl Media, the content would be exactly the way I want it; however, that amount of work is unsustainable for one person alone once you take into consideration all the other roles I play. The more successful you become and the more money you make, the more you will be able to pay for more resources and help.

PRODUCTIVITY DOES NOT DETERMINE YOUR SELF-WORTH

Certain time saps have a way of creeping back into our psyches, like feeling guilty for leaving work early to spend time with your kids or feeling like a failure because you didn't cross everything off your to-do list. It takes conscious work every day to harness your time and energy toward your most important goals, but often we are too hard on ourselves. We feel guilty or think less of ourselves when we feel we haven't worked hard enough, achieved enough, lived enough or taken enough Instagram-worthy pictures to show off our fabulous lives. We need to let go of this idea that our productivity is somehow tied to our self-worth. You shouldn't have to cross a million things off your to-do list to feel productive. Remember, you are only one person.

If you don't reach the success you originally envisioned (most people rarely ever do on the first try), know that you gain what you're meant to.

With each step forward you're still making progress and elevating. Instead of focusing on the things you didn't get done today, take a moment to celebrate all the things you did. Shut down the negative-feedback loop and self-critical voice in your head. The best way to combat doubts is to re-engage your faith

> "We need to let go of this idea that our productivity is somehow tied to our self-worth."

and meditate on the belief that everything is in perfect order and you're exactly where you're supposed to be. You will have to make tough decisions and ruthlessly prioritize certain goals over others without knowing the final outcome, which is why becoming attuned to your own instincts and listening to your gut is so important.

HOMEWORK

Ponder and answer these questions in your journal:

- How many leadership positions do you hold between your job and personal life? List all the roles you play at home, professionally, and socially.

- What are the things that really matter to you personally right now? If you have a partner, what are the things that really matter to him or her? From there, can you come together and agree on what matters for both of you to avoid conflict and disunity later on?

- Outline two to three priorities for your next elevation period and get intentional about the ROI you hope to achieve for each.

11

Humility

"Never look down on anybody unless you're helping them up."

—JESSE JACKSON, CIVIL RIGHTS ACTIVIST

Rachael Chong, the CEO of Catchafire, is one of the most extraordinary people I know. Founded in 2009 when Rachael was still in her twenties, Catchafire was built with the objective of providing "transformational volunteer experiences." The organization works with thousands of non-profits seeking pro bono services and matches them with professionals who want to give back by offering their skills and expertise. Today volunteers on Catchafire have donated more than $40 million in professional services, and Rachael has been named one of World Economic Forum's Young Global Leaders and *Fast Company*'s 100 Most Creative People in Business.[1] Impressive as all that sounds, the real reason I admire Rachael is that so much of her success is derived from her tremendous humility, one of the most significant leadership qualities. I've known her from the time she started the business in her twenties to where she is now as the leader of one of the most social-good driven businesses, so I know that she has always had an amazing ability to describe her powerful business proposition yet at the same time communicate from a place of humility—"I always want to improve and learn from you." Over the years this leadership quality has enabled her to gain critical introductions and advice from a stellar advisory board, receive critical rounds of financing from angels and funds, and learn essential managerial and organizational skills from CEO coaches to scale her resources. The one consistent thread is her ability to graciously ask for help. This is why humility is so important. When you are humble you recognize the wisdom that surrounds you and ask for help.

HOW HUMBLE YOU ARE DETERMINES HOW TEACHABLE YOU ARE

Life is a decades-long learning journey, and the world is your classroom. How humble you are determines how teachable you are. How teachable you are determines how successful you will be in life. You will never reach a point in your life where you know everything; there's always another layer of experience and knowledge you can gain. Every leadership position requires teaching, mentoring, and role modeling, but before we become teachers we must first become students so we can bring a solid foundation of knowledge and perspective to any situation. Great leaders don't bring a narrow, small set of knowledges to a situation; they bring a seasoned, open, and broad set of knowledges. Humility is recognizing your own limitations and being willing to receive what others have to teach you. It offers us a flexibility and an attitude that is conducive to learning unfamiliar concepts and stretching our perspectives. When you are humble you acknowledge that you have so much more room to develop, and this honesty allows you to gain. Rising high in your lifetime isn't solely determined by how hard you work, how much courage you have, or how great your vision is; how humbled you are as you climb plays a significant factor too.

"Humility is recognizing your own limitations and being willing to receive what others have to teach you."

Humans tend to think that our way is the right way. We are biased toward the unique background we come from, and without knowing it, we can judge situations and people because of it. Most people move through life evaluating things in family, relationships, work, politics, or situations against "their way" when they should be evaluating them against "what is the best way?" If you think it's your way or the highway or have so much self-assurance that it's difficult for anyone to convince you otherwise, then there's no flexibility. People like this will always be limited by what can they do and where they can go. They can't see beyond their current state, which limits their personal growth.

When we are humble, we are better listeners and observers. This is important because just as God sends you visions, blessings, and obstacles to draw you toward your extraordinary purpose and potential, God also sends you lessons and signs in the form of people and conversations that influence your opinions and broaden your knowledge. I live life viewing people, situations, and obstacles as seeds being planted in me that will bear fruit later. Being humble makes me open to hearing and seeing these messages. Humility opens doors because it gives you the freedom to ex-plore unfamiliar territories and see the miracles being sent your way—God doesn't mean for you to get through life alone.

Have you ever had a random coffee date with someone and your conversation inspired or led to something transformative? Every con-versation is an opportunity to learn and teach, so I do my best to convey a massive sense of humility in all my interactions—I don't act cocky like I know it all but instead expose and share the projects I'm working on and remain flexible and open—because I never know who might be able to help me. At a friend's baby shower I happened to talk to one of the host's colleagues, Sam, who is an investment banker focused on the cor-porate professional services and learning space. Coincidentally this was the area my business was headed in—offering corporate leaders mem-bership and development opportunities to further their gender and di-versity impact. Sam not only planted a few business seeds in my mind regarding how to focus my business but also made two important intro-ductions, one of whom has become a client we are growing with and the other has become a key strategic adviser. When you engage others with positive energy, have faith that everything put in front of you is for you, convey passion for your purpose and vision, and bring a humble and willing-to-learn attitude to conversations, it's tremendous how much impact can come your way.

Some of the most successful people are also the most humble because they are not afraid to ask questions and seek help. In order to do this they must show vulnerability and are confi-

> "When asking for help be as clear as possible about what help means. How can the specific person you're approaching help you?"

dent enough in themselves that they don't have to project a perception of perfection. They are okay with saying, "I am not where I need to be . . . I am not good at this . . . I am in a slump . . . I am struggling with X—can you help me?" When you really do need help, your friends and family can often sense that based on your energy, so you are better off showing that vulnerability. But I want to stress: when asking for help be as clear as possible about what help means. How can the specific person you're approaching help you? Make it realistic for the person. Make it easy for them to help you. If you're that person who is so uncomfortable with asking for aid, just go back to Part I when we talked about vulnerability as a leadership trait because if people, leaders of organizations, are not addressing their vulnerabilities, they will fall behind and hit code reds.

SEEK FIRST TO UNDERSTAND OTHERS

Leadership author and educator Stephen Covey referred to this as the fifth habit of highly successful people: we must seek first to understand, then seek to be under-

> "I live life viewing people, situations, and obstacles as seeds being planted in me that will bear fruit later."

stood. Becoming a better listener is critical for this. Covey points out, "If you want to interact effectively with people and influence them, you first need to understand them. We have a fatal social problem: we don't learn how to listen. People usually don't listen with the intent to understand, they listen with the intent to reply."[2] He explains the different kinds of listening people do.

Levels of listening:

- *Ignoring stage* (not listening at all)

- *Pretentive listening* (acting as if listening, but in fact he's not)

- *Selective listening* (selects what interests him from what's being said)

- *Attentive listening* (listens to everything but without being involved or affected himself)

- *Empathic listening* (listens to everything and puts himself in the place of the speaker)[3]

Think about just how different everyone's backgrounds and experiences are. Their cultures, upbringings, genetics, current circumstances, abundances, scarcities, talents, and core limiting beliefs are based on their past and present. When others project their political, professional, or personal beliefs on us, can we be more curious and fascinated than quick to disagree or judge? The way to better understand where others are coming from is to approach them with the right energy—send them a message that is supportive and curious—and become better listeners. James 1:19 says, "Let every person be quick to hear, slow to speak, slow to anger." I find this to be especially necessary with those you're closest to, like a family member or intimate partner. We tend to be most combative and immature with the people we can be brutally honest with.

Humility is also a critical leadership trait to bring to the workplace. I hear this story often from female corporate professionals who have a female coworker or senior manager who always seems to want to sabotage them. You expected to get this colleague's support as a fellow woman, but her attitude seems only to reinforce the stereotype that women are the first to hold each other back. She sends you emails pointing out flaws, throws you under the bus in meetings, and seems to always be against your recommendations and ideas. Now shift into her perspective for a minute: perhaps she comes from a different generation and was probably conditioned to compete against other women because there were so few slots for them compared to men; she's faced different adversities and hasn't gone through the personal growth work you have. Maybe her marriage is struggling at home, and she's overcompensating for her loss of security at home to the workplace. So before you react and vent—"OMG, she's such a bitch!"—can you perhaps offer compassion and grace toward this person? We just never know what insecurities or private events someone is going through—it's so easy to look at them from the outside and make assumptions and judgments about who they are. To step up your integrity and further differentiate yourself in the workplace, can you be mature enough to model humility and class in this situation? Can you approach this woman with softer, gracious, nonthreatening, and supportive energy to try to understand where she is coming from? This behavior will exude leadership, and your colleagues will notice and respect you more for it.

PEOPLE RESPECT HUMILITY
MORE THAN PERCEPTION

Beyond enabling you to learn more in life and to better influence people, humility also grows your reputation and the respect people have for you. As I mentioned, people who spend time around you at work, in your community, and at home will form their opinions about you based on your actions. We've all met our share of "Mr. or Mrs. Know It All," who leads based on their opinion and perspectives only. That's the person co-workers gossip about and roll their eyes around. They have the bad reputation of too much pride and making unilateral conclusions without truly hearing other sides. Though they walk around with confidence and determination, very few people actually respect and look up to them. Rather, we want to be the person who achieves great success by listening well and taking all input into consideration. That's the leader who doesn't convey that she knows everything (which is impossible) and instead asks the right questions and knows how to get everyone on the team working toward a common goal. Humble leaders have the best reputations because they take the time to listen and learn from others.

We all must be aware of one major thing that prevents us from being humbled: our impulse to maintain a perfect or impressive self-image. It's a tough balancing act because when people (management, colleagues, direct reports, clients, friends, social followers) perceive you to be "all that" and highly impressive, their perception of you does, in a way, help the path ahead get easier. The more others respect and admire you, the more opportunities come your way. The problem is that you can get caught up in maintaining the perception that you think you need to be successful, and then you focus on this more than your actual purpose. The ego takes over again, and more of your time gets spent on how to draft the perfect Instagram post than on the social good you've committed to. You become more focused on fabricating the authentic you than being the authentic you, which is *not* authentic. In this self-centric context we start marketing instead of being. We set targets and goals we're unable to meet, and we talk up a *big* game so others will perceive us in a great light. In reality there is so much you need help with, so much you're not sure of, so much wisdom you could benefit from, and so many introductions you need others to make. But you're unable to tell anyone and express humility because then you won't keep up with the image you've created. This is why many people walk through life with the terrifying, crippling fear: *What if others find out I am a fraud?*

People can usually tell when you're doing something just to win admiration and praise. But if you stay focused on your vision of making an impact on the world and align with your values instead of paying attention to what other people think of you, respect will naturally follow. I get it: perceptions matter to some extent. But there's a way you can garner both respect and humility.

My best advice for balancing perception with humility is to just stay focused on strengthening the pillars of this book, what you have learned in each chapter on purpose, vision, faith, and so on. Then just act and speak as the *authentic you*. If you stay focused on your why—your significant purpose here on earth and the good work that you're meant to do—then your impressive reputation will speak for itself. And pursue purpose not for what others may think of you but for what your higher power, source, or God may think of you. They are always watching and have your back.

LET THE UNIVERSE HUMBLE YOU

If you're still not humble enough to hear what I am saying, then allow your sheer existence and the universe to humble you. When you see your life through the outside-in lens, you will realize how miraculous and vast the world that you exist in is. You are just one of 7.3 billion humans who live on this planet, where one sun rises and sets to meet one moon and billions of stars. All 7.3 billion people experience reality differently based on their geographic destiny. You were conceived in your mother's womb and are yourself endowed with the means to mate with a partner and create another human being. You move through life unable to predict the future without any control over who you will meet and what you will encounter. The universe we live in is so mind blowing—how can you or I possibly think we know everything? What we do know is that what is possible and unknown is infinite; therefore, we must believe that there is an infinite amount of wisdom to be learned. No matter where you are now, humble yourself like crazy and realize how much more there is to learn about who you're meant to be and the universe you're in.

I do want to point out the difference between being humble and being insecure because people who lack confidence have no problem being humbled. The difference is that humility embodies confidence and security. Humble people are secure in who they are, what they stand for, and where their strengths lie and never think twice about wanting to learn more. Insecurity, however, means one lacks security and confidence. C. S. Lewis said, "Humility is not thinking less of yourself, but thinking of yourself less." I'm not telling you to think less of yourself or to diminish the accomplishments you've achieved; I'm saying you have nothing to prove and that will come through more if you can focus your attention on listening to others.

It's also interesting that researchers have observed that humility is more often displayed by women than by men. For instance, men are more likely to become entrepreneurs because they are better at disregarding market signals and criticism and more willing to fail multiple times before they achieve a level of success. Women, however, are more likely to be humble about their achievements and abilities and less likely to attribute their mistakes to specific circumstances.[4] This means that if you're a woman who already embraces humility, you may actually need to work on communicating your accomplishments and skills to others rather than striving to be too humble. If you're a man who struggles with humility, then you may want to practice actively listening to others, acknowledging others' accomplishments, and aiming to be more collaborative.

Without humility, you can't do the work of personal growth. Without personal growth, you can't go through professional development. Without optimal professional development, you will never be able to lead greatly. Without leadership ability, you will never be able to fulfill your purpose and realize your visions at your highest potential. Great leaders think of life as a constant learning experience and are always looking for opportunities to expand their minds and adopt new strategies. You could spend your entire life learning, and there would still be things that shock and amaze you. Ultimately we are here to learn as much as we can during our lifetimes.

HOMEWORK

Ponder and answer these questions in your journal:

- Try to gauge your barometer on humility. Do you tend to think you know it all, or are you great at receiving opinions and advice from others? Where can you be more humble?

- In conversation how much do you usually talk versus listen? When and where can you become a better listener?

- Could a lack of humility be blocking you from further development in your career or personal life?

12

Gratitude

"Acknowledging the good that you already have in your life is the foundation for all abundance."

—ECKHART TOLLE, SPIRITUAL TEACHER AND
THE AUTHOR OF *THE POWER OF NOW*

I want to reiterate one of my most significant pieces of advice. It's a simple concept but one of the hardest habits to maintain: you get what you focus on. If you focus on something you fear, you will get more fear. If you focus on what you lack, you will actually promote more scarcity in that area. As I've preached, you are all destined for infinite greatness—but *only* if you can train your mind to focus on and continually shift back to that which you want to manifest. One of the best tools to help you do this and combat scarcity is practicing gratitude. To practice gratitude is to see the silver lining in everything, to appreciate the foundation that supports us throughout our life's climb, to be humbled that we don't know everything, and to trust that the universe has bigger plans in store for us.

GRATITUDE COMBATS SCARCITY BY BUILDING AN ABUNDANCE MINDSET

According to author and life coach Martha Beck, "For the vast majority of world history, human life—both culture and biology—was shaped by scarcity. Food, clothing, shelter, tools, and pretty much everything else had to be farmed or fabricated, at a very high cost in time and energy."[1] Given the hostile history we come from, it's not surprising that humans are wired to approach life from a glass-half-empty mindset instead of a glass-half-full one. The problem with the scarcity mentality, however, is that it promotes zero-sum thinking—that is, that there are winners and losers, and one person winning necessarily means another person is losing. This manifests in feelings of never having enough money, status, possessions, or power.[2] When something very disappointing happens, our initial reaction is to feel like a victim or a loser: *Why does this always happen to me? I have the worst luck.* Or on the other end of the spectrum we just put ourselves down: *I'm not smart/talented/good enough. It's my fault this happened.*

> "To lead greatly is to assume an "abundance mindset" that moves you up the mountain faster because you are not saddled with the fear of losing what you already have."

Ironically, psychology research has revealed that people who have a scarcity mindset consume more "mental bandwidth" or brainpower by focusing energy on the area where they feel deprived.[3] This leads to bad decision making and shortsighted solutions that never truly address the root of a problem. Wasting time worrying about what you lack is not only inefficient but can also be detrimental to the other areas or goals in your life. We all have scarcities based on our upbringings and what our parents focused their mental bandwidth on (maybe they were always scrambling to make ends meet or constantly feared losing their job security). It's normal to be influenced and sometimes scarred by past trials.

Leaders who are hung up on scarcity end up trying to maintain the status quo instead of forging ahead and taking smart risks. They value "preservation rather than growth, familiar surroundings instead of new frontiers, and complacency over challenges," which eventually leads to stagnation or, worse, obsolescence.[4] To lead greatly is to assume an "abundance mindset" that moves you up the mountain faster because you are not saddled with the fear of losing what you already have.

Living in abundance allows you to identify new opportunities and acknowledge the efforts of others, and this in turn boosts your organization's morale and incentivizes individuals to be curious and innovative. If you focus on all the ways you have been blessed and lucky, you will get more of that good stuff.

My friend Sallie Krawcheck is the perfect example of this. Chances are you've heard her name. She was once known as the most powerful woman on Wall Street for her role as one of the few female CEOs at major financial institutions. But in 2008 she was forced out as CEO of Citigroup's Smith Barney unit and then let go again just three years later from her role as CEO of Bank of America's wealth management division.[5] Most people who go through a scenario like that—let alone twice—never bounce back. Instead of harboring resentment for being wrongfully terminated—in both cases Sallie had turned the company around and increased revenues significantly—or feeling like a failure, Sallie kept communicating and focusing on her gratitude for all she accomplished and experienced. During the many times I interviewed her, either on the S.H.E. Summit stage or for webinars, I could see that deep down inside she always knew there was something bigger to come out of those Wall Street events. Her ability to shift into an abundance mindset and focus on gratitude allowed her to create the space and attitude needed to think about her next move. Without these experiences, she never would have purchased 85 Broads and rebranded it to the professional women's network Ellevate. Then in 2016 she launched Ellevest, an investment platform tailored specifically to help women invest and take control of their financial well-being. She turned her pain into positive impact by empowering women in business and money.

SOFTEN TO ACCESS YOUR POWER

Because the macro-movement tells us to hustle harder and step up our game, a natural response is to just take on more and try to get it all done faster. As we learned in the Productivity chapter, extreme busyness can become a breeding ground for scarcity because there's no time for reflection or to pause to ensure that your actions are aligned with your purpose and what really matters. This is because hurry prevents connection, pulling us away from authenticity and the big picture of what we're trying to accomplish. Also, when we're in the frantic go-go-go mode of life, we can get bogged down in the details—bills to pay, meetings to attend, sick kids to take to the doctor—and we forget to appreciate the things that make us truly blessed.

In the Anusara yoga philosophy that I have studied, the first step to optimize your pose and experience is to "soften your heart." Whether you're in downward dog or cat-cow pose or you're preparing for a handstand—this action requires shrinking the space between your shoulder blades where your heart is. By doing this, you expand the internal and external space for your body and any pose to come, especially the most difficult ones.

This has become a metaphor for my whole life because really, in absolutely any situation, softening allows us to create space to connect back to what really matters or to recall our most powerful mantras and think about how we want to respond. Softening allows us to practice mindfulness. Softening allows us to access our power so we can choose to respond instead of react. We can choose to be thoughtful instead of irrational. When a colleague creates what you think is more unnecessary work for you, a family member says something that digs into your skin, a driver cuts you off on the highway, or your toddler is having a massive tantrum, these are all opportunities for you to first soften and then decide how you want to respond. You bring soft energy so you don't exacerbate the situation. If you respond with rigidity and aggressive energy, it will only add fuel to the fire and escalate the tension.

Practicing gratitude is one the best ways to soften because it directs your energy to positive thoughts. Right now I'm preparing to welcome my second child into the world via a C-section. In the middle of my first quarter of the year, the most important corporate fundraising and strategic planning period for my business, I will be caring for a very needy toddler, breastfeeding a newborn, and recovering from major surgery. I'm going to need to hire new sales and operations resources for the business in addition to more caregiving support for myself, my toddler son, and the newborn. On top of all this, we're contemplating moving back to a major city (New York City or Los Angeles) later in the year, not to mention my book launch and S.H.E. Summits taking place around the world. It's insane and paralyzing to think about! In moments of panic I ask myself, *How can I possibly do all this?*

But by proactively practicing gratitude, I'm able to shift my anxiety to positive thoughts and create the space for channeling my precious energy toward devising a plan to handle it all. I am grateful for so many blessings: John and I are so lucky we got pregnant as quickly as we did in our early forties; since 2012 I have moved major mountains each and every year with grace and success, and things have always worked out; S.H.E. Globl Media just finished its most profitable and impactful year ever and is poised to expand in the coming one; we can afford the extra help to assist us with childcare; John and I are both in unique entrepreneurial positions where we can make anything happen; I have a life partner who shares my values and goals, and together we will manage it all in accordance with what really matters to both of us; and I have a vast network of friends, clients, and team members who will support all these goals. Acknowledging what I'm grateful for gives me the power to focus my energy on devising the best plan for moving forward. It lightens my load so I can flow again and take advantage of all the miracles, angels, and blessings that God has already lined up for me.

> "Softening allows us to access our power so we can choose to respond instead of react."

PRACTICE RADICAL GRATITUDE DAILY

So how do you actually practice gratitude? There are so many ways to do this, ranging from journaling to meditating on what you're grateful for, but I'll share with you what I call my Radical Gratitude Prayer. As my inner naysayer tends to be the loudest in the morning, this is a common exercise I do the moment I wake up and notice any tension. It helps me start the day from a positive and glass-half-full mentality. I also access it whenever I start feeling overwhelmed with stress or negative emotions. No matter where I am—sitting at my desk, driving, before or after meetings—I just close my eyes and start by expressing thanks for the basic privileges I know so many in this world don't have, and then I work my way up to more specific circumstances. Wherever I feel the most scarcity is where I try to acknowledge my progress, successes, and accolades. Here's an example:

> *Dear God, thank you for all my blessings.* [I start with basic privileges that don't require much thinking.] *Thank you for my family I get to live this life with and the beautiful home we get to live in. Thank you for the oxygen we breathe, the clean water we have to drink, the foods we get to eat. Thank you for today's sunny weather, for the trees and the birds, for the miracle of nature. Thank you for the important work I get to do each day, the incredible team who moves the work forward to clients we get to serve. Thank you for the maturity, intelligence, and gift that every past obstacle has brought me. Thank you for all the struggles and the pain that I went through because now I realize why I went through them. Thank you for my son, Jackson, and for the little one on the way. Thank you for my loving husband and partner in crime, John. Thank you for taking care of my dad in heaven.* [I move on to my successes, what I have gotten done, what has worked out.] *Thank you for this book deal and the opportunity to teach so many with it* [this combats fear of it not being good]. *Thank you for the accomplishments X, Y, and Z that my company made this month* [this combats feelings of lack of progress]. *Thank you for the progress John and I made these two weeks on managing family responsibilities* [this combats any judgments I put on my husband and marriage]. *Thank you for my role as a US State Department speaker on women's empowerment and traveling to countries to empower women, for my global spokesperson deal with P & G, for my ability to quadruple our business in my first year of motherhood, for the opportunity to support very special corporate and entrepreneurial leaders from Deloitte, Prudential, Bacardi, Morgan Stanley, Lifeway, Johnson & Johnson, and thousands of S.H.E. community members in their specific gender-women's movements, which create a ripple effect of good for millions* [this combats my self-doubt that I am not enough].

Keep in mind that my process is a prayer, but you should obviously choose whatever format works for you; for instance, instead of addressing a higher power—"Thank you, God"—it can simply be an acknowledgment like "I am so thankful for xxx." Challenge yourself to practice your own radical gratitude prayer daily, either in the morning or whenever your energy runs low and the negative voices start to talk.

Often we forget that our problems are mostly first-world problems. Remembering the many, many things I need to be thankful for humbles me and reminds me that not everyone is as fortunate to have the basic necessities of life: safety, home, nourishment, love, and professional fulfillment. This remotivates me for my purpose and reminds me that I am one of the lucky ones meant to do something impactful with these privileges. The acknowledgment of how I have specifically been successful affirms for me that I can do this again and again, that the life I lead for this world is meant to be a history of successes.

GRATITUDE IS GOOD
FOR YOUR HEALTH

Gratitude not only puts you into an abundant state; it also has scientifically proven health benefits. For example, gratitude improves psychological health, and studies conducted by researcher Robert Emmons confirm that gratitude increases happiness and reduces depression. When you practice gratitude on a regular basis, you're less likely to experience toxic emotions like jealousy, frustration, and regret. It also has an impact on your physical health, as grateful people tend to exercise more and schedule regular doctor appointments.[6]

> "The impossible comes within reach when we focus on the glass half full."

Gratitude boosts self-esteem (you realize you have so much to feel good about), keeps stress at bay (you sweat the small stuff less), and can even strengthen your mental fortitude. A 2006 study on Vietnam War veterans discovered that those who experienced higher levels of gratitude were better able to recover from trauma and showed lower rates of PTSD.[7] Best of all, grateful people sleep better and longer. To take advantage of the full benefits of this habit, start your day by meditating on the things that enrich your life and be thankful for them.

Every day is a privilege, and we take that for granted. If you're overwhelmed by the professional goals you're working toward for the next six months to a year, if you suffer from depression and struggle to make it through the day, or if you're still trying to build your foundational habits and beliefs, gratitude will keep you centered and pull you through hard times. Life will always have meaning when there are things to be thankful for. By softening your heart you will open yourself up to learning from others (humility), relentlessly prioritizing the things that matter (productivity), strengthening relationships with friends and family (community), and understanding how the privileges you already enjoy support your faith. The impossible comes within reach when we see the glass half full.

HOMEWORK

Ponder and answer these questions in your journal:

- Do you typically see the world from a glass-half-full or a glass-half-empty mindset? Why?

- What things in your life do you take for granted and need to practice more gratitude for?

- Take a moment now to name and write down your three to five most common scarcities, then cross them out and write gratitude/abundance statements.

- What does practicing your radical gratitude prayer look like? Can you start this today and set reminders for yourself?

13

Grace

"To forgive is to set a prisoner free and discover that the prisoner was you."

—LEWIS B. SMEDES, THEOLOGIAN AND AUTHOR

We have learned that the size of your obstacles can determine the size of your greatness. How much faith you have determines how much support and lifting you get from God. How humbled you are determines how teachable you are. How grateful you are determines how happy and abundant you are. So what role does grace play in helping you reach your life's potential? How much grace you have determines your capacity to forgive, and how much you're able to forgive results in how much freedom from angst and frustration you will have in your lifetime. What do I mean by this?

GRACE IS FORGIVING OTHERS, EVEN WHEN THEY DON'T DESERVE IT

One consistent theme throughout this book has been the significance of people. Humans were created to be social beings, and we exist to relate with one another. Because so much of our heart and emotional reliance is tied to people, especially the ones closest to us like a partner, parent, child, or sibling, relationships can cause us to experience more negative feelings than anything else. Nothing can hurt us, frustrate us, and anger us the way other people can. This is where grace comes in. Grace means forgiving others even when you feel they don't deserve it. It is what sets you free from nega-

> "Grace means forgiving others even when you feel they don't deserve it."

tivity and resentment so you can give your highly precious energy and life force to your greater destiny and purpose. In the Productivity chapter I asked you to value your time and energy at $1,000 an hour because it's a limited resource and the only thing you have to advance what matters to you. When relational conflicts arise, you must access grace from your leadership toolbox and allow it to wash away the animosity it can awaken. Granting grace to others sets your time, energy, and life force free so instead of dwelling on past wrongs, you can be positive and healthy.

Not too long ago I had lunch with an old friend. She is a senior executive who has many years of experience in the nonprofit world and had just been fired from a job her mentor had spent months grooming her for, so she was justifiably upset about the entire situation. She felt that not only had she been wrongly terminated, but she had also been betrayed by the person who had brought her to the company in the first place. In some ways her layoff was a blessing in disguise because it was the first time in a very long time that she had quality time to spend with her kids, who were two and five years old. However, she didn't see it that way. We ended up spending most of our lunch focused on my friend's resentment for this woman who fired her. When you become consumed with anger because of something someone else has done against you, whether that slight is real or imagined, you hold yourself captive to all that pain and outrage. By punishing others for someone else's misdeeds, we also punish ourselves, and the seed of resentment continues to grow. Only with forgiveness are we able to move on and reset to our foundational beliefs and values. At the end of the day relationships are either growing closer or farther apart. They are never still. So know that the longer you wait to offer them grace, the farther apart those relationships will sadly become.

What happens when people, especially the ones we love the most, drive us nuts? We get angry and want to tell them off. It's not something I am proud to share, but I have been through my fair share of retaliation and interpersonal combat. When my husband complains to me about something I do that he also does, I have gotten defensive and told him he is a hypocrite. This has led to fights. In my last business, Shecky's, when my business partner would repeatedly make decisions that I felt were poor, I went off on him and insulted his intelligence and character. This has led to fights. A lot of managers and business owners experience this.

If you're managing a team and an employee does something wrong, your first impulse may be to call them out immediately to address the issue, but it's not really the most effective time. Think about whether it can wait for the next staff meeting or your weekly one-on-one with this employee, a quiet moment when he or she will be more receptive to your feedback.

> "Relationships are either growing closer or farther apart. They are never still. So know that the longer you wait to offer someone grace, the farther apart that relationship will sadly become."

The better way to respond to interactions like these is to reflect, not react. When something upsets us or sets us off, we often want to speak up about it right away. We want to share our feelings immediately to get it off our chest, but we're still emotional and can end up sounding pissed off and intense. Grace, like gratitude, is another way to soften. When we offer forgiveness, we create more space for a relationship or interaction to be successful. Grace becomes an act of prevention—preventing arguments, more frustration, and spiking blood pressure. One of my mentors says, "Relationships are never still; they are always growing further apart or growing closer together." When we feel someone has done us wrong, retaliation and fighting only pull two people further apart. If left unaddressed, we have the tendency to bottle up grudges and rage inside ourselves. Maybe we blame the other person for something we lack. Or we develop a victim mentality, and the desire for revenge and justice deepens. The result? We try to put other people behind bars for what they did, and in turn we put ourselves behind bars too. The longer we want to imprison someone, the longer we imprison ourselves. The longer we decide to be upset by something someone has done, the longer that negativity brews in us.

WHEN IN RELATIONAL CONFLICT,
VIEW THINGS FROM
THE OTHER PERSON'S PERSPECTIVE

Conflict is inevitable in any human relationship, so when it does arise, learn to see things from the other person's perspective. You might not necessarily know what hardships they have been through, how people have hurt them in the past, or why certain words and actions trigger a reaction. Difficult relationships usually have a lesson to teach us. My relationship with my mom has become more complicated over the years because, from my perspective, she is constantly expressing anger, anxiety, and negativity. For example, when it comes to how I am raising and caring for my one-year-old son, Jackson, she always finds something to criticize: "Jackson has food all over his face! What a poor child. Why is he eating with his hands? The pieces of food are too big. Why do you have him dressed in that shirt? Look, he just sneezed. You see, I told you to put his sweater on!" In reactive mode I'd simply yell back at my mom, and an unproductive argument would spiral out of control. But when I lead with compassion and soften my approach, I begin to see things from her perspective and become more sensitive to what's actually driving her negativity.

My mother's dad died when she was young, and her mom's family didn't treat her well. She came to the United States without a college education, married my dad, and then worked nonstop for forty years. She was an equal and substantial driver of the family's income, which helped put me and my brother through private school and allowed me to graduate college without a penny of debt. After she sold her business and retired, my dad got sick, and she ended up taking care of him for the next eight years. Because of the circumstances of her life, she had little time to tend to herself and nurture her dreams outside the family unit. Over the years, as my mom's obligations increasingly depleted her emotionally and physically, she became more negative in her outlook on life. Shifting into the outside-in mindset and seeing my mom's life from her perspective has been extremely humbling; understanding her burdens has made me more compassionate. When she does get negative or critical, I need to make it less about me and more about her circumstances. I need to realize that my perspective is not the only way to see things. Learning how to cultivate a positive relationship with my mom in recent years has been one of the greatest challenges of my life. It has exercised my grace, humility, and patience muscles all at once.

We must not forget that sometimes we also need to cut ourselves some slack and offer ourselves grace. Your internal self-critic will get bigger and louder as you scale more difficult stretches of the mountain; the more ambitious you are, the greater the risks, the larger your fears, and the more there is to get done. Rewriting the playbook and taking radical steps forward means the margin of error is also bigger, and you will likely fail many times along the way. Maybe you get upset with yourself for making bad decisions, for taking too long or not spending enough time on things, or for mistreating a person or mishandling a situation because you're under so much pressure. These are times when you need to extend grace to yourself, relax the high expectations you hold yourself to, and have compassion for your own limitations.

> "Grace adds an elegance and refinement to your character by opening up interactions with people and helping you to become more flexible and nimble."

Finally, there is another definition of grace: when someone is graceful like a dancer, they move with poise and agility. In the same way, grace adds an elegance and refinement to your character by opening up interactions with people and helping you to become more flexible and nimble. Grace enables you to turn obstacles, in the form of difficult relationships, into opportunities; when you give grace to others you project love and positive energy. And the more pleasant you are, the more persuasive you are. Even when you are upset, use words to build and lift people up, not to tear them down. Stop to ask yourself, *Can I speak in a way that doesn't offend but still gets my point across?* Be slow to speak and quick to listen. Remember that most people aren't going to be as developed as you because they haven't done the personal growth work. Just decide you're going to be the bigger person. Live up to your destiny by choosing the high road.

HOMEWORK

Ponder and answer these questions in your journal:

- Do you have an estranged relationship with someone whom you can forgive and start healing your relationship with? Who can you extend more grace to so you can free yourself from the friction?

- What are the tendencies or traps you fall into when you are with this person? Can you catch yourself next time and extend grace? Can you try to see it from his perspective?

- If you knew that everyone was doing the best they can, even when they do things that upset you, would that change your response and ability to offer grace?

14

Community

"I think we so often equate leadership with being experts—
the leader is supposed to come in and fix things. But in this
interconnected world we live in now, it's almost impossible
for just one person to do that."

—JACQUELINE NOVOGRATZ,
CEO OF ACUMEN AND
AUTHOR OF *THE BLUE SWEATER*

Keeping the significance of human relationships in mind, we now turn
our attention to the concept of community. You were meant to go through
life with the help, support, guidance, and company of other people. For
this reason it's important to choose wisely the relationships you invest
your time in because your community can both influence you and reflect
the kind of person you are. Ultimately you become the company you keep
because we are impressionable and often take on the characteristics, habits, thoughts, and energies of the people around us without even knowing
it. We are especially susceptible to this when we lack the strong foundational values that Part II of this book teaches us. Young people especially
need to watch out for this—no matter how much wisdom your parents or
other events have imparted to you, you still lack the volume and variety of
life experiences that come with age and allow you to develop a strong
value system. Your internal foundation of values is like your immune

system: how strong it is determines how much the people and content you encounter affect you. The more proactive you are about what you decide to let in or dismiss, the more successful you will be in building community.

YOU BECOME THE COMPANY YOU KEEP; ESTABLISH RELATIONSHIPS WISELY

When I think about where I was during those dark years at Shecky's I see that I was in a very unhealthy relationship with my business partner. Chris and I kept having the same arguments and battles—it was like being stuck in a vortex of repetitive negative patterns—and because he and I were like the parents of the company, our disputes and bad energy spread to the rest of the company and infected everyone else. I was stuck in a toxic culture that did not support me to be a better person. Often we can accidentally find ourselves in a scenario that brings out the worst in us. So I shifted the focus in my life and proactively surrounded myself with positive people, support groups, and activities. I started doing yoga and found ways to extract myself from the situation at the company by flying to other cities where Shecky's was throwing Girls Night Out parties. I had conversations with women doing amazing work all over the country and cultivated a new mindset and knowledge by reading voraciously. This is how I pulled myself out of a toxic situation and began building a community built on positive values.

"The ideal community is supportive, believes in you, and makes you feel good when you're with them."

Building a tribe is not just about befriending people. Don't just get to know people—get to know their souls. What kind of soul do they have? What experiences or skills do they have that you can learn from? Your energy also has to be reciprocated. The ideal community is supportive, believes in you, and makes you feel good when you're with them. Be highly strategic about who qualifies to be a part of your inner circle.

There is an old business adage that says you should hire people who are smarter than you if you want your company to thrive and succeed. The same holds true for your personal community, whether they are friends, family, or professional contacts. You don't want to be the smartest person in the room because then you'll have no one to stretch or challenge you. Surround yourself with role models who stand for something and are doing amazing work in the world that piques your curiosity. The whole point of role models is to teach you and give you an example to aspire to.

I love creating "next actions" for myself after spending time with someone who has motivated me to do something different. When we spend quality time with others and openly exchange our ideas and experiences, a friend may say something that causes you to feel awakened. You get *ahas* and think, *Wow, what you're saying speaks to where I am now and what I need. I love you!*

NOTHING STRENGTHENS COMMUNITY MORE THAN GENEROSITY

Generosity is the common theme in all these relationships. It is not only the quality of being kind and understanding but also an attitude that allows one to give and share openly without the expectation of being repaid. Adam Grant, Wharton professor and best-selling author, writes in his book *Give and Take*, "The more I help out, the more successful I become. But I measure success in what it has done for the people around me. That is the real accolade." You want to spend time with people who espouse a similar ethos. People who are generous and willingly give what they need to offer, whether it's time, resources or expertise. They volunteer their support without your even asking because they know what it's like to be in your shoes. But the *key* is knowing that you can't expect people to just come out of the woodwork and want to do things for you; people treat you well when they respect you, but you first have to earn their respect. What do you stand for? Is your character something that inspires them? Are you the kind of person who is always gracious? Do you also offer your help and resources to others? Are you a role model others can look up to?

I have often heard people complain about not being supported by their community when they have, in fact, done very little to earn their support. Their mindset is too self-centric: "My dream is xxx, and I really need help. Susan is in the perfect position to help me, and I don't understand why she won't. I don't know how many more ways I can hint at her." Or, "I have emailed Susan a few times and she won't get back to me." Well, perhaps you should look at the situation from her perspective. Susan has a lot on her plate, and given her role, everyone wants something from her. You're hinting at this favor in a way that makes it only about the thing you want. Remember: when you ask for help you should be coming from a place of humility and gratitude. Explain to Susan *why* what you're asking for is significant and how it would benefit others or something bigger than yourself. Communicate your request in a way that persuades Susan to answer, even relate it back her own work and the value she can contribute. If you stand for something bigger (i.e., your purpose), people will buy into your mission and become your champions.

If you want to establish powerful relationships, the feeling of generosity between parties has to be mutual. We should all proactively share our gifts and talents with others as they do the same for us. Community cannot survive on a take model; it works only when it's based on mutual respect and a symbiotic give and take. Women are typically better at building and maintaining friendships; they call friends up on the phone and meet in person regularly. Male friendships tend to be more transactional and based around shared activities like watching sports games or playing poker, which leads to fewer conversations about feelings or issues someone might be dealing with internally. According to one survey, men who identified someone as a close friend often had not spoken to that person, in years and in some cases the friend had passed away.[1] So when it comes to community, understand your own biases, and push yourself to break out of past patterns. The more vulnerable and honest you are, the stronger your relationships will be and the more you will get out of them.

HOW TO BUILD YOUR DOPE SQUAD

So how do you determine the qualities of the community your surround yourself with? Who do you prioritize dinners, lunches, coffee dates, phone calls, and weekend visits with? Not everyone in your life has to be a person who teaches you something. Other people might be there to inspire and motivate you. Sometimes we need motivation. Sometimes we need a good time. Sometimes we need a sounding board. Sometimes we just need support. You will find yourself calling on different friends in different life situations, which is why you should build a tribe, or what I like to call a dope squad, made up of all these different energies. Who you have dinner with, make social plans with, meet at events, or grab a coffee with matters. You might meet twenty new people every year, but who are the top three or four you're going to build deeper relationships with? The people in your community make up different circles:

- **Your Closest Tribe.** This circle has the smallest number of people because it only includes people you know on a deeply intimate level—you know each other's souls. This group is your support system and usually consists of family, intimate partners, BFFs (those who know your character and tendencies so well that they know your needs without having seen or spoken to you for a while), and lifelong mentors (those who not only "get you" and whatever it is you are sharing but also offer feedback in a way that is constructive).

- **Your Larger Tribe.** The people within this circle have similar interests and beliefs as you and share some common goals. You are often powerfully aligned to help each other achieve your purposes. Your larger tribe might include influential sponsors (those who are busy people doing important work in the world yet they make time for you, which immediately conveys that they want to listen to how you are and be ready to offer help) or generous givers (those who cherish your relationship so much that they offer up random acts of kindness, their gifts and talents, such as yoga sessions, acupuncture, beautiful meals, business session, etc.).

- **Your Network.** These are loose ties you have connected with on LinkedIn and Facebook or through mutual friends or colleagues.

Anyone you've met once or had at least one meaningful conversation with falls into this bucket. Your network usually includes people who are your cheerleaders (those who believe in you so much that they champion your cause but only after they understand and are moved by the meaning you represent).

So when you go about planning your week or months, consider the different circles of people in your community and where you need to invest more time in order to develop or nurture specific kinds of relationships. For example, if you've just moved to a new city and want to make friends, maybe you should focus on building a larger tribe by joining clubs or participating in activities where you can meet people with similar interests. If you're looking to change jobs, you should invest more time in growing your network.

Community is not only the people you surround yourself with; it's also the content you consume, the projects you pour your energy into, and the topics you spend time thinking about. What are you feeding your brain? Get intentional about the articles and books you read, the events and conferences you attend, and the activities you do during personal time. The newsletters you subscribe to, the podcasts you listen to, even the TV shows you watch are going to nourish and develop you. What kinds of things do you want to be exposed to and learn from? I spend time focusing on yoga immersion, listening to church sermons, and reading inspirational, self-help books because I want to surround myself with positivity. Whatever you allocate your time to, ask yourself what purpose it serves. How is a specific practice or study of an area of knowledge helping you work toward your goals? How is it developing you as a persona? Be intentional, but also diversify your activities and education. Our brains can't always be in hyper-learning mode. When I have a date night with my husband or we stay in to cozy up and watch a movie, it's just good, old-fashioned couple time.

> "Community is also the content you consume, the projects you pour your energy into, and the topics you spend time thinking about. What are you feeding your brain?"

Essentially you want to establish a community who enables you to move through life with a "me for we" mindset and inspires you to grow in integrity, character, humility, productivity, faith, and self-love with the goal of becoming your highest self.

HOMEWORK

Ponder and answer these questions in your journal:

- Make a list of the people in your community and the different circles they fall into. Which relationships do you want to strengthen? Can you set aside a few hours one day a week for calls or coffee dates with each of them over the next few months?

- What kinds of relationships are you currently lacking in your life and community? What will you do differently to start seeking them out?

- What kind of friend are you to your tribe and network? Are you a taker who often doesn't reciprocate? Or the opposite?

15

Self-Love

"Our deepest fear is not that we are inadequate. Our deepest fear is that we are powerful beyond measure. It is our light, not our darkness that most frightens us. We ask ourselves, 'Who am I to be brilliant, gorgeous, talented, fabulous?' Actually, who are you not to be? You are a child of God. Your playing small does not serve the world. There is nothing enlightened about shrinking so that other people won't feel insecure around you. We are all meant to shine, as children do. We were born to make manifest the glory of God that is within us. It's not just in some of us; it's in everyone. And as we let our own light shine, we unconsciously give other people permission to do the same."

—MARIANNE WILLIAMSON,
SPIRITUAL TEACHER AND AUTHOR,
FROM *A RETURN TO LOVE*

You've probably heard generic advice about the significance of self-love. Some people describe it as taking the time to nurture your own well-being and happiness or fostering more loving thoughts. Women especially struggle with self-love because they're wired to think of others before themselves. Indeed, women are more likely to feel guilty, to lack confidence in their own abilities, and to bear a heavier burden when it comes to balancing career and family.[1] Yet if you don't take care of yourself and find a way to overcome your internal adversaries, you'll never truly be able to care for and love others. As activist Parker Palmer says, "Self-care is never a selfish act—it is simply good stewardship of the only gift I have, the gift I was put on earth to offer to others."

SELF-LOVE IS STAYING FUELED FOR LIFE'S HIGHEST CLIMB

When you're committed to rising to your highest potential, you're operating at a different level from the average person. You already know that climbing to the summit will have its easier, breezier moments and that at other times you will hit the gnarly, rough patches of the climb that require endurance and determination. To bring our most mentally, physically, and emotionally fit selves to the climb, our buckets need to be full and our battery power fully charged.

> "To bring our most mentally, physically, and emotionally fit selves to the climb, our buckets need to be full and our battery power fully charged."

In order to maximize self-nourishment, we must cultivate the skill of radical self-love. I will mostly refer to self-love as a verb because I want you to get into the habit of loving yourself as an action.

Think of yourself as a powerhouse of an engine that is constantly delivering goods and services to your work, spouse, children, and friends. Your engine needs excellent-quality fuel to stay in tip-top shape and keep performing at this level—that fuel is self-love and can take many different forms. When your pipes fill up with negative thoughts and self-doubt (mind), you need to clean them out and fuel them with positive affirmations and what you love instead. Define your core-limiting beliefs, negative thought patterns, and destructive habits. Know your culprits so you can actively combat them and focus on the positive. Tony Robbins talks about how our physiology also affects our state of mind: we are what we eat; certain foods give us energy while others deplete it. When you have low energy or are malnourished, you need to prioritize changing your diet and feeding yourself healthier food. Exercise produces endorphins that help improve your mood and attitude along with other benefits.[2] When your pipes get physically weak or start breaking (body) you need to prioritize health and physical activity. When your pipes feel emotionally dried up, unappreciated, or lonely (heart), you need to call on some loving company, good-quality snuggling, or whatever emotionally nourishes you. Spend time with your intimate partner, children, and family.

KNOW YOUR SELF-LOVE ADVERSARIES

If we've all been preached to about self-love and we intellectually understand it, why is it still so hard to put into practice? We each have different tendencies and negative patterns that drain our battery. When we're aware of these damaging behaviors, we have a much better chance of not only halting them but also determining the best kind of fuel to counteract them with self-love. Mimi, my life coach, used to assign me an exercise in which I name my core-limiting beliefs as a way of owning them and quieting the noise when I need to. You can do the same. Body image could be Brenda the Body, comparison could be Carla the Comparer, and perfectionism could be Petra the Perfector. These adversaries will never disappear completely; they're always going to have a seat at the table, but the trick is learning how to manage your relationship with them. Here is a list of the most common patterns.

Guilt

At the end of day do you focus on what you didn't get done instead of celebrating what you did achieve? Do you give yourself a hard time when you leave work early to spend time with your family? Do you berate yourself if you stay at work late instead of spending time with your family? When you need some pampering—say, a spa treatment or some alone time away from people or when you need to increase expenditures on more help (childcare, housekeeper, assistant, etc.)—do you feel guilty for investing that extra money and time?

Body Image

Are you always insulting your body and the way you look? *Look how fat you are! You're so disgusting and lazy!* Do you take the time to do things that make your body feel fresh and rested, such as exercise, healthy meals, yoga, and time outdoors? Do you sometimes wish your body and its needs would simply disappear?

Fear of Offending Others

When you contact someone and they take a while to get back to you, do you feel like maybe you did something wrong? *Did I mess up? Was it something I said? Did I hurt their feelings?* When you're bad about staying in touch with someone and totally forget to respond to their call or message from a while back, do you feel like a horrible and inadequate friend or professional?

Perfectionism

As you tackle a big project, do you hear a voice in your head whining about how you should have been better prepared, critiquing the quality of your work? Do you feel disappointed with yourself because you know you can do better with more time and resources? Are you holding yourself to impossible standards that no one else could live up to anyway?

Comparison

Do you constantly compare yourself with others? *Am I as smart, successful, pretty, rich as X?* Do you feel that you are never enough because someone else is always doing something more impressive or making ten times the money? Do you say you'll be happy once you achieve Z, like other people in your circle?

PERSONALIZE A
STRATEGIC PLAN FOR SELF-LOVE

So what does self-loving consist of? It depends on what your needs and tendencies are, but I break it down into the activities or people who nourish your heart, mind, and body. You want to operate from a place of joy, excitement, and high energy. Different kinds of fuel give you different kinds of results. Because it's easy to misconstrue the concept of self-love as narcissism or selfishness, I want to take a moment here to point out that there are two kinds of self-love.

1. Loving yourself in a **self-centric way:** You're motivated to do things for yourself as an escape so you can feel nourished, healthy, happy, acknowledged, fulfilled, and successful outside of your normal roles. Often you desire pampering because of how hard you've been working; you feel your life is so difficult and you deserve to be spoiled once in a while because of all the burdens you bear.

2. Loving yourself in a **purpose-centric way:** You're motivated to do things for yourself so you can feel nourished, healthy, happy, acknowledged, fulfilled, and successful so you can recharge your battery, get back out there, and bring your best self to the purpose you're working toward.

Most people naturally fall into the first scenario of self-centric self-love. I was no exception. As the president of Shecky's, I lived to be pampered. Because I was so sick of the toxic situation at our office, I took full advantage of the fact that we curated guides to dining, beauty, and fashion in cities across the country where we held our Girls Night Out events. I remember thinking, *At least I'm getting this free spa treatment. At least I'm getting to eat in nice restaurants. At least I can take advantage of company perks.* I thought I was taking care of myself, but all I was really doing was masking the misery and unhappiness I felt about my career. Sometimes we go shopping or get a manicure to pep ourselves up, but it's just a temporary high. Maybe you forget about your unhappiness for a few hours, but eventually it shows up again. The problem with the self-centric self-love is that it treats the symptom and not the disease. You go on vacation or get cocktails to alleviate the depletion and stress, but the impact stops there.

When you love your purpose-centric self, you have clarity around the greater work you're trying to achieve, so self-loving, whenever you set time aside for it, has a greater purpose and meaning. In the Productivity chapter we discussed how *you*—your heart, mind, body—are the vessel through which you realize your life's greatness. Therefore, self-loving is being as good as you can to your mind, body, and heart. Now that I'm running S.H.E. Globl Media, I might have a bad day or an exhausting week, but if I plan a weekend spa trip, enjoy a date night with John, or take an afternoon off to read a good book, I know exactly why I'm doing it—to refresh my soul and refuel for the next stage of purpose. The positive impact I have the potential to make is so massive and important that I need to bring my most healthy and replenished self to it so I can do my best work. Purpose-centric self-love is like the breaks between school semesters. Any downtime I take is a quick burst of relaxation and rejuvenation because I know that's what my vessel needs, and I can't wait to jump back into the ring again at full throttle. Pausing for self-love is the calm before the storm, recharging before you're let loose again.

> "Leaders are those who can strike the proper balance between service to others and service to oneself."

The best way to incorporate self-love into your life is to make it a regular routine or habit. Personalize a strategic plan for self-love that will address your specific needs for your heart, mind, and body. We learned about prioritizing for elevation periods in the Productivity chapter; similarly, you're going to have different self-love needs for different phases of your life and should design self-love plans for specific elevation periods. For example, if you're going through a major life event like pregnancy, moving, taking care of young children, transitioning careers, or going through a major breakup, you need to go easy on yourself and your expectations. It's important for you to eat well, rest to keep your strength up, and find moments for yourself. Self-love can be physical or mental breathers such as getting up for a walk and clearing your head, catching up with a friend, indulging in something pampering like a massage or acupuncture, and taking a vacation with loved ones. Sometimes it can be as simple as making imperfection your goal for the day or celebrating small things as victories.

The climb to the top, where you reach your limitless potential, is long, hard, and riddled with obstacles. Life is not a sprint but rather a game of endurance, which is why taking care of your own needs is so important. You can't finish the race if your vessel is no longer functional. When you think about it, self-love is simply valuing yourself equal to your potential—what you already intrinsically are and were created to be. God knows how much you're worth. Do you? When we practice self-love we are saying, *I am worth it because I have so much important work to do in order to fulfill my purpose.* Leaders are those who can strike the proper balance between service to others and service to oneself.

HOMEWORK

Ponder and answer these questions in your journal:

- What is self-love for you? What do you typically need from an emotional, physical, and mental standpoint? What do you crave or need to recharge?

- What are your negative adversaries and tendencies to watch out for? How can you love yourself more in these areas?

16

Courage

"Courage is the most important of all the virtues, because without courage you can't practice any other virtue consistently. You can practice any virtue erratically, but nothing consistently without courage."

—MAYA ANGELOU, POET AND AUTHOR

When people think about the concept of courage, they might conjure up images of physical power like David and his improbable battle against Goliath or of General Patton leading US troops in World War II, but really, as counterintuitive as it may sound, being vulnerable can also be a great act of courage. As the second-to-last foundational pillar of your leadership development, courage is the ability to share your greatest pain, fears, and problems in the hopes of helping others. It is living with and overcoming discomfort.

COURAGE IS A GATEWAY TO INNOVATION AND DISRUPTION

Leadership requires great courage—the ability to do something that frightens you and helps you stay the course in the face of opposition. Change is difficult. Most people and institutions are happy to maintain the status quo because it suits their interests and keeps the powerful in power. If you're a change maker, you need to expect that instigating change is going to be hard. Whenever you are innovating or disrupting the norm, you need the courage to oppose worldviews, break away from the herd, and choose the unpopular or unknown path. That's why leaders are called trailblazers. They forge ahead based on the force of their convictions. Some people get knocked down once and give up. They build a wall around their life to keep the pain out. But doing that also keeps love and joy out. Those who lack bravery end up existing in survival mode, where scarcity and fear reign. It is only with courage that one has the resiliency and grit to get back up and keep going.

> "We all aim to be comfortable, but comfort is really the enemy of leadership because so many of our steps up the mountain require courage."

We all aim to be comfortable, but comfort is really the enemy of leadership because so many of our steps up the mountain require courage. Great leaders always put themselves in uncomfortable positions. If you're not uncomfortable, you're probably not innovating enough. You've got to rip those muscles in order to build them. Living through the discomfort and confronting it head-on should become your default.

BEING VULNERABLE IS THE GREATEST ACT OF COURAGE

When bad things happen in life we usually experience one of four emotions: anger (*Why is this happening to me?*), grief (*What have I lost?*), shock (*I can't believe this. What do I do now?*), or fear (*What's going to happen next?*). In situations like these our tendency is to go inward. If we lose somebody in our life or we're going through something devastating, we're wired to feel like we need to keep it all together on our own and be so strong. We feel weak if we need to ask for help, that people will think less of us, that it's embarrassing to be so needy. Men especially are taught to embrace the mask of masculinity, as we discussed in Chapter 3, and never show any sign of weakness. But what we really need to do is turn outward. Only when we are honest with ourselves about our darkest secrets and shame can we put ourselves in a position to receive help.

Professor and best-selling author Brené Brown writes in her best-selling book *Daring Greatly* that, "Vulnerability is not weakness, and the uncertainty, risk, and emotional exposure we face every day are not optional. Our only choice is a question of engagement. Our willingness to own and engage with our vulnerability determines the depth of our courage and the clarity of our purpose; the level to which we protect ourselves from being vulnerable is a measure of our fear and disconnection." Take a moment to meditate on what Brown is saying: our ability to be vulnerable determines the depth of our courage. It takes courage to share and open up and create community around you. Becoming a leader means not being afraid to reveal your vulnerabilities.

> "Being generous with your most vulnerable stories is also a great act of courage."

To this day it takes a lot of courage for me to share the fact that I had a miscarriage. I don't want to make other people feel uncomfortable by speaking about it, but I know that someone else in the room has gone through it, and by telling my own story I pave the way for someone else to tell hers. An audience member heard me talk about it at S.H.E. Summit 2016 and afterward decided to start a blog on wellness and fertility to share her own struggle with IVF. Now she's creating something to help others who need advice and is expanding the ripple effect.

Being generous with your most vulnerable stories is also a great act of courage. Everyone has experienced something painful or traumatic that upsets them or makes them feel ashamed. Perhaps you are suffering from depression, have been raped or sexually assaulted in the past, are in financial debt and falling deeper down the rabbit hole, struggling with fertility or some other feeling of shame. The social stigma around issues like these keeps you from speaking out, but just think about the number of other people struggling with and closeting the same issues who would be relieved and supported if you shared your story with them. The more we open up and communicate our deepest shame and imperfections, the more we give other people permission to talk about their issues too. And in *this* openness and dialogue pain is courageously shared for community to be cultivated and solutions to be discovered. It is in this transparent conversation and brainstorming that movements and movement drivers are borne out. Again, your pain can lead to your positive impact and purpose.

FEAR MEANS GO

If the idea of taking big steps toward your vision scares you, you're on the right track. Fear means go. No pain, no gain. No risk, no reward. The most memorable people in history—Martin Luther King Jr., Mahatma Gandhi, Rosa Parks, Steve Jobs, Richard Branson—walked through the fire to realize their dreams on the other side. Defeat fear by making your dream—the betterment you want to create—so big and bold that it drowns out the fear. The most successful people are successful because they had the courage to put themselves in the most uncomfortable positions. Humanity is in desperate need for you to solve a specific problem.

Sheryl Sandberg had proven herself in her career and was already worth hundreds of millions of dollars when she decided to write her book *Lean In*. She had more success than most people dream about. In fact, she could have walked away from it all and called it a day. But she didn't. Instead, she saw her role as COO at Facebook as an opportunity, a platform to drive awareness around a problem: the gender gap in corporate leadership. She saw firsthand how women were not leaning in and were instead opting out of the workforce for many different reasons, but she was comfortable in her own life and career, and it wasn't necessarily her responsibility to do something about it. By speaking out on the issue and writing a book about it, however, she put herself in an uncomfortable and controversial position. What she did was an extremely courageous act undertaken to advance gender equality and improve conditions for professional women. Sheryl started a conversation about something people weren't talking about and made the conversation mainstream. She single-handedly resuscitated the conversation on feminism and got the attention of all kinds of major media: TV networks, women's lifestyle magazines, business, politics, and so on. She didn't have to do it. So much media attention can be terrifying. Even now people still give her crap for it. They criticize her for being too privileged, too corporate. A lot of women say, "Please, Sheryl. Stop telling us to lean in." Still, she drew massive awareness to the topic and stood to lose a lot more than she would gain by staking a claim on such a controversial issue. It took some ballsy guts and bravery to do that, but that's what leaders do.

Or take Malala Yousafzai, for instance, who was shot by the Taliban in 2012 on her way to school for blogging about her views on girls' education in Pakistan. She survived and continued her activism undaunted, becoming an international symbol of girl power and the youngest person ever to receive the Nobel Peace Prize. Because she stood up for herself and the right of all girls to receive an education, Malala's story is a reminder that girls everywhere should and can demand better. One person—in this case a teenage girl from a conflict-heavy country—with the courage to act can make a difference.

> "By strengthening the pillars that make up your foundation, you are also expanding your capacity to act courageously."

You will surely face challenges where the road ahead is anything but certain. Bravery is what is needed when there are no guarantees you'll get the outcome you desire. In order to attempt greatness, you can't be afraid to fail. Again, I'm encouraging you to aim higher because of the important destiny the universe already has in store for you. Moreover, when you choose to be courageous, leadership qualities like perseverance, resilience, and confidence come naturally. And by strengthening the pillars that make up your foundation, you are also expanding your capacity to act courageously. All these traits feed off each other in a virtuous cycle: faith pulls you through obstacles, self-love recharges your energy, humility enables you to learn from the wise community you surround yourself with, gratitude makes you thankful for the things you already have and realistic about how you prioritize your productivity, and grace allows you to forgive and lift those closest to you when they need it.

HOMEWORK

Ponder and answer these questions in your journal:

- When was the last time you put yourself in an uncomfortable situation in order to stretch your courage?

- What do you need more courage in?

17

Mindfulness

"In this moment, there is plenty of time. In this moment, you are precisely as you should be. In this moment, there is infinite possibility."

—VICTORIA MORAN,
AUTHOR AND HOST OF *MAIN STREET VEGAN*

I bet I know what you're thinking: *Why is mindfulness the final foundational pillar for building personal leadership?* Well, if you view all the prior pillars as muscles you are learning how to flex and develop, then mindfulness is the daily, ongoing exercise that keeps these muscles limber for whatever comes next. Just as your body grows weak and eventually atrophies from lack of movement, your leadership pillars will grow weak and ineffective if you aren't mindful about practicing and improving them on a regular basis. Remember: your mind's tendency is to be centered in the ego. You start out in life as the person hogging the spotlight on stage and caring about what others think of you. That is the self-centric default.

To lead great lives and attain meaningful achievements, you need to get into the habit of practicing mindfulness. The dictionary defines mindfulness as "the quality or state of being conscious or aware of something" and "a mental state achieved by focusing one's awareness on the present moment, while calmly acknowledging and accepting one's feelings, thoughts, and bodily sensations." Practicing this daily means bringing yourself into a state of awareness several times throughout the day so you are always shifting back into the best version of yourself—the extraordinary being you are in God's eyes. Mindfulness enables you to shift back to seeing yourself from the outside-in lens in order to realign negative self-talk and thoughts with what is positive and abundant. You might consider these as the "talk back" statements that you can save to respond to the core-limiting beliefs you established in the Self-Love chapter and combat other negative patterns. Tony Robbins has put tremendous emphasis on what he calls "shifting your state" as a way of directing the actions that are a direct result of your thoughts. He explains,

> Shift your focus. Find new and empowering meanings. Model those who succeeded before you. Take control of your state. You are controlled by your rituals. Your life comes from your rituals. Some put you in state and some take you out of state. If you do the right thing at the wrong time, you get pain. Learn how to change your state. Control your own conditioning. Your shift in perception will generate a shift in thinking. And a shift in thinking will give rise to a change in attitude and subsequent performance. Do this often enough and you will be an ultra-successful achiever yourself.

You see, people move through life with the assumption that good habits like "feeling confident" and "doing the right thing" should come automatically. Subconsciously or not, we react when things don't go our way by asking ourselves, *Why did I do that again? What is wrong with me that I just keep repeating this bad habit?* Intellectually we know that positive thinking is best for us, but in practice we falter because our ego is like an almighty devil; it wants us to depend on it so that self-centric thinking becomes our default. Therefore, we have to spend our whole lives—yes, our *whole* lives—working hard to cultivate better mental and emotional habits. As I mentioned in the Resilience and Courage chapters, comfort is the enemy because it makes us self-satisfied and lazy. Life is meant to be a span of hard, fulfilling work that breaks you out of your comfort zone over and over again so you can grow and rise to your highest potential. You never really learn what you're made of until you get pushed to the brink.

MINDFULNESS IS THE WARRIOR IN YOUR HEAD FENDING OFF THE ENEMY

The mind, like any resource or organization, needs managing. Mindfulness is learning how to manage your mind to be an ally, not a critic. It's very easy to become a slave to the thoughts in our heads. We all—and I repeat, we ALL—have core-limiting beliefs so we need tools to manage them. I like to name the critical voices in my head, critics like Brenda the Body-Basher and Carla the Comparer, so that when she starts nagging away, I can identify who she is and put her in a closed room. Critical voices can get so loud that you can't hear your spirit anymore and you lose your way. Noise causes stress and worry, and stress is like the years of wear and tear on your car that's slowing it down, wearing through the brake pads and overheating the engine. Similarly, negative thoughts not only distract you and slow you down but also harm you mentally, emotionally, and physically by introducing a vicious cycle of bad habits. Therefore, it's critical to find the time for mindfulness. We grow powerful when we are at peace and quiet. Being in a calm, cool, and steady state allows us to get in touch with our gut instinct, which is how God directs you when your instinct aligns with the purpose-centric values you've committed to. But if we are busy all the time, we lose that connection with the right values. We lose that connection with why we are here and what really matters.

> "We grow powerful when we are at peace and quiet. Being in a calm, cool, and steady state allows us to get in touch with our gut instinct."

Here are some examples of mindfulness practices you can use to shift into the ideal mental state and optimize your days; they will strengthen each of your personal leadership pillars:

1. In the morning, before you tackle the day's tasks, get mindful about your **purpose** and think about *why* you are here to ensure that today's activities will be aligned to serve your purpose.

2. As you tackle the tasks on your to-do list, get mindful and ask yourself, *Does this current activity really move the needle toward my big **vision***? *Are these steps big enough, or am I getting caught up in the small stuff?*

3. On the days you worry about the magnitude of all there is to do and execute for your big vision, get mindful and access **faith** in your higher power that is lifting you and your work. Trust and believe that there is a spiritual power watching over you and your mission who wants you to succeed.

4. When obstacles block your path as you climb to the next elevation, exercise **resilience** by remembering that obstacles exist for you to turn them into opportunities. Ask yourself, *Is this obstacle meant to direct me, protect me, humble me, or mature me? What is the lesson or message hidden inside of it?*

5. As you encounter people every day online, on the phone, and in person, get mindfully proactive about the **energy** you project, read, receive, and reject. That way you can radiate and feed yourself the best social messages possible and avoid toxic energy that will stifle your climb.

6. To master **productivity** in your busiest seasons when life responsibilities come at you from every direction (parenting, partner, work, social, health, money, home, etc.), mindfully step back and ask yourself, *What are the priorities that REALLY matter most during my current elevation period?* Recalibrate your schedule and activities to align with this list.

7. When other people give you advice as you're scaling the course up the mountain, mindfully embrace **humility** and be open to asking for help and getting honest feedback and suggestions—even if they are hard to hear. Remember: you don't know it all. Reflect on outside opinions and discern which advice to incorporate so that you don't miss out on any miracles in the wisdom others can offer.

8. If you're starting to feel scarcity in a life area or heading down a common rabbit hole, start focusing on the full portion of the glass and feel **grateful** for all that is going right and well. Appreciate what you already have: family, health, shelter, financial security, friends, education, and so on. You are beyond blessed.

9. As you engage in a difficult conversation with a loved one, partner, or frustrating colleague, get mindful about offering **grace** to this person, even though he might not deserve it. See the situation from his perspective, and learn to let go and surrender to love. Otherwise you will imprison yourself, and who has the energy for that?

10. When you're making plans for the days and months ahead and a million people want to schedule appointments with you, get mindful and step back to consider which relationships in your **community** you really want to invest in right now. Check in with your priorities and be more strategic about whom you invite in the various circles that make up your community.

11. When your inner critic gets loud and noisy, get mindful and catch the negativity as it's happening in order to shift back into positive **self-love**. Realize that your core-limiting beliefs are going to hold you back rather than nourish you for the climb. Listen to your own needs, and customize a self-love strategy to nurture your body, heart, and mind.

12. If you start to feel frustrated and exhausted, that you want to give up because the road ahead is too hard or too terrifying, remind yourself that God wants you to have uncommon **courage**. Innovation and disruption exist on the other side of uncommon courage. Embrace the discomfort, and summon all your bravery as you serve a purpose much bigger than yourself.

We've been given an incredible gift as sentient beings: by changing the inner attitudes of our minds, we have the power to change the outer aspects of our lives. Thoughts are the most powerful tools we have. If you feed the beast negative thoughts, he will thrive and expand. When you create the space and time to be alone with your thoughts, you discover, understand, and cultivate what's already inside of you. Sometimes

"By changing the inner attitudes of our minds, we have the power to change the outer aspects of our lives. Thoughts are the most powerful tools we have."

you just need to get away for that "me time" and go somewhere quiet where you won't be interrupted or distracted in order to find your inner voice. Think of it as a vacation for your mind.

PRACTICE MINDFULNESS THROUGH THE ACTIVITY THAT WORKS BEST FOR YOU

Mindfulness can be any activity that allows you to connect back to the principles of meditation, prayer, journaling, mantra repetition, prepaving (see below), yoga, reading, running or preprogrammed tech alerts. These efforts allow you to shift into states of relaxation, positivity, abundance, and success so you can optimize your state and ignore the negative patterns holding you back. Remember: your thoughts become things. Whatever energy and attitude you project, the universe reflects it back onto you. Choose a mindfulness practice that serves your needs in any given moment. When you're feeling lazy, choose an activity that will inspire and motivate you. When you're feeling disheartened, access positive mantras. When you're feeling unproductive, celebrate your successes and everything you did to get them done. Whatever your method for practicing mindfulness, make sure it creates the time and space for you to have a conversation with your source. Here are some of the methods I turn to often and the different ways in which I use them. Experiment and try different methods to find what works best for you.

Mindfulness Activities

- *(Meditation)* The most common form of meditation is organic breathing: sitting in a quiet place, closing your eyes, and focusing on the breath to connect with your source. The goal is to replace unconscious breathing with conscious breathing. When we do this, our bodies flow in the present. Sit for five to ten minutes to inhale and exhale. Breathe into the very top of your head. Exhale through to the tips of your toes. Your exhale is the universe's inhale and vice versa. Send breath to the area of your body that feels tense. Just hang out and get comfortable with yourself. For me mornings are an especially good time to meditate because the ego is loudest then. This is my most important daily practice.

- *(Meditation)* Meditation can also be used to chant specific mantras. One I like to concentrate on is the Four S's: *I am significant. I am spirit. I am self-love. I am service.* By repeating affirmations like this and meditating on them every day, you can disempower whatever is against you, verbalize your intentions, and consciously shift your thoughts back into that powerful, extraordinary, mindful state. If you need to work on humility, for example, repeat the mantra, *Humility is how teachable I am.* I have provided mantras at the end of each of the chapters in this section for exactly this purpose.

- *(Prayer)* Traditional prayer often consists of sending a wish or words of gratitude to your higher power: *Dear God, please let me find the strength and patience to be a good parent. Thank you for granting me good health and keeping my family safe.* In fact, 55 percent of Americans say they pray every day, and 20 percent of people who are religiously unaffiliated also say they pray daily.[1]

- *(Prayer)* Another form of prayer is simply having a conversation with God or life source. God wants to maintain a deep relationship with each of us, so the more we share, the more direction and guidance we receive. I like to pray out loud by speaking directly to my source, and I often stumble onto answers in the process of praying. For example, I might share the following: "Dear God, 2016 has been an extraordinary year. My vision for 2017 is so huge, it's so overwhelming—double revenues, double impact, create a foundation to scale better. But as I pray to you, I'm rooting back into you and know that this is the path you've laid out for me. All the success has already been paved for me—you're just waiting for me to grab it."

- *(Journal or email)* Prepaving, which is something my former coach, Mimi, taught me how to do, is a simple exercise where you write down your intentions and what you want to have happen in the near future as if they have already occurred. For instance, if your goal is saving money for a down payment on a house, then you might write something like, "Big news! I've finally reached my savings goal of $50,000 and have enough for the down payment on a beautiful two-bedroom home. I close escrow on the house next month!" You can prepave on a daily, weekly, monthly, or even yearly basis by journaling or writing emails to yourself. I have gone through periods when I need to keep mentally fit each day, so I write myself an email every night. When you go back and read some of your prepaves, you'll be amazed how many of your intentions came true.

- *(Journal or email)* Sunday Learning and Celebrations is a ritual where I reserve time on Sundays (or any downtime when you are winding down and preparing for the week ahead) to recap all the things I have learned or accomplished in the past week—for example, I signed a new sponsor for S.H.E. Summit, I got to spend quality time with Jackson every day, I had a wonderful date night with John, and so on. This is also a chance to write down lessons you may have learned from difficult interactions or other obstacles so you are always reflecting on the things that happen for you.

- *(Visual reminder)* Leave yourself reminders, positive affirmations, mantras, or quotes that you really love in places where you'll see them every day. You can display them as your screensaver on electronic devices (smartphone, tablet, computer) or stick Post-it Notes where you will see them the most (office wall, bathroom mirror, refrigerator door).

HOMEWORK

Ponder and answer these questions in your journal:

- Which leadership pillars do you struggle with the most and, therefore, will need to be the most mindful about?

- What mindfulness practices are best suited to your personality and lifestyle? Set aside ten minutes to do a mindfulness activity every day, ideally around the same time, for thirty days.

PERSONAL LEADERSHIP MINDFULNESS MANTRAS

Now that you have learned about the thirteen foundational pillars of personal leadership, the next step is to implement and practice them in your daily life. Remember: they are the foundation for how you will reach your highest potential and lead change in the world. It's a rough world out there, and your tree needs to be rooted firmly when the storms come. To take advantage of the rest of your life and live to your fullest, I implore you to plant deep roots for your pillars and do the work.

We each have personal tendencies and areas that require more work than others. Hopefully the homework in each chapter of Part II has helped you identify and reflect on your strengths and weaknesses so you can proactively address areas that need more development. One way that I continually address issues or patterns I am struggling with is through mantras. It may seem cheesy at first, but trust me: they work. For example, if you're feeling overwhelmed by everything you need to get done and stressed about being productive, write a Post-it Note or email to yourself with the mantra, *Today I focus on today.* This will help you to consciously refocus your mind whenever it starts to wander and panic about being productive.

To make it convenient for you to remember these personal leadership habits and principles, I've gathered mantras specifically tailored to each pillar that you can tap into whenever you're feeling particularly low or challenged. Feel free to add your own mantras into the mix as well. You can meditate on mantras in the morning, use them as phrases to repeat to yourself when you're on a run, print them out and stick them on your fridge or mirror, send yourself alerts on your smartphone calendar, add them to relevant sections in your journal, post them on social media using InstaQuote, or even make them into artwork for your bulletin board—whatever works best for helping you to synthesize and absorb the lesson they contain.

PURPOSE

- Everything has happened FOR me, not to me, so that I can discover and fulfill my holistic purpose.
- I do not live my life in the world; I lead my life for the world.
- My holistic purpose is my life's assignment from God.
- My source is X and where my purpose draws its strength.
- I am driven by the impact I can make, not by my personal image.

VISION

- Visions have been and are often cast on me; I will no longer abandon them.
- If I see the invisible, I can do the impossible.
- I vision big so I can take big steps.

FAITH

- My faith widens my possibilities.
- The stronger my faith is, the less I will struggle and worry.
- Faith pulls me through problems, not around them.
- Wherever I have scarcity, I place more faith.

RESILIENCE

- Obstacles are growth opportunities if I pause to see the lesson.
- Obstacles are like obstacle courses meant to build my leadership muscles.
- How can this obstacle build me or mature me?
- Is this obstacle protecting me or directing me?
- Obstacles shape my character so I can become the great leader I'm meant to be.

ENERGY

- *Energy is the invisible messaging that nourishes or weakens me. I am thoughtful about what I allow in.*
- *I am intentional about the energy I project.*
- *If I give positive, I receive positive.*
- *My attitude is the physical expression of my energy.*

PRODUCTIVITY

- *I invest my time in what matters right now.*
- *I focus on priorities in elevation periods.*
- *My time is worth $1,000 an hour, and I am clear on the ROI of the time I invest.*
- *Productivity does not determine my self-worth.*

HUMILITY

- *How humble I am determines how teachable I am.*
- *Humility allows me to receive important miracles and messages.*
- *Without humility, leadership is impossible.*
- *I work on becoming a better listener.*
- *I work on getting better at asking for help.*

GRATITUDE

- *Gratitude enables me to soften so I can create the space to receive more.*
- *Gratitude enables the abundance mindset I need to achieve success.*
- *I get what more of what I focus on.*
- *Being grateful is good for my health.*

GRACE

- *Grace is forgiving others even when I don't think they deserve it.*
- *Grace preserves relationships for the long haul.*
- *Grace gives me freedom and helps me surrender all that is negative.*
- *I channel grace and surrender as much as I can.*
- *When in conflict, view things from the other person's perspective.*

COMMUNITY

- *I am on this planet for people, to be in relationship with others.*
- *I become the company I keep, so I must establish relationships wisely.*
- *My community is the crew who I lean on as I venture uphill.*
- *Nothing strengthens relationships more than generosity without expecting anything in return.*
- *Anything I consume intellectually and emotionally is also a part of my community.*

SELF-LOVE

- *Self-love is staying fueled for my life's highest climb.*
- *Self-love is nourishing my heart, mind, and body.*
- *I personalize a self-love strategic plan for my needs.*
- *Self-love is valuing myself equal to the greatness that God does.*
- *I am beyond enough, and I am beyond worth it.*

COURAGE

- *The more courageous I am, the more I can innovate and disrupt as a leader.*
- *Vulnerability is the greatest act of courage.*
- *I live in the discomfort and have uncommon courage.*

MINDFULNESS

- *Mindfulness is the act of surrendering and letting go of all that does not serve me.*
- *Mindfulness is focusing my mind, body, and heart on what serves and empowers me.*
- *Mindfulness is connecting back to God (or spirit, the universe, nature, etc.).*
- *Mindfulness is plugging into the source of my higher power.*
- *Focusing on my breath is my most accessible tool to get mindful.*

PART III

HOW TO THRIVE IN
THE MACRO-MOVEMENT

Now that Part I has convinced you to join a new breed of leaders in the making, what I call S.H.E. Leaders, and Part II has walked you through the pillars you must master in order to build a strong foundation (yes, you have your work cut out for you with all those homework assignments), this final section of the book, Part III, shows you how to put all these learnings into practice. It teaches you how to treat your whole life as the organization you are leading so that *all* your life areas thrive as you lead change in the world as well as how to practically pursue your purpose based on where you are at this moment in your life.

The reason I'm ending the book with these chapters is because they offer realistic strategies for executing everything you have just learned. When we think about reaching our highest peak and acquiring tremendous success, we often land on a path that is exhausting, depleting, and causes some part of our lives to suffer or burn out. I know so many accomplished people, especially women, who end up going down this road. Technology has made people in the world do more, and there is a level of busyness to everyone's lives that didn't exist just decades ago. I find that when I catch up with friends and acquaintances, most people convey how overwhelmed they are. This is especially true for the hyper-ambitious person who wants to be a trailblazer and lead change in the world. On the one hand, this is a great thing—we're seeing people inspired to do it all. But on the other hand, it's critical that we strive for success in a way that is lighter, enjoyable, and ultimately more sustainable. When we learn how to manage our entire lives in an integrated manner, success comes so much easier.

That's why it's so important to put the faith pillar I've taught you into practice. You enable the universe to partner with you on tackling your enormous vision when you have faith. Moreover, by pursuing your purpose and staying in the "me for we" mindset, you position yourself to serve and lift others. The more you follow the principles in this book and think about how you can help and impact others, the easier the climb is going to be and the more the universe is going to do the heavy lifting for you.

18

Treat Your Whole Life as the Organization You Are Leading

"Happiness is not a matter of intensity but of balance and order and rhythm and harmony."

—THOMAS MERTON,
THEOLOGIAN AND AUTHOR

The final way we need to shift our thinking about leadership is to not only apply the term to our career and social impact but also to start thinking about our *whole life as the organization we are leading.* Earlier we discussed research that says feminine qualities are a new form of innovation and that the twenty-first century is a generation driven by feminine traits. Well, having a more holistic definition of leadership is, in many ways, a more feminine approach. Leadership in and of itself needs to embrace a more 360-degree view of our lives in order to incorporate all the bodies of work that make up our livelihoods and compete for our time and attention. I call this *whole-life leadership.* I've also talked extensively about how the purpose-centric lifestyle places our obsession more on *how to lead our life for the world* instead of *how to live our life in the world.* This chapter is about ensuring that you add the word *whole* in that phrase: *How can I best lead my whole life for the world?*

ONE DEPARTMENT CAN SLOW DOWN AN ENTIRE ORGANIZATION

You see, the flip side of the macro-movement and the downside of everything I've been pitching you on—rising to your highest potential and leading big change in the world—is the danger of over-committing yourself to the point where other important parts of your life become neglected and start to suffer. If you were a farmer, it would be as if you were fertilizing only certain portions of your crops while forgetting to tend to the crops that bear the most fruit. Over time the neglected crops jeopardize the entire harvest, leading to irreparable damage. Or if your life were an organization and every life area was a department in the organization, then think about how one poor-performing department could slow down the whole company. I hear too many stories from women and men about how they have pursued their goals so intensely in one or two life areas, to the exclusion of everything else, and it led to major health issues, financial depletion, divorce, and fertility challenges. The obsession to get your business or movement off the ground might not be so rewarding if you end up going through a bitter divorce because you didn't prioritize your marriage enough or in a major financial debt situation because you neglected income generation or money management.

Take, for example, some of my friends who have over-focused on their careers:

- One friend devoted most of her energy to building a very successful business for the last two decades, but after selling her business at age forty, she wanted to get on having a family and children quickly. She started dating a lot, but no suitors made the cut, and her biological clock was ticking, so she decided to go the route of artificial insemination. She is the mother of a beautiful boy today, but often she tells me how she wishes her son were growing up with a father, laments the pressures of solo parenting, and states that she regrets not having invested more time in her romantic life during her thirties.

- Another friend, forty-seven, similarly put her focus on a career at a big law firm and climbing the ranks to senior partnership. She got engaged to her fiancé seven years ago, and for seven years they still have not gotten married because hundreds of thousands of dollars have gone into IVF and fertility treatments instead. Today they are finally considering adoption, but she has shared with me that her upbringing placed priority on career because she was a part of the first generation of American women in her family who could be powerful and highly paid in the workplace.

- There's my thirty-seven-year-old guy friend who works in government. He's been so obsessed with his political career that he didn't realize he was putting it before his wife and daughter. In the last few years he has repeatedly canceled date nights with his wife and missed parenting events at his daughter's school. He struggled to show up as both a husband and father. It was no surprise, then, that his wife asked for a separation last year.

Then there are examples of people who neglect a certain part of their lives for deeper reasons. Perhaps there is lack of education, self-worth, or confidence in some area. Sometimes we get so busy with what we know how to do too well—taking care of others before ourselves, focusing on building something new, or getting to an elusive goal—that we unintentionally or subconsciously neglect the sometimes mundane but necessary things we have to do to maintain and sustain our lives like healthcare, personal finances, mental well-being, and our closest relationships.

- One of my girlfriends, who is all about love and doing good in the world, decided years ago to launch a social innovation conference and media business. She threw herself into this endeavor full force, not realizing how much went into it all, from booking venues to securing speakers. She ended up mortgaging her home and depleting her savings to get her business off the ground. Over the years she's been able to get back on track financially, but investing more time in her financial education and foundation at the beginning would have avoided a tremendous amount of stress. More often than not, leaving financial planning and organization to the very end stunts an organization's growth because it stunts the leader. Financial stress can be paralyzing.

- I know a woman who started a successful online retail business. She was so consumed with operations and brand building that she had her husband manage all the money as CFO. But years into the business she happened to take a look at the accounting books and noticed the numbers didn't add up. To her shock, she discovered that her husband had been embezzling money from the company into his own account. She had to hire private investigators to prove it, followed by many lawyers to work on the lawsuit. Luckily a major company wanted to buy her business around the time this all went down, which helped her recuperate financially. This is another lesson why people, especially women and those who run their own businesses, need to take control of and understand their finances.

- Then there's my friend who gives most of her time to caring for others and often puts herself last. Her life is devoted to taking care of her four-year-old daughter; her breadwinner husband who also needs a lot of attention, love, and support; and private clients for whom she works as an interior designer part time. She's also that person who is always helping or going above and beyond for friends, parents, siblings, and many others. The perception of her life to others might be that she's got it made—with a luxury apartment, name-brand wardrobe, and lavish vacations. But a year ago she started having episodes of low energy and physical weakness. One morning she woke up and could not physically move her body. Turns out she was very anemic because she did not prioritize her own health and wellness needs more.

Couples often put their relationships last when it comes to all the other life responsibilities they may have: income generation, children, keeping the home in order, and getting food on the table. This is especially common for people with young children who are still adjusting to the life-altering responsibilities of parenting. I see moms prioritize their children before their spouse, especially when their spouse opts out of the caregiving due to professional pressures or just lack of interest. Sometimes when the partner does try to help, the primary caregiver can be critical or overly particular about how he or she wants things done. But I also see scenarios where the breadwinner or both working parents prioritize work over relationship time because they have a great deal of pressure to financially produce in a life stage with increasing expenses. I also see those who put more energy into keeping up with the Joneses and ensuring that their home and everything else looks perfect before they sit down for the long-overdue therapy conversation their marriage desperately needs. All these things can chip away at an intimate relationship and cause you to grow apart and stop communicating, which could eventually lead to an affair, irreconcilable differences, or divorce. Having a thriving relationship is critical for ensuring that your home, children, and individual careers also thrive. It requires investing quality time in your partnership and seeking the right counseling if you can't resolve issues on your own.

> "It can be really easy to get caught up in trying to do it all."

You know all these people. One of them might even be you. With the excitement of today's macro-movement, it can be really easy to get caught up in trying to do it all. Moreover, the stress of forfeiting one major area of your life in order to focus on another, like career or childcare, can lead to fatigue and burnout. The effects of stress on the body—physical pain, mood swings, weight gain or loss, high blood pressure—can be debilitating and even lead to more serious conditions, such as a heart attack. A 2015 survey shows that 34 percent of adults report that their stress increased over the last year and that women's average stress levels continue to be higher than men's.[1]

To prevent this kind of imbalance from the get-go, you want to strategize and define how to *lead your whole life* well in an integrated way, not just one aspect of it. This means that when you set your goals for the season, year, or next five years, make sure to include goals for every category that matters to you. Also, to make sure you don't miss something, talk to other friends and people you admire to learn what their categories are. Read books by authors who specialize in this subject, or even hire a life coach to go through the exercise with you. Go back to my chapter on Community to cultivate relationships you can learn from.

DEFINE YOUR LIFE'S ORG CHART

We must live with a *whole life leadership* mentality and aim to work hard at creating a harmonious equilibrium where *all* areas of our lives can thrive as we rise. To do this, think of yourself as the CEO of an organization (your whole life) whose responsibility is to manage all the departments (the various areas of your personal life) that allow your organization to run smoothly and thrive. This means taking a 360-degree approach to leadership, where all departments are clearly identified. By treating your whole life like an organization, you take everything into consideration and have a bird's-eye view of everything that needs to get done, which means you're never completely neglecting any of your life's departments.

Often, as we get older, our responsibilities multiply in the form of mortgages to pay, children to raise, and households to manage. It's hard to keep track of everything if your priorities are siloed into different areas. Before I started S.H.E. Globl Media and became immersed in women's empowerment and leadership work, I still viewed my work and personal lives as two separate things. This didn't work out very well—it was as if I was running two separate organizations that never communicated or coordinated with each other. This resulted in a herniated disc and back injuries as well as the very toxic environment and low self-image I have already told you about. So when I decided to launch S.H.E. Globl Media I made a conscious decision to keep the company lean and nimble. For me, employing more people meant more people to manage and more complexities to hash out. I also knew that I wanted my next business to be a remotely run business because my partner and I were ready to start a family. Finally, I concluded that if I was going to dedicate more than 50 percent of my time and life toward work, it had to be purpose-centric and drive change in a meaningful way. When I had this level of clarity around how I wanted to live my life, it allowed me to stop seeing my work and my personal life as separate realms. Being able to integrate all the areas of my life into one entity made it more manageable to lead.

To be clear, I am not talking about work-life balance, which has become an overused and unpopular term.[2] Whole-life integration, rather, is a more practical and sustainable strategy because it encompasses the entirety of your life's departments. When you integrate all areas of your life, you can more realistically plan for the near future in the elevation periods I discussed in the Productivity chapter and decide how to prioritize your top two to three departments in an increment of time.

Here are the departments that I consider most important, but you should customize and order your list of departments to reflect the demands and dynamics of your own life:

Personal Well-Being and Health

- Your body, mind, and heart make up your vessel, the engine that powers you through life. You have only one vessel, so it is of primary importance that you take good care of it, set boundaries, and know when to set aside time for self-love.

Marriage and Intimate Life Partnership

- The person you choose as your spouse or romantic partner is the most important decision you will ever make. If your life is the organization you're leading, then the person you marry is your business partner for life. He or she is going to be the cocaptain of your ship, and together you'll navigate through careers, financial planning, raising children, taking care of family, and giving back to the community. The healthier and happier you two are, the more successful your individual careers are going to be and the more successful your kids will be, and the same goes for the other areas of your life.

Children and Parenting

- Becoming a parent is one of the most profound experiences of our lives. It's what we were put here to do—to procreate and usher in a better future for humankind. That said, it's so easy to compare and judge yourself as a parent and worry about whether you're doing the right thing for your children. Remember that we all have different stories and a mixed bag of skills. We are each better at some things and worse at others. As long as you are guided by love and good intentions, chances are you will do just fine as a parent and learn a lot along the way.

Career and Vocation

- Your work is not only a huge part of your identity; it also consumes an enormous part of your life. If you're awake for fourteen to eighteen hours each day and then work eight to ten hours, that means you're spending anywhere between 50 and 70 percent of your waking time on your career. If you're not happy, fulfilled, or satisfied, reflect on how you might change course.

Purpose and Social Impact

- The impact you are meant to make in this lifetime is the reason you are here. It may take a different form and structure, as you learned in the Vision chapter, depending on your specific circumstances and experiences, but understand that your personal potential is ultimately tied to your efforts to serve and lift others. When you follow the path of purpose, you are rewarded tenfold by the good work you do, and everything starts to fall into place.

Financial Well-being

- So many people neglect their finances. Everyone wants to make a lot of money, but too many spend it recklessly and get themselves into massive debt. Women especially need to take control of their finances, as they make less on the dollar compared to men but live longer. We all have different relationships with money and how we value it. The key to managing your financial well-being is understanding and acknowledging your history with money. Generally we inherit our financial outlook and habits from our parents and the people we grow up around.

Social Community and Other Close Relationships

- Good relationships are like your extended family in life. We're born to be in relationships with each other, to build friendships and join communities that support and nurture each other through good and bad times. Develop relationships with people who inject you with various forms of positivity. After spending time with them, you should walk away feeling inspired, excited, educated, energized, ignited, supported, or just plain *good*. Avoid people who are overly critical and self-obsessed—they will deplete your energy and leave you feeling bad.

Physical Home and Living Foundation

- The environment you surround yourself with can have a powerful effect on your well-being and state of mind. This is the place you come home to, that shelters you. Your home should nourish you and make you feel good, so take the time to create a beautiful space where you feel comfortable and at peace. Ultimately it's also a reflection of who you are.

You may have more departments in your life. Perhaps you're a son or daughter who is caring for an aging parent or relative. Or you may have other passions and hobbies that make up another department of your life like playing music or traveling. When you lead your life from a 360-degree lens, your actions and achievements will feel more integrated. Each department will start working more synergistically with one another, and though some will fall behind during life's unpredictable events, that lagging department will still be in your sight clear enough for you to jump in when it needs extra love and attention. You're not going to give every department your full leadership attention at all times. You will instead divvy up and allocate your time based on your judgment of what needs the most attention when, just as you do with prioritizing specific goals for specific elevation periods. The important thing is taking stock of your whole life and using the leadership pillars from Part II to manage it all. You are the sum of your parts, and the whole cannot thrive unless all your individual parts thrive as well.

"You are the sum of your parts, and the whole cannot thrive unless all your individual parts thrive as well."

19

Lead from Where You Are

"Tell them about how you're never really a whole person if
you remain silent, because there's always that one little
piece inside you that wants to be spoken out, and if you
keep ignoring it, it gets madder and madder and hotter and
hotter, and if you don't speak it out one day it will just up
and punch you in the mouth from the inside."

—AUDRE LORDE, POET AND CIVIL RIGHTS ACTIVIST

YOU ARE ALREADY WHAT YOU SEEK

Now that you are on the path to clarifying and executing your purpose,
your first thought might be that you'll need to make a massive career
change or life shift. That may be true; perhaps that thought is the universe
calling you to make a change. But before you jump to that conclusion,
know that pursuing your purpose doesn't necessarily mean undergoing
massive changes.

We often think the answers we're searching for are far away and can be
found and sorted out only after doing a lot of hard work and making big
changes or worse, big sacrifices. I felt this same way during the last few
years I was at Shecky's. When things got bad, at first I avoided considering
new career opportunities because I thought that if I left, not only would I be
flushing all those years of work down the toilet but I'd also need to start

from scratch and overhaul my professional identity and comfortable lifestyle. I had a team and resources at Shecky's, and the thought of rebuilding everything again, from brand legitimacy and clientele to websites and press, seemed exhausting. I'd begin again with nothing. Plus, at thirty-five I felt I should have been further along and more established, not starting over.

In reality, I didn't realize something huge. All the time and energy I was putting in—trying to fix my business partnership, those eight- to ten-hour days at work; traveling to and putting on a happy face at client sites and events around the country; complaining to John, family, and friends about how unhappy I was; and the overall angst and toxicity of the job— all of that could have been put toward building something new. More importantly, I also didn't understand yet that whatever new thing I built, I would *not* be starting from scratch—I'd be building a new business based on everything I had already accomplished.

Looking back, S.H.E. Globl Media and my entire women's empowerment career have been built on my previous personal and professional network, business experience, skills, obstacles, and my instinct for what I felt was missing for women. Of course, I didn't have all the resources and clarity to be successful overnight, but I could rely on what I did have to help me get what I was still missing.

Of course, now that you know my story, you may think that leaving my role at Shecky's and starting a new venture *was* a big change and a lot of work. This is not to say that it wasn't! What I want to reinforce, though, is that you are likely already on the path to living and working for your purpose. Maybe you just haven't seen it yet. Many of us feel we need to take an extreme measure to contribute to our purpose, without taking into consideration the sacrifices or drawbacks that might come with such a dramatic move; instead, we should take a cue from the monk and activist Thich Nhat Hanh, who once said, "What you seek is seeking you." Believe it or not, you already have all the abilities, knowledge, and expertise needed to move your purpose forward. Once your new purpose and vision are clear, the trick is to focus and put that new purpose-centric plan into action immediately. Sometimes this does require taking a few steps back so you can leap forward up the mountain. But take stock of where you are. Could your purpose-centric plan already be within your reach?

You already have everything you need to steer your life to a purpose-centric path. You may not have the clients, website, brand, or resources yet, but you have the skills and networks to attain these things sooner than you think. You may not have the management buy-in, team support, or budget approval now, but you have the creativity, perseverance, and relationships to gain the traction you need to get it off the ground. God did not give you the powerful vision you have without

> "Believe it or not, you already have all the abilities, knowledge, and expertise needed to move your purpose forward."

first equipping you with the skills and abilities to manifest it. The strategy is to live in abundance, not scarcity, and believe that you have already received everything you want—and allow that positive attitude to manifest the best-case scenario. Again, refer back to the Faith chapter when you find yourself needing to strengthen that muscle.

CHOOSING YOUR BEST PATHWAY TO PURPOSE: ENTREPRENEURSHIP, INTRAPRENEURSHIP, OR HYBRIDPRENEURSHIP

As we learned in Part II, purpose is the specific work you want to accomplish—the specific gap you want to close, the specific white space you want to fill, the specific people you want to help—and vision is the structure through which you serve this purpose, whether it's a purpose-centric project, job, career, or vocation (discussed in the Vision chapter). Now it's time to think about the various pathways available for you through which to execute your purpose and vision.

Across the thousands of women we've activated through S.H.E. conferences and programs I have seen three main pathways: entrepreneurship, intrapreneurship, and hybridpreneurship. Each of these models is built on top of the word entrepreneurship because purpose-driven work requires the same spirit of innovative thinking and risk taking. Just as an entrepreneur often needs to put in countless *unpaid* hours of work in the early stages of a venture, purpose-driven work is often not monetizable in the beginning. Entrepreneurs also face many rejections when it comes to raising capital or winning customers, which requires more resilience and persistence. (If it were easy to start a business, everyone would do it, right?) Purpose-driven initiatives and businesses often face many nos before they get to their first yes. Finance expert and author of *The Entrepreneurial Instinct*, Monica Mehta, defines it this way: "The entrepreneurial instinct is the mental toughness that is required to make something from nothing. It is the mindset that allows you to take smart risks, thrive in ambiguity, and bounce back from failure."[1]

On the next few pages I explain each of these pathways and give examples to help you think about your own situation. Regardless of which path you take, a few key elements will remain the same: all "preneurs" need to be self-starters who don't wait for others to step in; put themselves in uncomfortable, riskier situations; and invest the unpaid time needed to get something off the ground because they are driven by the good or product they want to create more than anything else.

Entrepreneurship

In the context of purpose-driven pathways, I define an entrepreneur as someone who fulfills their purpose through leading or coleading his or her own organization, which can be for-profit or nonprofit. Whether you're leading a quickly growing start-up, building a small to mid-size charity, or operating a freelance business of one, the same entrepreneurial skills come into play: managing a profit-and-loss statement, raising funds, hiring talent, and creating demand for or participation in the product, service, brand, or cause. And if you haven't noticed, entrepreneurship is trending, especially among millennials, 67 percent of whom say their goals involve starting their own business.[2] Some even call entrepreneurship the new women's movement because women have been starting businesses at a higher rate than men for the last twenty years.[3] And according to a 2015 report, 27 million working-age Americans have started or are running their own businesses.[4]

With an MA in public policy and a PhD in child and adolescent development, Gary Barker spent years researching issues of gender justice and became convinced that the only way to end violence and achieve equality is to engage men as "voices for change."[5] Gary founded Promundo in 1997, a nonprofit based in Brazil that was one of the first organizations to work directly with men and boys to promote positive masculinity and solidarity with the issues women and girls face. Now, many would not refer to Gary as an entrepreneur because his organization is a nonprofit, but I would label his pathway as entrepreneurship, or social entrepreneurship, because the skills required to build and lead Promundo were not too different from what's needed to run a for-profit organization. Starting his own enterprise made sense for Gary because there were very few existing organizations at the time that understood the innovative approach he wanted to take toward gender equality. He applied his research knowledge and went on to raise money to build and sustain the organization through sponsors like national and local governments, aid organizations, and individuals.[6] Now, twenty years later, Promundo has done work across continents in places like the favelas of Rio de Janeiro, the Democratic Republic of Congo, and inner cities in the United States.

Social entrepreneur is another term that can be used for the purpose-driven self-starter. Consider Geena Rocero, supermodel and founder of Gender Proud. She got her lucky break at twenty-one after she was discovered by a photographer, and she spent the next twelve years building a successful career as a fashion model. Then, in 2014, she gave a TED Talk titled, "Why I Must Come Out," when she revealed her identity as a transgender woman who was born as a boy.[7] The overwhelmingly positive response she received from the talk spurred her to create Gender Proud, an advocacy organization and production company that aims to uplift transgender communities around the world. The entrepreneurial path was the right choice for Geena because she'd already had experience as a model-entrepreneur, only this time her specific mission was to support and strengthen representations of transgender people. The organization she launched and the business model she came up with support that mission.

For me personally the entrepreneurial path was the only way. I grew up in an entrepreneurial family, watching my parents build their restaurant businesses from scratch. My mom would say, "Claudia, to own your independence, you need to own your own business one day." My risk aversion to entrepreneurship was also low because I saw my parents eat risk for breakfast every day. Hundreds of thousands of dollars were borrowed for each restaurant from banks and the banker friends my dad made bartending on Wall Street, and it would always take a minimum of three years to pay those funds back with interest. That was a lot of money in the 1970s to 1990s. Even more risky, when my mom's restaurant lease was up at the Empire State Building in 1990, she began looking for another business to invest in. At the time my mom had developed a close friendship with a Greek store owner next door, Angelo, who owned several shoe-and-leather repair shops in the city. He had hit a difficult time a year back, and she lent him $200,000 to be repaid with interest. As she was seeking the next business to get into, Angelo offered her his new storefront on the lower level in the famous 666 Fifth Avenue building. Without any knowledge of leather goods repair or fixing shoes, she took on the venture. If you lived in New York City between the 1990s to 2000s during the *Sex and the City* era, when dropping a G on pair of Choos or two wasn't out of the ordinary, you probably remember Angelo's Shoe Repair at 666 Fifth Avenue. She not only ran that business for nine years; she also became famous as NYC's shoe repair woman and was voted "Best Shoe and Leather Repair" in local publications like *New York Magazine* and the *New York Post* for multiple years in a row.

> "If you're the kind of person who wants to move at your own bold, fast pace and build an organization according to your rules, then entrepreneurship is for you."

Watching her and my father focus on the gain instead of the pain in business, especially during my high school and college years, motivated me to start my own business as soon as I could. My father would say, "Claudia, when you run a business, worry more about making the money than spending it." So it's no surprise I started my first business, iLounge, a dot-com networking event business, at twenty-three years old. I just focused on the "making and creating" over the spending, and that mindset spearheaded what has now been an almost twenty-year entrepreneurial path.

If you're the kind of person who wants to move at your own bold, fast pace and build an organization according to your rules, and if you can live without the security of structure and a regular paycheck, then entrepreneurship is for you. You might have a great idea for an innovative product or service, but unless you have an appetite for risk and a singular conviction in your own abilities, entrepreneurship is going to be a hard path. Remember: it's not just about starting something; it's about the long-haul commitment to building an organization. The media platform you dream of starting, the social impact app you want to launch or the sustainable fashion business you're hoping to design may all be great ideas, but the real test is whether you're willing to commit to eating, drinking, and sleeping your venture for the next three to ten years of your life. Often this is what it takes to get something off the ground. You need to be able to live in the unknown and rely on your conviction to keep you going.

Intrapreneurship

The entrepreneurial path is definitely not for everyone. Entrepreneurship has become so trendy and popular, but I actually warn corporate professionals—especially women—not to get sucked into how glamorous the entrepreneurial path may seem. When it comes to celebrating today's change agents who are driving change in the world, everyone from mainstream media publications to social innovation conferences tend to profile entrepreneurs or organization founders more than those who actually work for large corporate conglomerates. Outlets like TED, Makers, Summit.co, SXSW, and countless others offer so much insight into the people and stories behind today's movements, but corporate leaders and professionals seem few and far between in the hipster, social change business world. It's no wonder I meet so many young people and women who lose passion for their work inside a large company and feel their only purpose-centric path is to go off on their own. Or they start building something on the side while they're in corporate jobs, devising the right plan and timing to leave. Research also shows that women and men are increasingly leaving corporate America; more than 2 million Americans voluntarily quit their jobs each month.[8]

Now more than ever people crave meaningful work that inspires and fulfills them, not just a paycheck.[9] Still, you need to be very thoughtful about jumping the gun and quitting your job right away. Your finances, current seniority or position, and sense of security are all very important parts of your career, just as much as following your purpose is. So if you are currently working within a corporation, don't feel the need to throw your life into a frenzy until you have really thought through the pros and cons of the corporate path. This may actually be the perfect position from which you can lead change as an intrapreneur.

If you have spent many years or over a decade in corporate life; have already been climbing the ranks or are at a somewhat senior level; have strong, established networks inside the company, especially with management; see clear areas where the company can make a greater impact for its people, profit, and/or product; and the adversity, frustrations, and disappointments you have experienced are major concerns in the grand scheme of things (considering how much more personal growth work we all need to do to strengthen our leadership pillars of courage, vision, obstacles, faith, grace, and the others), then I ask you to consider whether an intrapreneurial path will allow you to better move your purpose forward.

Intrapreneurs fulfill their purpose through an organization they work for as an employee, but they do not own or co-own the organization. They generate change from the inside-out by working within their existing corporate infrastructure. Like entrepreneurs, intrapreneurs need to be resourceful and progressive, but unlike entrepreneurs, they must do so while working within the confines of their organization. This also takes patience and compromise. But when you stop to think about all the customers a large corporation touches externally and all the employees they touch internally, executing your purpose from inside an established company, especially one with a global footprint, is quite an extraordinary opportunity. The best part is that you can pursue your purpose—aspire to be an impact intrapreneur or corporate change agent driving a movement—and do so with the security of health insurance, a consistent paycheck, and other benefits that should not be taken for granted.

If you're feeling the corporate blues or believe fulfilling your purpose will be impossible inside a corporate environment, here are some ways to get you thinking about the corporate world in a different light.

ACTIVISM AND MOVEMENTS ARE NEEDED INSIDE COMPANIES. The current corporate workplace paradigm could use more innovation and initiatives started by women and men internally, especially when it comes to empowering diverse groups to thrive both inside their industry culture as well as outside in their marketplace. For example, can you change the way a product or service is developed and marketed to solve an external issue better? Can you start or innovate an internal employee network or program to create more community and conversation around a specific improvement needed for the company? Can you make the case for funding a new division or paid role that will innovate a long-standing issue? One obvious area that needs corporate change is requiring businesses to offer parental leave and workplace flexibility: 43 percent of women with children are opting out and leaving their careers, oftentimes never returning to the workforce.[10] Women also cite short maternity leaves and the cost of childcare as some of the reasons they remain at home with young children, yet nearly three-quarters of full-time homemakers say they would consider returning to the workforce if more flexible hours were available to them.[11] Think about the negative impact that women dropping out of the workplace has had over the years, not just for a nation's GDP and social and business innovation but also for female self-esteem, identity, and the imbalance of economic power. A survey conducted by Deloitte reveals that although 50 percent of respondents—male and female—say they would rather have more parental leave than a pay raise, fewer than half feel their company fosters an environment where men feel comfortable taking parental leave.[12] "Parental leave is about much more than recovering from a medical event. It's about bonding with a new child—and that goes for fathers as well as mothers," says Deepa Prushothaman, who heads Deloitte's Women's Initiative.[13] When men don't take advantage of parental leave benefits even when they have them, this societal issue is only perpetuated. This is just one cause where corporate professionals can bring about profound change. Imagine the millions of people you can impact by focusing on an area like this within your current company.

THERE ARE MORE BENEFITS, RESOURCES, AND SECURITY INSIDE COMPANIES. Once you decide the purpose you want to move forward, you can pursue it with the security of a solid paycheck, health and retirement benefits, colleagues and personalities whom you're already familiar with, and some knowledge of where you gain more support. Again, you already have an existing role in the company to leverage, and if you've already invested years at the firm, why not go after a new purposeful achievement that will give the years you've been there only more meaning? I have met women who've given fifteen years of their life to an industry or company and finally want to jump ship for the entrepreneurial path; instead, can you consider that maybe the fifteen years of frustration you've had at the company have happened for you so you can lead a change for the company and your industry? In my consulting work with corporate clients I often see people get demoralized very quickly when confronted with one or a few rejections or signs of resistance to their newfound missions and movements, which to me seem like a walk in the park in comparison to the magnitude of barriers entrepreneurs overcome. It can be a war zone for us entrepreneurs sometimes. Remember: it took me several years to gain the revenue traction for S.H.E. Globl Media that I expected to get in year one. And I was doing it without the stability of a consistent paycheck and benefits.

IF WOMEN CONTINUE TO LEAVE THE CORPORATE WORLD, THERE WILL BE FEWER FEMALE ROLE MODELS TO LEAD CHANGE AND INSPIRE OTHERS, AND THE GENDER GAP WILL TAKE LONGER TO SHRINK. We cannot emphasize enough that if women continue to leave the corporate world at the rate they have (as I said earlier, 43 percent of women with children opt out), not only does workplace gender parity in pay, leadership roles, race, and other diversity categories get further delayed, but we also end up losing the people to fuel projects and programs of change as well as the role models for younger women and men to look up to, both inside and outside a company. I would love to see the rise in corporate impact intrapreneurs launch movements from inside corporate walls, a media landscape that features more corporate titles next to news headlines that read like "Meet the Corporate Trailblazers Changing the World" and for more corporate faces to grace the cover of *Fast Company*'s Innovation issue as well as "Thirty Under Thirty" and "Forty Under Forty" lists.

Someone who embodies a typical intrapreneur is Marlene Gordon, North America vice president and general counsel at Bacardi. She came from humble beginnings, growing up in rural Jamaica without running water or electricity, went on to law school at Northwestern University, and climbed the corporate ladder as a woman of color to become the chief legal counsel for the North American region of the world's largest privately held, family-owned spirits company.[14] To say that Marlene is impressive would be an understatement. I first met her in 2014 when she had just become head of Bacardi's Women in Leadership (WIL) initiative in North America. Because she was so passionate and committed to running this program—which is a volunteer role she plays in addition to her responsibilities as vice president of general counsel, where she serves as a strong business partner and member of the North America Leadership Team, managing the legal services and support to the regional president and senior leadership—she is now leading the company's global Women in Leadership initiative that impacts around six thousand global employees. Moreover, she excels at reaching across the gender divide to get men involved by chairing committees and speaking at events. In 2016 Bacardi hosted its own S.H.E. Summit Bacardi conference in Miami, with over four hundred attendees, and now plans to follow up with a second summit after the major impact that the first conference achieved for its employees and South Florida's business community. She even secured Bacardi's global CEO, Mike Dolan, to speak at S.H.E. Summit 2016. which was a huge feat. When a global CEO of that stature participates in something like this, it sends a clear message about the company's commitment, from the top down, to gender equality. Marlene is the epitome of what it means to be a S.H.E. intrapreneur: a purpose-centric corporate professional driven by doing good for people inside and outside the organization.

Personally I am in awe of the potential impact corporate professionals have to lead change, yet they often opt out or don't see the opportunity because they lack exposure to inspiring role models who would encourage them to innovate within their own corporate workspace. The possibilities of intrapreneurship have so captivated me that I have completely shifted S.H.E. Globl Media's business to focus on activating corporate leaders to become tomorrow's change makers in the gender equality and women's macro-movement. If you already sit inside of a company, especially if you've been there or in the same corporate industry for many years, why not stay and leverage your knowledge and position to improve the system, which could in turn affect thousands to perhaps even millions of people?

> "If you already sit inside of a company, why not stay and leverage your knowledge and position to improve the system?"

Intrapreneurs put their deep institutional knowledge toward understanding how an organization can empower people inside or outside their company. Corporations are massive vehicles for social change and doing good because of the number of people they employ and customers their products and services touch. An excellent example of this is when the person in charge of a marketing campaign at an organization has the opportunity and budget to create content that teaches and impacts people positively. That person is an intrapreneur utilizing her role within a company to broach topics that are important to its brand and its customers, similar to the Always and Dove marketing campaigns we talked about earlier. If you're in product development and see that a large segment of your consumers is working mothers, perhaps you can innovate and design a better product that will serve their lives better. What's more, intrapreneurs usually know better than anyone else the problems and pain points within an organization because they have experienced them firsthand. As an intrapreneur you hold invaluable insights from years of working at an organization, and you know how to navigate the corporate workplace toward a solution. Whether it's setting out to change the company's culture, recruiting the right leadership support behind an important program, or developing a better service for customers, consider what you can do to help the company retain its people and innovate its value in the world.

Finally, if starting an initiative feels too daunting, start with something more manageable like mentoring one or a few junior team members. Take them under your wing and support them to develop the skills and traits that will take their careers to the next level. As you rise within an organization you will have the opportunity to groom and lift others with you; in fact, you're going to need talented people on your team, so it behooves you to mentor and sponsor the next generation of leaders.

Hybridpreneurship

Not all of us fit into the entrepreneurship and intrapreneurship paradigms; instead, you might be a mixture of the two and many other things: someone who has the flexibility to split her time between various endeavors, whether that means freelance work, volunteering her time and services, or being a full-time stay-at-home mom or dad. In fact, some research tells us that 40 percent of the American workforce is projected to ditch full-time jobs to be freelance or contingent by 2020.[15]

Hybridpreneurs fulfill their purpose through a web of projects that may be interconnected or discrete; they are a hybrid of the more traditional entrepreneur and intrapreneur roles because they can be working both inside an existing organization and doing their own thing on the side independently. Hybridpreneurs can be independent one-man/woman shows without entities and teams. They walk to the beat of their own drummer and cherry-pick the paying and nonpaying gigs that align best with their lifestyle and interests. If you're an independent publicist, for instance, and your mission is to help promote female role models, you might decide that you're going to work with women only. Or you might be a freelance writer whose purpose is the environment and climate change so you write articles about environmental policy and decide to volunteer part time on a political campaign because the candidate has taken a strong position on the environment. Maybe you're a stay-at-home dad who runs a consulting business on the side, and because of a life-changing trip to South America, you develop a new mission of impacting change in underdeveloped countries and decide that, moving forward, you're going to work with companies investing in development projects in the third world. You could be a freelance producer who works on social good commercials and music videos (part of your purpose is supporting artistic expression), but your main passion project is a documentary on women refugees because your father came to the United States as a refugee and highlighting women's issues is also a deep part of your purpose. As you can see, the possibilities are as diverse as your interests. Being a hybridpreneur allows you to pursue whatever moves you.

Hybridpreneurs can also balance big, full-time corporate jobs with multiple external projects and roles. Carla Harris is an inspiring example of this. She has held a powerful corporate post at Morgan Stanley for more than twenty-seven years, and as vice chairman of Wealth Management and senior client adviser at Morgan Stanley, she has been finding ways to drive change internally for just as long. For example, she was instrumental in kicking off Morgan Stanley's first-ever Senior Multicultural Leaders Conference in 2016 and found purpose in the company's philanthropic arm by chairing the Morgan Stanley Foundation for ten years. But she also has extremely impressive identities and roles outside of her professional career and pursues projects to check her purpose box even further. Her passion for singing and teaching others has pushed her to become an accomplished gospel singer, public speaker, and author of the book *Expect to Win*. She can now draw on the hard-won wisdom she's gained from the corporate world to empower others who are just beginning their careers and professional journeys. On top of that, in 2013 President Barack Obama appointed her to chair the National Women's Business Council, a service role that tapped into her expertise in business. Who better to advise on the state of women in business than someone who's seen it firsthand? In the macro-movement landscape, Carla's not only driving the movement to empower women in the corporate world; she is also doing great work for women entrepreneurs. As a hybridpreneur Carla brings her whole self to her leadership, whether it's in the executive boardroom or on the stage at Carnegie Hall.

If most of your time goes to parenting but you have other projects or causes you're committing substantial professional time to, hybridpreneur is also a title you can own. Let's talk about full-time and part-time care-givers for a moment. The work parents do is so often overlooked, yet moms and dads are perhaps the most important change agents we have. Raising a child is no small undertaking. Parents—moms especially—tend to dismiss their roles when they say, "I'm just a stay-at-home mom [or dad]." Really, your job as a parent is one of the most important jobs in society. As a caregiver you are developing and bringing up our next generation of citizens. The lessons you teach and the values you instill in your children will have an immense effect on shaping the future of society.

I meet countless parents—mostly mothers, but some fathers . . . and I would like to see more dads!—who spend the majority of their time with kids yet at the same time are either dreaming of starting something or thinking about getting involved in purposeful or volunteer work, if they aren't already doing these things. If you're a parent, I want to encourage you to own that desire for something more. First, recognize your own significance, abilities, and the massive role you play as a parent. Second, really own taking on something else, whether it's dabbling in something new (there are all kinds of structures for this, as we discussed in the Vision chapter) or starting out small. Whatever it is you decide to do to fulfill your purpose in the social realm (in addition to parenting in the personal realm), own the fact that you're doing many things and proudly call yourself a hybridpreneur. Don't talk down your value or shrink your identity just because you're not getting a paycheck; instead, celebrate being a hybridpreneur who is making an impact for the spectrum of purposes that matter most to you.

My former Smith College roommate Diana is a burgeoning hybridpreneur. After working in the corporate world for six years and earning her MBA from Duke University, she left to raise her three kids over the last ten years. Now that her children are all in school, she finally has some extra time to think about her identity and purpose beyond being a mother and wife. So she has begun taking on work as a freelance marketing consultant and is volunteering on a regular basis for Fugees Family, a non-profit devoted to integrating and educating child refugees in their new host countries.[16] All of these pursuits allow her to fill her purpose bucket while exploring paths she might want to follow further when the time is right. When asked, "What do you do?" she can proudly say, "I'm a hybrid-preneur! I juggle my time between raising my three kids, development and fund-raising for a nonprofit that empowers child refugees, and marketing consulting for women-led start-up companies." Do you see the difference between this and "Oh I'm just a stay-at-home mom who volunteers at a nonprofit and dabbles in some marketing consulting on the side"?

DO A PERSONAL RESOURCE ASSESSMENT TO DISCOVER YOUR PATHWAY

We've covered three main options for how you can delve into purpose-centric work based on where you are now. If you're still not sure where to start, begin by doing the Personal Resource Assessment, an inventory check of all your current resources. Based on your current status, what talents, resources, and relationships do you have that you can build on? Be thoughtful about the knowledge and assets you have at your disposal that could help you move your purpose forward faster while still providing enough security and minimizing stress.

Spend time with these questions, and be thoughtful and realistic about your answers. Put them down on paper and talk them through with your partner, mentor, or a close friend who knows you well and has your best interests at heart. The answer you seek will come to you—just listen to your instincts, which are really your higher power guiding you.

TALENTS. What are you really good at? What do you love to do? What comes easily or natural to you? Is it business development and convincing people to invest in what you pitch? Is it the ability to develop powerful programs and convince many people to participate?

EXPERIENTIAL KNOWLEDGE. What kind of professional experiences do you have? Think about the product launches, client wins, major projects, events, and teams you have worked on: What knowledge can be applied to new scenarios?

NETWORK. Who of your existing community can help you get your project off the ground? How can they collaborate or help you? How might your new movement directly benefit them?

FINANCIAL WELL-BEING. What's your financial situation and appetite for risk? If you're single, what kind of savings or nest egg do you have? If you're married, does your partner have a secure corporate gig with family insurance and benefits, or is his/her path entrepreneurial or higher risk too? Do you have kids to support?

TIME AND SCHEDULE. What is your lifestyle and level of life responsibilities right now? How much time do your family, job, and other nonnegotiable circumstances demand of you? Do you have any special needs related to health or family that require more emotional energy?

CREATE YOUR OWN
"THIS IS HOW I RISE" PLAN

Congratulations, you are almost at the final chapter and have learned the blueprint for how to reach your highest potential and lead change in the world! But before you move onto the conclusion, I want to make sure you walk away with clear action steps. Now is a great time to reflect on previous chapters and define what you need to do most based on your personality and patterns in order to claim the extraordinary destiny that is your birthright. Choose the steps where you are most lacking or unclear, and create a sample list like the one below. Just as one needs to create a strategic plan for her business or a big project, think of this as writing out your personal leadership or life's strategic plan. Customize each bullet for what you need most and get ready to see your life transform. You will experience more joy and fulfillment, and you're going to blow your mind away with all that you will accomplish and become.

1. **Embrace the Outside-In Perspective.** I see my life from the universe's perspective. I can no longer try to understand things

just from my own narrow perspective. When things happen or I experience conflict that I don't agree with or can't make sense of, I must try to see it from God's eyes and not my own. I don't know it all and there's a much bigger force out there.

2. **Have Greater Faith.** I need to start walking by faith and not by sight. I must trust in the invisible and continue to trust that my gut is guiding me.

3. **Picture the Mountain as Your Life's Potential.** Whenever I lack confidence, I visualize my life as the mountain and realize how extraordinary my birthright is—that everything has happened for me to live out this destiny.

4. **Define Your Holistic Purpose.** God gave me my unique gifts and experiences for an extraordinary purpose. Right now in my life I think this means X in the personal realm and Y in the social realm. Therefore, I am courageous in following my instincts and take bold steps towards my destiny. In the social realm I am going to tackle X in the macro-movement landscape. Being here on this earth is not just about me and my family.

5. **Choose an Accessible Pathway.** My Personal Resource Assessment guides which pathway I will take—entrepreneurship, intrapreneurship, hybridpreneurship—that is based on where I am now and is best suited for my personality, network, and desires.

6. **Build Your Foundational Pillars of Personal Leadership.** To be successful in this pursuit I must undergo extensive personal growth and leadership development. I hone in on the qualities I am the weakest in, and keep leveraging my journal to do so.

7. **Treat Your Whole Life As the Organization You're Leading.** I define the departments that make up my life right now and prioritize what matters most according to the life stage I am in.

8. **Set Goals by Elevation Periods.** My vision is doable and realistic by creating short-term phases of work and priorities. For the next three months my focus is only X, Y, and Z.

9. **Connect, Educate, and Activate.** Every year I will grow in my leadership and impact by investing in greater connections, education, and activation. This is how I can make greater progress on my life's mountain.

You get the picture. Grab that journal you started in Part II, start customizing your "This Is How I Rise" plan, and you'll be on your way to becoming the leader God intended you to be with a whole-life-thriving strategy. But don't stop here. The conclusion of this book is the most important message I need to give you, so turn the page now.

Conclusion

All Roads Lead to Character

"Your circumstances are temporary. Your character will last forever."

—RICK WARREN, PASTOR AND AUTHOR

Sometimes in life we go through traumatic events or difficult experiences that put our lives into perspective and clarify our true priorities like never before. No matter what we do, we can't predict what's going to happen next or when our time on earth will be up. Every day is precious, which is why we need to constantly reassess what truly matters and decide how we're going to lead our lives. A similar kind of reckoning happened for me in August of 2016 when my father passed away at eighty-six. It was the first time I had ever lost someone really close to me. This book is dedicated to him, and his character has inspired this concluding chapter, so I want to share the Facebook post I wrote about him two days after he passed:

> First, we want to thank all of you who prayed or sent light to our father, Wallace Wai-Hung Chan. The past few years, though, he had many health issues, including liver cancer; he was really doing well under our mom's care. Everyone was always amazed at how cool and stable he was with so many illnesses and past tumultuous hospital events. His life force was miraculously strong and resilient. But a month ago, on an ordinary

day, just like that, he took a fall at home . . . that would lead to one last insanely heroic fight lasting for four weeks.

You see, Wallace Chan was extraordinary in generosity, charisma, compassion, creativity, vision, honesty, loyalty, perseverance, and EN-DURANCE. These qualities made up his extraordinary life—he came to America in the 1960s to study history with $7 in his pocket . . . eventually meeting buddies while bartending on Wall Street who loaned him money to open a wildly successful Chinese restaurant called Kirin (a Chinese mythical creature that brings prosperity and serenity). Eventually he met my mom, and they went on to open four more restaurants, including the first Chinese restaurant in the Empire State Building. All this enabled my brother, Robert, and I to have the quality education and privileges we did as Asian Americans living in a much less diverse world then (I was just one of two Asians in the American private schools I attended growing up). An only child, Wallace Chan, was also born premature, but he was so tough that my grandparents (both government officials) called him the "little lion." His whole life stood for stamina, integrity, and character.

Fast forward to now. After a heroic journey of operation rooms, ER to ICU and back—he finally got to come home on Thursday night, August 26, and passed peacefully just a few hours later at 5:25 a.m. Wallace Chan was a lion who entered this world HARD CORE, and that is how he left it—a dramatic, heroic final battle, followed by the ending he wanted. We are devastated by the earthly loss of his tremendous life force and presence, but we feel beyond blessed to have had so many years with him and know that his spirit lives on in and around us. We're going to CELE-BRATE his life by working even harder to represent his exceptional character. And as Wally was always a social man who loved attention and gatherings (Rob says, "If you know myself and Claudia, you pretty much know my dad"), we invite friends to join us at his wake this Thursday, September 1, at NG Fook Funeral Home (36 Mulberry Street, 3–7 p.m.).

Marianne Williamson says, "If the universe is a house and we are the lamps, it is the electricity (the us and we) that lights up the house and not the lamp (me)." Thank you for being a part of our electricity.

Love, the CHANS

Losing Dad and, specifically, seeing his dead body for the first time was by far the most devastating event to happen in my life. In the midst of all the shock and sadness, I needed a way to cope. I had to stop seeing things from my personal perspective and instead try to look at it from God's perspective. That's when I began to see earthly existence from the outside-in, a perspective I introduced to you at the start of this book. If I looked at things through the outside-in lens, from God's perspective, what was the meaning of my father's life to God and society? What was his time here on earth all about? What would his legacy and stamp on our world be? All my mind wanted to do was run through the four weeks of hospital events and how, if we had done things differently, we could have saved his life or minimized his physical suffering. Instead of focusing on how he died and all the "what ifs," I pushed my heart and mind to focus on the meaning of my dad's life and to accept that this was his time according to his higher plan and destiny. Inevitably, this would force me to define the meaning for my own life and all of humanity. Why are we all here? We wake up every morning mentally running through our tasks for the day, but in reality, is completing our to-do lists really God's purpose for our lives? So what is the bigger-picture meaning for our lives?

> "What matters most at the end of this life is the character you shape while you are here on earth."

In preparing for his wake and eulogy, my brother, mother, and I spent hours going through old photos from his life. It's interesting to realize that when you think about your parents or any family member, you think about who they are *right now*—what they look like and their personalities. Your perception of them is shaped by your present relationship because it's easy to forget the older stories that made up their lives before you were born or what your relationship was like with them years or decades ago. Well, as I reflected on his life memories and photos, one word kept standing out to me: *character.* As I wrote in my Facebook post, my dad was and had always been an incredible and exceptional character.

This led me to realize that what matters most at the end of this life is the character you shape while you are here on earth. Remember: our birthright is to be extraordinary, and extraordinary character is what we should all aim for. But it is not something we are born with or learn in a classroom; instead, we spend our entire earthly life developing character by going through the life experiences that have filled the pages of this book. Every experience is a test, and every time we pass a test (serve, do the right thing, have integrity, etc.) blessings eventually come to us. Every time we fail a test, the things we want get delayed. And nothing builds our character more than the hardest tests.

BE A PERSON OF EXTRAORDINARY CHARACTER

The dictionary defines character as "the mental and moral qualities distinctive to an individual," so you can think about character as the combination of your internal ethics, traits, and values that dictates your outward behavior. Teaching you the thirteen foundational pillars of personal leadership development has been my attempt to shape and influence your internal moral and ethical code. The *purpose* you choose, the *visions* you pursue, the *resilience* you build, the *faith* you depend on, the *productivity* you master, the *energy* you permit, the *humility* you practice, the *gratitude* you acknowledge, the *grace* you offer, the *community* you grow, the *self-love* you grant yourself, the *courage* you demonstrate, and the *mindfulness* you cultivate—every experience and situation are a test to see whether you can make a better decision based on your last experience. In the process of making good and not-so-good decisions, relishing in the wins and enduring the losses, you will need to choose what your personal character stands for when you decide how to respond to specific situations, as people are often tempted with the easy way out. Like all the values discussed in this book, character and integrity are not qualities you just wake up with one day—you need to do the work. Fight down your core-limiting beliefs. Constantly augment and improve your toolbox of strategies. Build healthy habits and daily routines that support your values. Life is a never-ending journey of tests and opportunities to develop and mature your character. How extraordinary your character is depends on your moral fortitude and how well you live up to it. Another word for this is *integrity*—how well you stick to your character's ethical codes.

Oprah Winfrey says, "Real integrity is doing the right thing, knowing that nobody's going to know whether you did it or not." Sure, there are many times when you can get away with not doing the right thing because you think no one else knows, but your actions are something you have to live with. If you see someone drop a $20 bill and pocket it instead of returning it, you might reason, *Whatever—nobody knows*. But the truth is that you know. The universe knows. God knows. And that negative stuff will build up and catch up with you.

> "Every experience and situation are a test to see whether you can make a better decision based on your last experience."

Remember that your birthright is extraordinary and your potential is limitless. At the beginning of life you start out as a helpless newborn, but from there you're meant to grow and *rise*. Everything happens for you so you can wake up your own remarkable promise and discover your purpose for the greater good. Remember: the two most profound experiences in life are birth and death, yet you're able to prepare for only the second one, and that preparation is not guaranteed. My point is that you were created for extraordinary character and leadership; whether it actually happens is what you decide to do after finishing this book.

Becoming a person of extraordinary character is living the full-blown purpose-centric life that embodies all the points I have made in this book: having a "me for we" mindset, seeing yourself and others from the outside-in lens, and leading your whole life not in but *for* the whole world. We spend so much of our lives worrying about finances, careers, and things we need to accumulate to be happy. Our barometer for success is comparing how we're doing with everyone else—people we know and understand only on a surface level. Securing success and happiness for yourself alone is an empty and lonely quest, not to mention that you can't take your million-dollar home or fancy car with you when you die. The universe doesn't care about how much money you made or how many fancy awards and accolades you gained; it cares about the character you became, how well you treated other people, and whether you left any aspect of the world better than when you found it.

I have also been greatly impacted by the question I shared from Bill Hybels in the Purpose chapter: What will you do that will outlive you and all of those earthly accomplishments? And now I pose it to you. Let's say you live to be ninety years old and are forty years old today. What will you do over the next fifty years that will have a lasting impact on the world and humanity? Go back to your homework from the Purpose chapter to start defining this answer, and if you need motivation for why you should care, refresh your memory on why every single one of us can and must lead in the macro-movement from Part I. What you achieve and the quality of character you shape is that peak on your life's mountain, and this book is your how-to guide for *rising* to the summit.

Extraordinary character is not just what you did but also what kind of person you were. As I prepared the eulogy for my father's wake, I also thought about what people would say about me one day at my funeral. I don't know about you, but I want to be known for being generous, honest, good, courageous, kind, humbled, impactful, patient, graceful, faithful, loyal, and many more positive attributes. I want to have raised extraordinary human beings who leave their destined mark on the universe. I want to have inspired and activated countless leaders who will then multiply more leaders. I want to have been known as a difference-maker and a barrier-breaker because I believe that is what the universe intended when it gave me the talents and experiences of my life. So what kind of legacy do you want to leave behind?

WHY YOUR LEGACY MATTERS

I want to provide you with three more reasons why you should commit to the calling of this book and the significance of becoming a person of extraordinary character.

First, cultivating character is about honoring your parents' legacy and your entire family lineage. Of course, I had read about and learned this lesson before, but it wasn't until I actually experienced the loss of my dad that it really hit home for me. I realized that I was my dad's legacy. I'm carrying on the Chan family name. To justify his life and his existence, I need to make my life and what I achieve on this planet meaningful. I want to make my dad proud by continuing his legacy of integrity. In this way I'm using the pain of his loss to motivate me to do what I hope to accomplish during my earthly life. The same goes for my mom and her family's legacy. As I looked through my dad's childhood photos, I remembered stories about his parents and ancestors. Just as we strive today for a better future for our families and children, our ancestors made even greater sacrifices—surviving wars and famines, crossing oceans and continents—to give us better opportunities. We forget that we are a product of centuries of heritage and countless people whose blood we still carry in our veins. We owe it to them to lead lives that honor their memory.

Second, cultivating character is also about how you influence and shape the people you leave behind. Just as your parents and ancestors paved the way for you, you have the power to shape the character of the children you raise, the mentees you advise, the leaders you multiply, and the many others whom you inspire with your actions and being. Think of all the millions of people who have been influenced by leaders like Mahatma Gandhi, Martin Luther King Jr., Oprah Winfrey, and Gloria Steinem. You too can touch other people and impact the lives of hundreds, thousands, or even millions. As Maya Angelou said to Oprah after hearing about the girls' boarding school she wanted to start in Africa: "You have no idea what your legacy is. Your legacy is every life that you touched. Every voice you gave to the voiceless. Every person whose life changed because they watched your show."[1]

Third, if you are spiritual in any capacity and believe your being or consciousness or existence will surpass earthly life, then I ask you again to consider that what you do and who you become while you are here will influence the quality of your spiritual life after your earthly body is gone. As many spiritual leaders have noted, "We are not human beings on a spiritual journey. We are spiritual beings on a human journey."

Buddha says, "Every morning we are born again. What we do today is what matters most." What you decide your character will be from today forward matters most for all of the reasons above. Whatever happened yesterday that you are not proud of, let it inform your path forward. This entire book has guided you toward becoming a person of extraordinary character and developing the qualities that define the greatest of leaders. Again, can you be the next Gloria Steinem, Martin Luther King Jr., Richard Branson, Malala Yousafzai, Rosa Parks, or Mother Teresa? Who are you not to be? The ball is now in your court; the next step is in your hands. What actions will you take to alter your life's course and reach the incredible destiny that is yours to claim?

So S.H.E. leaders (SHEs and HEs WHO EMPOWER THE WORLD), let's get back to gender equality for a moment. Is it possible for each of us to root our leadership in the macro-movement to get our planet's people on equal playing fields? Because if I'm driving a movement and you're driving a movement, we inspire others to drive movements—well, that's when the ripple effect happens, and before we know it, millions are driving movements. As we each take on very specific purposes unique to who we are, it's inevitable that we will stumble upon and mobilize each other and collaborate. Collaboration then drives acceleration so that maybe, just maybe, we don't actually need to wait more than one hundred years to achieve gender equality and other realms of social progress. Maybe we can see this in our lifetime. The universe is great at delivering miracles when its people are focused on improving it. I want to live in a world where my son and daughter have equal opportunities, safe environments, and healthy resources to thrive and succeed, a world where their mother and father had something to do with that. Do you want that too?

To conclude, here's my current plan on how I will rise and lead change in the social realm. After you read mine, will you think about yours?

- My purpose is to start and drive movements that will advance social good and gender equality.

- My pathway to do this is entrepreneurship.

- My vision and structure to do this is through my S.H.E. Globl (www.SHEGlobl.com) organization and movement, which offers conferences like S.H.E. Summit (www.SHESummit.com), leadership curriculum and advisory workshops, and now this book to spread my message even wider.

- My work focuses on inspiring a new breed of leaders and change agents.

For now this is a big part of my purpose and vision, and my hope is that after you turn the final page of this book, you will seek and ponder your own. Remember that you are already what you seek, so the truth is already in you or not far off. THIS IS HOW WE RISE—working together in solidarity and finding unity in our great diversity while each of us pursues our own submovement. I think this is the perfect community that God intended for the universe. It is not how we start but how we finish that matters, and when we rise, we lift the whole world with us.

ACKNOWLEDGMENTS

This book would not be possible without my incredible book team. Leila Campoli, you were my destined agent; thank you for being so efficient, resourceful, involved, and helpful throughout the whole process. Katie Salisbury—I just could not have done this without your support in writing and editing. Thank you for your talent and patience and for going above and beyond and bringing calm and positive energy throughout the whole process. Claire Schulz, thank you and the entire Da Capo team for getting the significance of this book and the impact it can make for feminism, gender equality, and social change.

I am indebted to all the spiritual teachers in my life who helped me understand the world and my purpose from God's perspective: pastors Keith Boyd, Bill Hybels, and Rick Warren. I have so much more to learn. To my husband, John Wagner, thank you for bringing me to Trinity Church in NYC when we started dating in 2008 because that's when my spiritual journey began.

Thank you to my first life coach Mimi Duvall, who was pivotal in helping me transition out of Shecky's in 2011 and was my greatest cheerleader when I launched S.H.E. Summit in 2012. Thank you to Jackie Glick for all the years of therapy in my twenties and early thirties; you taught me how to connect the dots of my past to my present so I can better understand what shows up. Thank you to Rha Goddess for being an influential mentor and collaborator—I hope we continue to raise purpose-centric leaders side by side for years to come.

I am also grateful to the role models and authors who inspired my leadership journey: Sheryl WuDunn and Nicolas Kristof, Stephen Covey, Oprah Winfrey, Sheryl Sandberg, Tony Robbins, and Jane Wurwand.

Thank you to my S.H.E. Summit and S.H.E. Globl team members over the years who brought real heart and dedication to my vision and mission. Katie Livornese, it takes a very special person to understand all aspects of this business and help manage under my direction with unwavering passion and loyalty—you're going to soar and it's been an honor to mentor you. Margaret White, I couldn't ask for a more brilliant program director and passionate team member than you—you were my S.H.E. champion and dream-believer for so many years, and I will never forget that. Lauren Curiotto, Jennifer Weber, and Alexandra Cristofer—you provided so much support in the early days, thank you. Thank you, Nathalie Banker and Dermalogica for being my first S.H.E. Globl client and getting what I was building when it was just a PowerPoint proposal.

Thank you to my tribe of sisters and friends who have had my back and been there for me when I needed it the most: Kathleen Griffith, you're my soul-sister forever! Thank you for your generosity and always knowing what I need, even before I ask. Dael Cohen, you're my other brother and other therapist in addition to a great lawyer. Agapi Stassinopoulos, your spirit lights up the world, and I am so blessed to have your light in my life. Reshma Saujani, I continue to be in awe of you as a movement creator and leader; thank you for always saying YES and asking, "How can I help?" when you're so stretched; I pray others lead with your conviction and integrity. To my college and high school besties Diana Fleming, Ellen Shallman, Lauren Reiner, and Joy Grossman, thank you for always being there for me through life's most celebratory and difficult events. Thank you, Betsy Hitzmann and Aimee Raupp, for supporting my motherhood journey—what a profound experience it's been. And to the nannies and au pairs who have cared for my children—Lynn, Carolina, Rhonda—and all the people that work in childcare: your role is beyond significant in society because you keep working moms in the workplace! Society must value more of what you do.

Thank you to my friends at Grace Presbyterian Church in Water Mill, New York—you've been such a significant community to my family since we moved to the East End of Long Island in 2013.

To my family again . . . Daddy, I miss you so much; thank you for teaching me to marry for love and to follow my heart, modeling integrity, and being the best man and character I know. "I la li forever!" Mom, it was your extraordinary love, relentless hard work, business savvy, and mentorship that propelled me to entrepreneurial success. You have always been my greatest role model of how strong and capable a woman can be, and I would have never started a women's empowerment business if it weren't for you. I am forever indebted to you and Dad. Rob Chan, I am the luckiest sister to have you as my big bro; you keep me in check like no one else. You're a guardian angel for me but also for Jackson and Arya. To my mother-in-law, Doris Wagner, you're the purest soul and most loving person I know; thank you for showing me people like you exist, and of course for raising such a great son. John, Jackson Wallace Wagner, Arya Chan Wagner (and Connor)—thank you for being my greatest joys in the world.

Thank you to the obstacles and the most complicated relationships in my forty-two years of life—you've built my endurance and character like no other.

Thank you, God, for continuing to guide me to discover what I am on this earth to do.

NOTES

INTRODUCTION

1. Sheryl Sandberg, "Transcript and Video of Speech by Sheryl Sandberg, Chief Operating Officer, Facebook," Barnard, May 18, 2011, https://barnard .edu/headlines/transcript-and-video-speech-sheryl-sandberg-chief -operating-officer-facebook.

CHAPTER 1: WHY YOU CAN AND MUST
LEAD CHANGE IN THE WORLD

1. Drew Desilver, "U.S. Voter Turnout Trails Most Developed Countries," Pew Research Center, August 2, 2016, www.pewresearch.org/fact-tank/2016 /08/02/u-s-voter-turnout-trails-most-developed-countries.

2. Carl Bialik, "Voter Turnout Fell, Especially in States that Clinton Won," FiveThirtyEight, November 11, 2016, https://fivethirtyeight.com/features /voter-turnout-fell-especially-in-states-that-clinton-won.

3. Paul Clolery, "Troubling Numbers in Volunteering Rates," The NonProfit Times, February 27, 20014, www.thenonprofittimes.com/news -articles/troubling-numbers-in-volunteering-rates.

4. Deidre McPhillips, "Across the World, Where Are the Voters?," Best Countries, July 1, 2016, www.usnews.com/news/best-countries/articles /2016-07-01/across-the-world-where-are-the-voters.

5. Anna Johansson, "5 Fears You'll Need to Overcome to Be an Effective Leader," Entrepreneur, December 23, 2016, www.entrepreneur.com/article /254107.

6. Gené Teare and Ned Desmond, "The First Comprehensive Study on Women in Venture Capital and Their Impact on Female Founders," TechCrunch, April 19, 2016, https://techcrunch.com/2016/04/19/the-first -comprehensive-study-on-women-in-venture-capital.

7. Simon Constable, "Women, Especially, Are Failing Financial Literacy," Wall Street Journal, June 14, 2015, www.wsj.com/articles/women-especially -are-failing-financial-literacy-1434129899.

8. "Invest Like a Woman," Ellevest, www.ellevest.com/personalized _portfolios.

9. Carol Hanisch, "The Personal Is Political," Carol Hanisch, (February 1969), www.carolhanisch.org/CHwritings/PIP.html.

10. "An Insight, an Idea with Sergey Brin," World Economic Forum Annual Meeting, January 19, 2017, www.weforum.org/events/world-economic-forum -annual-meeting-2017.

11. Liz Wiseman, "Are You a Multiplier or a Diminisher," HR Exchange, September 21, 2010, www.humanresourcesiq.com/hr-talent-management /articles/are-you-a-multiplier-or-a-diminisher.

12. Stephanie Watson, "Volunteering May Be Good for Body and Mind," Harvard Health Publications, October 29, 2015, www.health.harvard.edu /blog/volunteering-may-be-good-for-body-and-mind-201306266428.

13. Philip Moeller, "Why Helping Others Makes Us Happy," *U.S. News & World Report*, April 4, 2012, http://money.usnews.com/money/personal -finance/articles/2012/04/04/why-helping-others-makes-us-happy.

CHAPTER 2: GENDER EQUALITY AND
THE PRIORITY TO LIFT WOMEN

1. Rachael Combe, "At the Pinnacle of Hillary Clinton's Career," *Elle*, April 5, 2012, www.elle.com/culture/career-politics/interviews/a12529/at-the -pinnacle-of-hillary-clintons-career-654140.

2. John Gerzema and Michael D'Antonio, "The Athena Doctrine: Feminine Qualities Will Rule the World," *Daily Beast*, April 12, 2013, www.thedailybeast .com/witw/articles/2013/04/12/the-athena-doctrine-the-future-is-feminine .html.

3. John Gerzema and Michael D'Antonio, *The Athena Doctrine: How Women (and the Men Who Think Like Them) Will Rule the Future* (San Francisco: Jossey-Bass, 2013), 7.

4. Ibid., 2, 10.

5. DeAnne Aguirre, Leila Hoteit, and Karim Sabbagh, "How to Keep the Promise of the Third Billion," Strategy+Business, February 26, 2013, www.strategy-business.com/article/00137?gko=5d83b; "The Third Billion," Strategy&, www.strategyand.pwc.com/global/home/what-we-think/third _billion?utm_source=printinvite&utm_medium=vanity&utm_campaign =ThirdBillion.

6. Global Poverty Project, "Introduction to the Challenges of Achieving Gender Equality," Global Citizen, October 12, 2012, www.globalcitizen.org /en/content/introduction-to-the-challenges-of-achieving-gender.

7. "Facts and Figures: Ending Violence Against Women," UN Women, www.unwomen.org/en/what-we-do/ending-violence-against-women/facts -and-figures.

8. "Gender and Water, Sanitation and Hygiene (WASH)," Eastern and Southern Africa, UNICEF, www.unicef.org/esaro/7310_Gender_and_WASH .html.

9. "77.6 Million Girls Are NOT Going Back to School," Girl Rising, http://girlrising.com/blog/39-million-girls-are-not-going-back-to-school.

10. "Gender, the Environment and the Sustainability of Development," Economic Commission for Latin America and the Caribbean, www.cepal .org/en/publications/5886-gender-environment-and-sustainability -development.

11. Morgan Stanley, "Gender Diversity Continues to Work," Global Qualitative Research, September 26, 2016, www.womencorporatedirectors .org/WCD/docs/new-content/MS--%20Gender%20Diversity%20Investment %20Strategy%209-26-16.pdf.

12. Michael Kimmel, "Why Gender Equality Is Good for Everyone Men Included," TED, May 2015, www.ted.com/talks/michael_kimmel_why _gender_equality_is_good_for_everyone_men_included#t-545942.

13. Seth Archer, "Companies with Women in Leadership Roles Crush the Competition," Business Insider, June 17, 2016, www.businessinsider.com /companies-with-women-in-leadership-roles-perform-better-2016-6.

14. "Companies with More Women Board Directors Experience Higher Financial Performance, According to Latest Catalyst Bottom Line Report," Catalyst, www.catalyst.org/media/companies-more-women-board-directors -experience-higher-financial-performance-according-latest.

15. Harriet Hall, "We Knew It! New Study Shows Feminism Can Help Men Live Longer," Stylist, June 17, 2015, www.stylist.co.uk/life/gender-equality -might-make-you-live-longer-feminism-women-mortality-life-expectancy.

16. Pauline Rose, "Why Girls' Education Can Help Eradicate Poverty," Reuters, September 25, 2013, http://blogs.reuters.com/great-debate/2013 /09/25/why-girls-education-can-help-eradicate-poverty; "Women Too Often Omitted from Peace Processes, Despite Key Role in Preventing Conflict, Forging Peace, Secretary-General Tells Security Council," UN Security Council, United Nations, October 25, 2016, www.un.org/press/en/2016/sc 12561.doc.htm.

17. Eileen Appelbaum, Heather Boushey, and John Schmitt, "The Economic Importance of Women's Rising Hours of Work," Center for American Progress, April 15, 2014, www.americanprogress.org/issues /economy/reports/2014/04/15/87638/the-economic-importance-of -womens-rising-hours-of-work; "The Case for Gender Equality," Global Gender Gap Report, World Economic Forum, 2015, http://reports.weforum .org/global-gender-gap-report-2015/the-case-for-gender-equality.

18. Cecile Fruman, "Why Gender Equality in Doing Business Makes Good Economic Sense," World Bank, November 17, 2016, http://blogs.worldbank.org/psd/why-gender-equality-doing-business-makes-good-economic-sense.

19. "Feminism," Dictionary.com, www.dictionary.com/browse/feminism.

20. Oliver Cann, "It's Back to the Future as Women's Pay Finally Equals Men's . . . from 2006," Global Gender Gap Report, World Economic Forum, 2015, http://reports.weforum.org/global-gender-gap-report-2015/press-releases; Donna Leinwand Leger, "170 Years from Now, Women Will Earn as Much as Men," USA Today, October 25, 2016, www.usatoday.com/story/news/2016/10/25/women-gender-equity-170-years/92716982.

21. The Rockefeller Foundation and Global Strategy Group, "Women in Leadership: Why It Matters," May 2016, www.globalstrategygroup.com/wp-content/uploads/2016/05/Rockefeller-100x25-Report.pdf.

22. "25 Surprising Stats to Share on Women's Equality Day," August 26, 2012, The New Agenda, https://thenewagenda.net/2012/08/26/25-surprising-stats-to-share-on-womens-equality-day.

23. Ibid.

24. Jessica Grose, "The Lenny Interview: Melinda Gates," Lenny, April 1, 2016, www.lennyletter.com/politics/interviews/a322/the-lenny-interview-melinda-gates.

25. Sustainable Development Goals, "Goal 5: Achieve Gender Equality and Empower All Women and Girls," UN, http://www.un.org/sustainable development/gender-equality/.

26. Elle Covington, "On Women's Equality Day, a Very Brief Timeline of Feminist History in America," Bustle, August 26, 2015, www.bustle.com/articles/106524-on-womens-equality-day-a-very-brief-timeline-of-feminist-history-in-america.

27. Sister Marches, Women's March, www.womensmarch.com/sisters.

28. Kaveh Waddell, "The Exhausting Work of Tallying America's Largest Protest," Atlantic, January 23, 2017, www.theatlantic.com/technology/archive/2017/01/womens-march-protest-count/514166; Sarah Wildman, "The Women's March Has Now Reached as Far as Antarctica (Really.)," Vox, January 20, 2017, www.vox.com/policy-and-politics/2017/1/20/14335430/womens-march-antarctica-seven-continents-60-countries.

29. Jeffrey Wright (@jfreewright), Twitter, November 9, 2016, https://twitter.com/jfreewright/status/796398258226610176?lang=en.

30. Claire Cain Miller, "Female-Run Venture Capital Funds Alter the Status Quo," New York Times, April 1, 2015, www.nytimes.com/2015/04/02/business/dealbook/female-run-venture-funds-alter-the-status-quo.html?_r=2.

31. Iris Vermeren, "Men vs. Women: Who Is More Active on Social Media?," Brandwatch, January 28, 2015, www.brandwatch.com/2015/01/men -vs-women-active-social-media.

32. "Single by Choice: Why Fewer American Women Are Married Than Ever Before," *Fresh Air*, NPR, March 1, 2016, www.npr.org/2016/03/01 /468688887/single-by-choice-why-fewer-american-women-are-married -than-ever-before.

33. Rebecca Traister, "The Single American Woman, *New York Magazine*, February 22, 2016, http://nymag.com/thecut/2016/02/political-power-single -women-c-v-r.html.

34. "Executive Order 13506 – Creating the White House Council on Women and Girls," The White House, March 11, 2009, https://web.archive .org/web/20161110153152/https://www.whitehouse.gov/the-press-office /executive-order-creating-white-house-council-women-and-girls.

35. "Shinzo Abe," HeForShe, www.heforshe.org/en/impact/shinzo-abe.

36. "Paul Kagame," HeForShe, www.heforshe.org/en/impact/paul -kagame.

37. Sarah Karmali, "#HeForShe: The Men Supporting Gender Equality," *Harper's Bazaar*, October 3, 2014, www.harpersbazaar.co.uk/culture/culture -news/news/g31993/heforshe-the-men-supporting-gender-equality.

38. Chava Gourarie, "Fashion, Politics, and Feminism: The Women's Magazines for a New Generation," *Columbia Journalism Review*, September 17, 2015, www.cjr.org/the_feature/feminism_fashion_politics_womens_news.php.

CHAPTER 3: INCLUDING, ENGAGING WITH, AND EMPOWERING MEN

1. "Men's Issues and Problems," Good Therapy, www.goodtherapy.org /learn-about-therapy/issues/men-issues.

2. Janet Sigal and Maureen Nally, "Cultural Perspectives on Gender," *Praeger Guide to the Psychology of Gender*, ed. Michele A. Paludi, 27–41 (Westport, CT: Praeger, 2004), 31.

3. Jeffrey Stoffer, "How Men and Women Handle Money Differently," DailyWorth, June 19, 2015, www.dailyworth.com/posts/3663-how-men -and-women-handle-money-differently-stoffer.

4. Lea Winermand, "Helping Men to Help Themselves," *Monitor on Psychology* 36, no. 6 (june 2005): 57, www.apa.org/monitor/jun05/helping .aspx.

5. Laura Donnelly, "Women Far More Likely than Men to Seek Counselling for Anxiety," *Telegraph*, January 15, 2014, www.telegraph.co.uk/news/10574941 /Women-far-more-likely-than-men-to-seek-counselling-for-anxiety.html.

6. "Men's Issues and Problems."

7. Betsy Bates Freed and David Freed, "Aversion to Therapy: Why Won't Men Get Help?," *Pacific Standard*, June 25, 2012, https://psmag.com/aversion -to-therapy-why-won-t-men-get-help-7998d34f1d4e#.k3ybbrxoh.

8. Audrey Nelson, "Why Don't Many Men Show Their Emotions?," *Psychology Today*, January 24, 2015, www.psychologytoday.com/blog/he -speaks-she-speaks/201501/why-don-t-many-men-show-their-emotions.

9. Thomas G. Fiffer, "The 3 Things a Man Fears Most: An Exposé of the Male Psyche," Good Men Project, June 5, 2014, https://goodmenproject .com/ethics-values/the-3-things-a-man-fears-most-fiff; http://www .yourtango.com/experts/charles-orlando/what-scares-men-expert.

10. Connor Beaton, "How Real Men Deal with Grief and Loss," ManTalks, December 5, 2016, http://mantalks.com/men-deal-with-grief.

11. John Bingham, "2.5 Million Men 'Have No Close Friends,'" *Telegraph*, November 14, 2015, www.telegraph.co.uk/men/active/mens-health /11996473/2.5-million-men-have-no-close-friends.html.

12. Gerald Schoenewolf, "What's Up with American Boys?," PsychCentral, March 2016, http://blogs.psychcentral.com/psychoanalysis-now/2016/03 /whats-up-with-american-boys.

13. Jeff Guo, "Poor Boys Are Falling Behind Poor Girls, and It's Deeply Troubling," *Washington Post*, November 23, 2015, www.washingtonpost .com/news/wonk/wp/2015/11/23/why-girls-do-so-much-better-than-boys -in-school.

14. Emine Saner, "The Dating Gap: Why the Odds Are Stacked Against Female Graduates Finding a Like-Minded Man," *Guardian*, November 10, 2015, www.theguardian.com/lifeandstyle/2015/nov/10/dating-gap-hook -up-culture-female-graduates.

15. "Suicide Statistics," American Foundation for Suicide Prevention, https://afsp.org/about-suicide/suicide-statistics.

16. Peter Baker, "The Shocking Facts Behind Men's Declining Health," Good Men Project, February 17, 2016, https://goodmenproject.com /featured-content/the-shocking-facts-behind-mens-declining-health-bbab.

17. Kim Parker and Gretchen Livingston, "6 Facts About American Fathers," Pew Research Center, June 16, 2016, www.pewresearch.org/fact -tank/2016/06/16/fathers-day-facts.

18. Ibid.

19. "Parental Leave Survey: Less than Half of People Surveyed Feel Their Organization Helps Men Feel Comfortable Taking Parental Leave," Deloitte, June 15, 2016, www2.deloitte.com/us/en/pages/about-deloitte/articles/press -releases/deloitte-survey-parental-leave.html.

20. Kristen Bellstrom, "How Fatherly Plans to Corner the Market on Millennial Dads," *Fortune*, April 8, 2015, http://fortune.com/2015/04/08/fatherly-millennial-dads; Mackenzie Dawson, "My Mommy Blog Ruined My Life," *New York Post*, May 29, 2016, http://nypost.com/2016/05/29/my-mommy-blog-ruined-my-life.

21. "About Us," Fatherly, www.fatherly.com/about-us.

22. "About Us," Good Men Project, https://goodmenproject.com/about.

23. Alanna Vaglanos, "How This Former NFL Player Became a Feminist Activist," *Huffington Post*, May 23, 2016, www.huffingtonpost.com/entry/how-this-former-nfl-player-became-a-feminist-activist_us_573cbb6be4b0aee7b8e8be0f.

24. The MENtour, http://thementour.com; The MENtour, "It's a Big Day for the MENTOUR," Facebook post, The MENtour, September 22, 2016, www.facebook.com/thementour/posts/1658607057785909:0.

CHAPTER 4: CALLING ON A NEW BREED OF LEADERS

1. Dean Takahashi, "WearRevolar Wants to Take On 'Rape Culture,'" VentureBeat, January 4, 2016, http://venturebeat.com/2016/01/04/startup-revolar-wants-to-take-on-rape-culture.

2. Lean In Collection, Getty Images, www.gettyimages.com/collections/leanin.

3. Lean In Circles, Lean In, http://leanincircles.org/?_ga=1.17189501.518851908.1478370993.

4. "Our Epic Battle #LikeAGirl," Always, www.always.com/en-us/about-us/our-epic-battle-like-a-girl.

5. David Griner and Roo Ciambriello, "Hugely Popular 'Like a Girl' Campaign from Always Will Return as a Super Bowl Ad," AdWeek, January 29, 2015, www.adweek.com/news/advertising-branding/hugely-popular-girl-campaign-always-will-return-sunday-super-bowl-ad-162619.

6. Partners, Girls Who Code, https://girlswhocode.com/our-team/#partners.

CHAPTER 5: PURPOSE

1. Vi-An Nguyen, "5 Best Quotes from Oprah Winfrey's Inspiring Harvard University Commencement Speech," *Parade*, May 31, 2013, http://parade.com/18717/viannguyen/5-best-quotes-from-oprah-winfreys-inspiring-harvard-university-commencement-speech.

2. Rick Warren, "Your Pain Often Reveals God's Purpose," Pastor Rick's Daily Hope, Novemeber 25, 2014, http://pastorrick.com/devotional/english/your-pain-often-reveals-god-s-purpose.

3. Heather Saul, "Ashley Graham: The Size 16 Model Calling for an End to 'Plus Size' Labels," *Independent*, January 29, 2016, www.independent.co.uk /news/people/ashley-graham-size-12-model-barbie-ferreira-end-to-plus-size -labels-a6841431.html.

4. Plus Is Equal, http://plusisequal.com.

5. Juno Dawson, "Juno Dawson: Join Our New Transgender Columnist on Her Amazing Journey," *Glamour*, January 5, 2016, www.glamourmagazine .co.uk/news/features/2016/01/05/juno-dawson-columnist-on-transitioning -into-a-woman-part-1.

6. Patrick Strudwick, "Internationally Bestselling Author Comes Out as Transgender," *Buzzfeed*, October 24, 2015, www.buzzfeed.com/patrick strudwick/internationally-bestselling-author-comes-out-as-transgender ?utm_term=.jqLQKNaa7#.kcwzk377d.

7. "Lisa Nichols," Motivating the Masses, www.motivatingthemasses.com /about/lisa-nichols.

8. Oprah Winfrey, "Winfrey's Commencement Address," *Harvard Gazette*, May 31, 2013, http://news.harvard.edu/gazette/story/2013/05/winfreys -commencement-address.

9. Ben Schiller, "These Sensors Raise the Bar of Accountability for Water Charities," Fast Company, January 11, 2016, www.fastcoexist.com/3055110 /these-sensors-raise-the-bar-or-accountability-for-water-charities.

CHAPTER 6: VISION

1. "What Percentage of Our Lives Are Spent Working?," Reference, www .reference.com/math/percentage-lives-spent-working-599e3f7fb2c88fca.

2. Sanaya Roman, *Personal Power Through Awareness* (Tiburon, CA: H. J. Kramer, 1986), 11.

3. Doug Sundheim, "Do Women Take as Many Risks as Men?," *Harvard Business Review*, February 27, 2013, https://hbr.org/2013/02/do-women-take -as-many-risks-as.

CHAPTER 8: RESILIENCE

1. Stephen Joseph, "Posttraumatic Growth," *Psychology Today*, February 8, 2014, www.psychologytoday.com/blog/what-doesnt-kill-us/201402/post traumatic-growth.

2. Jim Rendon, "Post-Traumatic Stress's Surprisingly Positive Flip Side," *New York Times*, March 22, 2012, www.nytimes.com/2012/03/25/magazine /post-traumatic-stresss-surprisingly-positive-flip-side.html.

3. Jacoba Urist, "What the Marshmallow Test Really Teaches About Self-Control," *Atlantic*, September 24, 2014, www.theatlantic.com/health/archive/2014/09/what-the-marshmallow-test-really-teaches-about-self-control/380673.

4. Ibid.

CHAPTER 9: ENERGY

1. Robert E. Fisher, *Quick to Listen, Slow to Speak: Living Out the Language of Love in Your Family Relationships* (Wheaton, IL: Living Books, 1987), 91.

2. Wayne Dyer, "You Are God," Dr. Wayne W. Dyer, October 2014, www.drwaynedyer.com/press/you-are-god-in-depth-conversation-with-dr-wayne-dyer.

CHAPTER 10: PRODUCTIVITY

1. Perry Marshall, "The 80/20 Rule of Time Management: Stop Wasting Your Time," *Entrepreneur*, www.entrepreneur.com/article/229813.

CHAPTER 11: HUMILITY

1. Nicole Reiff, "What Is Catchafire?," Catchafire, https://catchafireblog.org/what-is-catchafire-b2d4730a3891#.iqgekc8op.

2. Donna Doss, "The Seven Habits of Highly Effective People – Stephen R. Covey," Book Summaries, http://booksums.blogspot.com/2008/04/seven-habits-of-highly-effective-people.html.

3. Ibid.

4. Sgabjar Vedantam, "Why Are Women Less Likely to Become Entrepreneurs than Men?," *Hidden Brain*, NPR, September 8, 2015, www.npr.org/2015/09/08/438473573/why-are-women-less-likely-to-become-entrepreneurs-than-men.

CHAPTER 12: GRATITUDE

1. Martha Beck, "Wait! Stop! It's All Too Much!: How to Keep from Being Overwhelmed," Oprah.com, www.oprah.com/spirit/Martha-Becks-Advice-on-How-to-Keep-from-Being-Overwhelmed.

2. "John C. Maxwell: 6 Tips to Develop and Model an Abundance Mindset," Success, March 4, 2015, www.success.com/article/john-c-maxwell-6-tips-to-develop-and-model-an-abundance-mindset.

3. Amy Novotney, "The Psychology of Scarcity," *Monitor on Psychology* 45, no. 2 (February 2014), 28, www.apa.org/monitor/2014/02/scarcity.aspx.

4. Christopher Hawker, "Lead with Thoughts of Abundance, Not Scarcity," *Entrepreneur*, December 1, 2015, www.entrepreneur.com/article/252840.

5. Jessica and Ashley Lau, "Krawcheck Seen Bidding Final Adieu, to Wall Street," Reuters, September 9, 2011, www.reuters.com/article/us-krawcheck -move-idUSTRE7887ES20110909.

6. Amy Morin, "7 Scientifically Proven Benefits of Gratitude," *Psychology Today*, April 3, 2015, www.psychologytoday.com/blog/what-mentally -strong-people-dont-do/201504/7-scientifically-proven-benefits-gratitude.

7. Ibid.

CHAPTER 14: COMMUNITY

1. Ronald E. Riggio, "How Are Men's Friendships Different from Women's?," *Psychology Today*, October 9, 2014, www.psychologytoday.com /blog/cutting-edge-leadership/201410/how-are-men-s-friendships-different -women-s; Lisa Wade, "American Men's Hidden Crisis: They Need More Friends!," *Salon*, December 7, 2013, www.salon.com/2013/12/08/american _mens_hidden_crisis_they_need_more_friends.

CHAPTER 15: SELF-LOVE

1. Rebecca Holman, "Do Women Really Have More to Feel Guilty About than Men?," *Telegraph*, November 22, 2013, www.telegraph.co.uk/women /womens-life/10467289/Guilt-do-women-really-have-more-to-feel-guilty -about-than-men.html; Kim Parker, "Despite Progress, Women Still Bear Heavier Load than Men in Balancing Work and Family," Pew Research Center, March 10, 2015, www.pewresearch.org/fact-tank/2015/03/10 /women-still-bear-heavier-load-than-men-balancing-work-family; Katty Kay and Claire Shipman, "The Confidence Gap," *Atlantic*, May 2014, www .theatlantic.com/magazine/archive/2014/05/the-confidence-gap/359815.

2. "Exercise and Depression," WebMD, www.webmd.com/depression /guide/exercise-depression#1.

CHAPTER 17: MINDFULNESS

1. Michael Lipka, "5 Facts About Prayer," Pew Research Center, May 4, 2016, www.pewresearch.org/fact-tank/2016/05/04/5-facts-about-prayer.

CHAPTER 18: TREAT YOUR WHOLE LIFE AS
THE ORGANIZATION YOU ARE LEADING

1. "2015 Stress in America," American Psychological Association, www.apa.org/news/press/releases/stress/2015/snapshot.aspx.

2. Laura Vanderkam, "Work-Life Balance Is Dead—Here's Why that Might Be a Good Thing," *Fortune*, March 6, 2015, http://fortune.com/2015/03/06 /work-life-integration.

CHAPTER 19: LEAD FROM WHERE YOU ARE

1. Dan Schawbel, "How to Train Your Mind to Become Entrepreneurial," *Forbes*, September 30, 2012, www.forbes.com/sites/danschawbel/2012/09/30 /how-to-train-your-mind-to-become-entrepreneurial/#78c07088311d.

2. Jeff Desjardins, "Millennials Are on Track to Become the Most Entrepreneurial Generation Ever," *Business Insider*, September 3, 2016, www.businessinsider.com/millennials-on-track-to-become-most -entrepreneurial-generation-ever-2016-9.

3. Nalaie MacNeil, "Entrepreneurship Is the New Women's Movement," *Forbes*, June 8, 2012, www.forbes.com/sites/work-in-progress/2012/06/08 /entrepreneurship-is-the-new-womens-movement/#4adc4eb76922.

4. Leigh Buchanan, "The U.S. Now Has 27 Million Entrepreneurs," *Inc.*, September 2, 2015, www.inc.com/leigh-buchanan/us-entrepreneurship -reaches-record-highs.html.

5. Kalyani Rao, "His Unique Organization Engages with Men to Promote Gender Justice and End Violence Against Women," Promundo, July 15, 2015, http://promundoglobal.org/2015/07/15/his-unique-organization-engages -with-men-to-promote-gender-justice-and-end-violence-against-women.

6. "About Us," Promundo, http://promundoglobal.org/about.

7. Geena Rocero, "Why I Must Come Out," TED, March 2014, www.ted .com/talks/geena_rocero_why_i_must_come_out.

8. Alan Hall, "'I'm Outta Here!' Why 2 Million Americans Quit Every Month (And 5 Steps to Turn the Epidemic Around)," *Forbes*, March 11, 2013, www.forbes.com/sites/alanhall/2013/03/11/im-outta-here-why-2-million -americans-quit-every-month-and-5-steps-to-turn-the-epidemic-around /#557b7c67f9fe.

9. Helena Kleine, "Why I Left My Corporate Job for a Career with Meaning," The Changer, October 1, 2015, http://thechanger.org/community /why-i-left-my-corporate-job-career-meaning.

10. Paulette Light, "Why 43% of Women with Children Leave Their Jobs, and How to Get Them Back," *Atlantic*, April 19, 2013, www.theatlantic.com /sexes/archive/2013/04/why-43-of-women-with-children-leave-their-jobs -and-how-to-get-them-back/275134.

11. Claire Cain Miller and Liz Alderman, "Why U.S. Women Are Leaving Jobs Behind," *New York Times*, December 12, 2014, www.nytimes.com/2014 /12/14/upshot/us-employment-women-not-working.html.

12. Hall, "'I'm Outta Here!'"

13. "Parental Leave Survey: Less than Half of People Surveyed Feel Their Organization Helps Men Feel Comfortable Taking Parental Leave," Deloitte, June 15, 2016, www2.deloitte.com/us/en/pages/about-deloitte/articles /press-releases/deloitte-survey-parental-leave.html.

14. Monika Gonzalez Mesa, "Self-Determination and Drive Take Gordon to Top Legal Post at Bacardi," *Daily Business Review*, September 1, 2016.

15. Jeremy Neuner, "40% of America's Workforce Will Be Freelancers by 2020," *Quartz*, March 20, 2013, http://qz.com/65279/40-of-americas -workforce-will-be-freelancers-by-2020.

16. "Our Mission," Fugees Family, www.fugeesfamily.org/our-mission.

CONCLUSION: ALL ROADS LEAD TO CHARACTER

1. "Full Remarks: Oprah Winfrey," YouTube, June 7, 2014, https://www .youtube.com/watch?v=C2s-1050fWE.

BIBLIOGRAPHY

Calhoun, Lisa. "30 Surprising Facts about Female Founders." *Inc.*, July 6, 2015. https://www.inc.com/lisa-calhoun/30-surprising-facts-about-female -founders.html.

Catalyst. "Statistical Overview of Women in the Workforce." 2016. http://www .catalyst.org/knowledge/statistical-overview-women-workforce.

Catalyst. "Women CEOs of the S&P 500." 2017. http://www.catalyst.org /knowledge/women-ceos-sp-500.

Confidence Coalition. "The Facts." 2017. http://www.confidencecoalition .org/assets/1442/8-2 13_facts_on_cc_2013.pdf?1377879930152.

Dishman, Lydia. "The State of the American Entrepreneur in 2015." Fast Company, May 29, 2015. https://www.fastcompany.com/3046773/hit-the -ground-running/the-state-of-the-american-entrepreneur-in-2015

Dove. "Our Research." 2013. https://www.dove.com/us/en/stories/about-dove /our-research.html.

Entrepreneur. "Women Entrepreneurs." From the Center for Women's Business Research, 2004. https://www.entrepreneur.com/page /216029.

Go Girl Finance. "Women and Finance: The Facts." 2016. http://gogirl finance.com/women-and-finance-facts/.

Gross, Jessica. "The Lenny Interview: Melinda Gates." 2016. http:// www.lennyletter.com/politics/interviews/a322/the-lenny-interview -melinda-gates/.

Heart of Leadership. "Pressure & Perfection." 2017. http://www.heartof leadership.org/statistics/.

Henson, Rich. "11 Surprising Statistics about Women in the Workplace." Resourceful Manager, 2015. https://www.resourcefulmanager.com /women-workplace-statistics/.

Kristof, Nicholas D., and Sheryl WuDunn. *Half the Sky: Turning Oppression into Opportunity for Women Worldwide.* New York: Vintage, 2010.

Nextshark. "Startling Statistics Reveal the Sad Truth about Women's Confidence in the Workplace." 2015. http://nextshark.com/startling -statistics-reveal-the-sad-truth-about-womens-confidence-in-the -workplace/.

Schwartz, Tony. "Overcoming the Confidence Gap for Women." *New York Times*, June 12, 2015. https://www.nytimes.com/2015/06/13 /business/dealbook/overcoming-the-confidence-gap-for-women .html?_r=2.

The Money Post. "Young or Old, Few Feel Ready for Retirement." 2016. http://themoneypostblog.com/resources/statistics/.

UN Women. "Facts and Figures: Ending Violence against Women." 2016. http://www.unwomen.org/en/what-we-do/ending-violence-against -women/facts-and-figures.

US Department of Labor. "Women's Bureau: Data & Statistics." 2017. https://www.dol.gov/wb/stats/stats_data.htm.

Warrell, Margie. "For Women to Rise We Must Close 'The Confidence Gap.'" Forbes, January 20, 2016. https://www.forbes.com/sites/margiewarrell /2016/01/20/gender-confidence-gap/#11a4beee1efa.

World Health Organization (WHO). "Maternal Mortality." 2016. http://www.who.int/mediacentre/factsheets/fs348/en/.

INDEX

ABOUT THE AUTHOR

Claudia Chan is a recognized expert on leadership and a social entrepreneur dedicated to activating individuals and organizations to lead change in the world and advance gender equality.

She is the founder of the award-winning global leadership conference, S.H.E. Summit, which has made advancing women's leadership accessible and actionable. Each year, the event connects, educates, and activates women's empowerment champions; speakers have included Deepak Chopra, Kelly Clarkson, Morgan Stanley's Carla Harris, Sallie Krawcheck, Gabrielle Bernstein, Soledad O'Brien, and UN ambassador Samantha Power, among others. She also leads S.H.E. GLOBL, a corporate initiative that helps Fortune 1000 companies modernize and accelerate their diversity initiatives with the goal of achieving gender parity by 2030 through various programs and services.

A sought after speaker on how women and men can and should create a more equal world, Claudia is referred to as the "Richard Branson of Women's Empowerment" by *Fast Company* and named one of 2017's "20 Most Influential Moms" by *Family Circle*. In 2015, Claudia became an official U.S. Department of State speaker and has visited countries such as South Korea for countrywide speaking tours to educate women on how to empower themselves and others in their communities. She was the 2015 global spokesperson for Gillette Venus #UseYourAnd empowerment campaign, a movement encouraging women to celebrate their multidimensionality.

Prior to launching S.H.E. Globl Media, Claudia was president and co-owner of the popular women's entertainment company Shecky's for ten years. Claudia is a lifelong New Yorker, proud alumnae of Smith College, mom of two, and an equal partner with her husband, John.

To learn more about how organizations
and people work with Claudia, visit
CLAUDIACHAN.COM

To order copies of *THIS IS HOW WE RISE*
for your organization's employees,
please email
office@SHEGlobl.com